A NEW ANTHROPOLOGY OF ISLAM

In this powerful, but accessible, new study, John R. Bowen draws on a full range of work in social anthropology to present Islam in ways that emphasize its constitutive practices, from praying and learning to judging and political organizing. Starting at the heart of Islam – revelation and learning in Arabic lands – Bowen shows how Muslims have adapted Islamic texts and traditions to ideas and conditions in the societies in which they live. Returning to key case studies in Asia, Africa, and Western Europe to explore each major domain of Islamic religious and social life, Bowen also considers the theoretical advances in social anthropology that have come out of the study of Islam. *A New Anthropology of Islam* is essential reading for all those interested in the study of Islam and for those following new developments in the discipline of anthropology.

JOHN R. BOWEN is the Dunbar-Van Cleve Professor in Arts and Sciences at Washington University in St. Louis. His fieldwork in Indonesia, France, and England, on topics ranging from poetics and political history to civil law reasoning and everyday forms of Islam, has spanned over thirty years. He has published widely on his research interests, and his *Islam, Law and Equality in Indonesia* (Cambridge, 2003) won the prize for Best Work from the Law and Society Association.

NEW DEPARTURES IN ANTHROPOLOGY

New Departures in Anthropology is a book series that focuses on emerging themes in social and cultural anthropology. With original perspectives and syntheses, authors introduce new areas of inquiry in anthropology, explore developments that cross disciplinary boundaries, and weigh in on current debates. Every book illustrates theoretical issues with ethnographic material drawn from current research or classic studies, as well as from literature, memoirs, and other genres of reportage. The aim of the series is to produce books that are accessible enough to be used by college students and instructors, but will also stimulate, provoke, and inform anthropologists at all stages of their careers. Written clearly and concisely, books in the series are designed equally for advanced students and a broader range of readers, inside and outside academic anthropology, who want to be brought up to date on the most exciting developments in the discipline.

Series editorial board

Jonathan Spencer, University of Edinburgh
Michael Lambek, University of Toronto and London School of Economics

A New Anthropology of Islam

JOHN R. BOWEN

CAMBRIDGE
UNIVERSITY PRESS

University Printing House, Cambridge CB2 8BS, United Kingdom

Published in the United States of America by Cambridge University Press, New York

Cambridge University Press is part of the University of Cambridge.

It furthers the University's mission by disseminating knowledge in the pursuit of education, learning and research at the highest international levels of excellence.

www.cambridge.org
Information on this title: www.cambridge.org/9780521822824

First published 2012
Reprinted 2013

Printed by CPI Group (UK) Ltd, Croydon CR0 4YY

A catalog record for this publication is available from the British Library

Library of Congress Cataloging in Publication data
Bowen, John Richard, 1951–
A new anthropology of Islam / John R. Bowen.
   pages   cm. – (New departures in anthropology)
Includes bibliographical references and index.
ISBN 978-0-521-82282-4 (hardback) – ISBN 978-0-521-52978-5 (pbk.)
1. Islamic sociology.   2. Anthropology of religion – Islamic countries.   I. Title.
BP173.25.B69   2012
306.6'97 – dc23   2012010632

ISBN 978-0-521-82282-4 Hardback
ISBN 978-0-521-52978-5 Paperback

To my parents

Contents

Acknowledgments

A work such as this one, intending to analyze a dimension of social life by synthesizing others' works on the topic, is necessarily part of a collective endeavor. For that reason, I will not single out the individual scholars whose works have contributed to my thinking, but rather thank the collective body of all those who have been trying to advance understanding of Islam as it is lived and understood by Muslims. Most of you are cited herein. It has been an honor and a pleasure to be part of this group.

The pleasure is all the greater for the ways in which Islamic studies and social anthropology have grown closer over the past generation. If in the past the former guarded the temple of high scripture, and the latter the thicket of contextualized knowledge, today we work together to trace practices of referring to the Islamic tradition in diverse and often competing ways. We bring together the tools of philology and fieldwork, pay attention to the magisterial reading and the marginal citation, study in the palace court and the law court. I once was called "a real anthropologist" by an old-school theologian, as a way of saying that I listened to the wrong people, ignorant villagers and poorly trained jurists, and could not be bothered to distinguish between "good" and "bad" readings of texts. Other scholars were denounced as "Orientalists" for focusing on writings of the intellectuals of the distant past, those who had produced the canonical "good" readings. Today, more often we combine forces to see how villagers and intellectuals use the writings of those distant intellectuals, and how intellectual production draws on everyday habits of life.

Or at least so I presume in writing this text: that "anthropology" now includes close textual readings and archival work, and that "Islamic studies" extends to ordinary understandings of the Islamic tradition. If this text has readers, then, on good pragmatist grounds, the presumption can be said to hold.

In working from one realm of social life to another, I draw abundantly on my own work, partly because I know it best and partly because doing so provides a degree of case-continuity across multiple domains. Some of the examples appeared in works already published; let me acknowledge in particular the publishers of *Muslims Through Discourse* (Princeton University Press, 1993), and of two articles: "On Scriptural Essentialism and Ritual Variation: Muslim Sacrifice in Sumatra and Morocco" (*American Ethnologist* 19: 656–71, 1992), and "Islamic Adaptations to Western Europe and North America: The Importance of Contrastive Analyses" (*American Behavioral Scientist* 55: 1601–15, 2011).

Notwithstanding what is said above about individuals, let me thank Michael Lambek and Jonathan Spencer for their patient and enthusiastic encouragement of this work, and, somewhat later but with equal enthusiasm, Richard Fisher and Lucy Rhymer of Cambridge University Press. And above all, for literally making this possible: my parents.

Note on transliteration

I give a close transcription of major Arabic terms at first usage, and thereafter use a simplified form. Please see the Glossary for these terms.

ONE

ᕗ

How to think about religions – Islam, for example

One day while driving home from work, I turned on National Public Radio, as I often do, and landed right in the middle of a story on women in Saudi Arabia. A Muslim woman was speaking about the well-known prohibition of women driving in that country; she argued that this and other constraints on women's freedom were "part of Saudi culture, not Islam." The NPR narrator began her summary with, "In this traditional Islamic culture . . ."

It is tempting to ascribe features of social life in certain societies to their "Islamic culture," to a way of life that follows from their religious beliefs. Older ways of thinking in Islamic studies (Lewis 1988) were built around this kind of reasoning. Sometimes we do the opposite, as the Muslim woman interviewed did, when she contrasted Islam to the regrettable facts of "Saudi culture." Neither way of speaking admits to reciprocal linkages between religion and particular cultural frameworks. For the one, Islam is only a matter of culture; for the other, it is only a matter of religion.

Unfortunately, these two ways of speaking tend to dominate public discourse about Islam in North America and Europe. I recall a recent series of gatherings at a Unitarian church in St. Louis with several representatives of the largest local mosque, an outreach group that had found its work multiplying after 9/11. I attended these meetings and was impressed with the liberal and consistent vision of Islam these men and women presented, one that emphasized verses of the Qur'an (*Qur'ân*) that speak of toleration and the high status of women. When members of the audience asked one speaker, a woman doctor, why, then, women could not drive in Saudi Arabia, the doctor gave the same response as had the radio interviewee: this rule comes from Saudi culture, not from Islam, because Islam teaches that women should work, trade, study, and so forth. She and her colleagues presented "Islam" as a set of rules and values, which even many Muslims failed to understand.

However opposed these two perspectives might seem – one that assumes that Islam has its own, rather backward culture, another that claims it to be independent of (and superior to) any particular culture – they share one feature: both perspectives assume a single object called "Islam." They often assume that we can find that object directly in scripture. Those urging a positive view of Islam quote verses of the Qur'an about the respect due to mothers, or a verse about "no compulsion in religion"; those seeking to condemn it quote verses about killing one's enemies. In both cases, scholars, religious leaders, and radio commentators move directly from a particular text to statements about Islam in general.

Now, if a public figure in Europe or North America were to infer from the Bible's accounts of divinely sanctioned massacres the idea that Judaism and Christianity preached genocide, Jews and Christians alike would point out that such texts must be seen in the broader compass of God's plans for his people. Some might treat such passages historically, others allegorically, still others as a message that was superseded by the gift of Jesus to humanity. The unfortunate public figure would be invited to look at the lives and teachings of Jews and Christians in order to understand how people work in the world with inspiration from their sacred texts. And that person's days in public life would be numbered.

But seldom do masses of listeners or readers condemn the same sort of inferences when Islam is the topic. The usual response is the one that I heard at the Unitarian church: defenders of the religion fall back on an essentialist apologetics for Islam in general. This kind of response seldom satisfies an intelligent public for very long: how can you say that "Islam means peace" if so much violence seems to come from it? That response is not an unreasonable one, but it calls for an approach that makes everyday interpretations and practices more central to understanding Islam.

Here enter anthropologists, who specialize in examining ordinary lives. Although we (for I am one) used to spend most of our time focusing on people who eschewed the large-scale faiths, many of us now turn our comparative lenses on Muslims and Christians, as well as on Hindus, Buddhists, Taoists, and Jews. And increasingly, we place those studies at the center of our discipline, and place anthropology at the center of Islamic studies. Or so goes the argument of this book, namely, that anthropologists, along with fellow-travelers from history and religious studies, have developed new ways of approaching Islam.

Those new ways start by taking seriously the idea that Islam is best seen as a set of interpretive resources and practices. From Islam's resources of texts, ideas, and methods comes the sense that all Muslims participate in a long-term and worldwide tradition. From Islam's practices of worshipping, judging, and struggling comes the capacity to adapt, challenge, and diversify. So far, so good, but specific to what I am calling a "new anthropology of Islam" is the insistence that the analysis begins with individuals' efforts to grapple with those resources and shape those practices in meaningful ways. Many anthropologists studying Islam today start from the socially embedded chains of human interpretation that link today's practices across societies and over time. Indeed, I choose to begin the next chapter with the trope of the *isnâd*, the chain of genealogical authentication of Islamic traditions. Whether with respect to politics, prayer, or purification, Muslims justify what they do by tracing contemporary understandings back to originating and authenticating acts.

This way of looking at Islam thus starts from people drawing on textual traditions to inform social practices, and it allows us to engage in two complementary analytical strategies. The first is "focusing inward," by deepening our understanding of intentions, understandings, and emotions surrounding specific practices, usually with a great deal of attention to individual testimonies and histories. What does it mean for a woman or man to follow the command to "submit" that is contained within the very term *islâm*? Can one strengthen a sense of agency and power through submitting to God? How do leaders of social movements call on Islamic allegiances to mobilize followers?

But at the same time we follow a second strategy, one of "opening outward" to the social significance of, and conditions for, these religious practices. Often we do so across social boundaries, to broaden our understanding of why ideas and practices take this form here, and that form there. What features of the social environment – social movements, political pressures, new forms of communication – lead more individuals to seek meaning through submission in prayer? How do urban and rural settings in, say, Egypt present different possibilities and constraints from, say, Lebanon, Indonesia, or Germany?

This notion of what anthropology brings to the table is broad enough to include much of what historians, sociologists, and religious scholars do when they, too, keep in their analytical lenses both the contingent and contextual nature of interpretation and action, and the importance to Muslims of living in an Islamic world that transcends particular times and places. This new anthropology of Islam has placed an increased emphasis on religious texts and ideas, but only as they are understood and transmitted in particular times and places. Far from ignoring scripture, anthropology increasingly seeks to understand how particular Muslims come to understand and use particular passages. What distinguishes anthropologists from an older generation of textual scholars is that we are as interested in how a Pakistani farmer, an Egyptian engineer, or a French Muslim theologian sees the Qur'an as we are in the knowledge held by a traditional Muslim scholar.

Does affirming the multiplicity of interpretations mean that Muslims cannot share in this anthropology of Islam? I believe that this is far from being the case. Muslims have always faced squarely the diversity of views within the tradition, recognizing, for example, that the distinct legal schools provide valid, though differing, answers to questions about theology, social life, and ritual practice. Although many Muslims would argue that their own particular view of their tradition is the correct one, such claims hardly make them any different from Christians or Jews, or, for that matter, lawyers or philosophers. Many Muslims would state further that only God knows which of many views is correct, and that only on the Day of Judgment will humans learn the answers – and that this is why the Prophet Muhammad promised two merits for the judge who makes the right decision and one merit for the judge who honestly arrives at the wrong one.[1]

But much of what everyday Muslims take from religion is not about grand questions of theology or jurisprudence, but about much more proximate matters, such as healing a child through reciting scripture, marrying or divorcing in an Islamic manner, or sacrificing correctly and efficaciously to God. As they have developed ways to do these things, Muslims living in particular places have adapted Islamic traditions to local values and constraints, and these adaptations have given rise to vigorous debates among Muslims over what is or is not correctly Islamic.

Let me give a brief example of how adaptations have created diversity, an example I will explore more fully in Chapter 6. Sufi members of devotional orders carried ideas about grace and sainthood throughout the world. In southern Asia, they added these ideas to pre-existing forms of devotion at shrines dedicated to holy people; so effective was the meld that Muslims could worship at these shrines together with people whom today we would call "Hindus." In Africa, these ideas fit into

---

[1] For a recent, sweeping account of the development of the Islamic legal tradition that takes full account of these legitimate, pluralizing processes, see Hallaq (2009). For a recent collection of essays around the questions of pluralism in Islam, see Hirji (2010).

a pre-existing social framework based on lineage structures, creating practically effective Sufi orders. Some engaged in large-scale production of cash crops; others carried out military campaigns against colonial powers.

Some observers, Muslim and non-Muslim, might find these developments to be contrary to the "true" Sufi spirit, or perhaps even contrary to Islam in general. What should the anthropologist say, be he or she Muslim or otherwise? I think that the student of such developments (Muslim or non-Muslim) ought to trace processes of adaptation and ought to illuminate the debates over authenticity thereby engendered. Indeed, anthropologists, historians, and religious scholars find themselves converging on these questions, even if, historically, each has only fitfully pursued this path.

Until relatively recently, many scholars had other disciplinary priorities, whether those were finding the culturally distinctive features of each society, tracing the development of political institutions, or examining the texts of Islamic "high culture." Few of us in anthropology emphasized the ways in which Muslims endeavor to transcend the limits of their own society even as they live in it, how they try to organize their lives around their understandings of "high texts," and how these texts – the Qur'an, the hadith (*hadîth*), and the wealth of devotional, legal, and political writings that Muslims have produced – are always grasped locally.

Things began to change in the late 1960s and early 1970s, when several younger anthropologists, including Dale Eickelman (1976, 1985), Michael Fischer (1980), Michael Gilsenan (1973, 1982), Lawrence Rosen (1984), James Siegel (1969), and Abdul Hamid el-Zein (1974), described the production of Islamic traditions within particular social contexts and through particular cultural understandings. They built on work carried out on patterns of authority in Muslim-majority societies, most prominently by E. E. Evans-Pritchard (1949), Ernest Gellner (1969, 1980), and Clifford Geertz (1968), but also on other scholars of Islam, especially

Albert Hourani (1962) and Wilfred Cantwell Smith (1957). Others were carrying out parallel innovations in the anthropology of other religious traditions, among them Stanley Tambiah (1970) for Buddhism and Milton Singer (1972) for Hinduism.

For many of us beginning our graduate studies in the United States at that time, a major inspiration came from the comparative studies carried out by Clifford Geertz. In his *Islam Observed* (1968), Geertz set up a maximal cultural contrast – Morocco vis-à-vis Java – to try and grasp the specificities of Islam. Islam emerged not as what was left when you subtracted culture, but as a set of processes through which Muslims, rural and urban, North African and Southeast Asian, drew on elements of their shared tradition in ways that made sense to them, in that place and at that historical moment. A counterpoint was provided a bit later by Talal Asad (1986) – a second importance influence on my own thinking – when he urged us to focus our anthropological lenses not on a cultural matrix – the Moroccan culture that creates Moroccan Islam – but on the powerful religious figures who authorize some interpretations of the Islamic tradition and suppress others.

Some may see these two approaches – Geertz's cultural emphasis, Asad's political one – as irreconcilable opposites; I prefer to note that, taken together, they pointed toward something like what I have sketched above: an approach to Islamic traditions that takes seriously both religious thinking and social frameworks. I find that the analytical tensions and dissensions emerging from contemporary debates within anthropology – Is religion symbols or discipline? Is it coherence or fracture? – have themselves generated an impressive set of new work on the processes and practices surrounding the Islamic tradition. Over the past twenty-odd years, many of us have taken the twin tensions – one between cultural specificity and a shared Islamic tradition; the other between an Islam of individual creativity and one authorized by religious leaders – as generating our empirical and analytical framework. The framework has "worked" analytically because it corresponds to the lived conditions of many Muslim believers, for whom Islam lies between the particular and the shared, and between the creative and the imposed.

More was to come in the anthropology of Islam, however, because we also began to take better account of transnational connections and global movements, dimensions downplayed in the work carried out in the late 1960s and 1970s. For many of us, these connections surfaced in the midst of our fieldwork. I was working in the Gayo highlands of Sumatra in the 1980s when I was astonished to find that in 1928, a handful of religious poets had their work printed in Cairo as *al-Tafsir al-Gayo*, a Gayo scriptural interpretation written in Arabic script. This book was the first, and for decades the only, printed Gayo-language text (and still the only one in Arabic script). The religious poets working in the highlands were able to have their work printed in Egypt because they belonged to active networks of study and publication devoted to promoting modernist views of Islam. These Malay- and Arabic-language networks stretched from Cairo and Mecca to Johor and Java.

By the 1990s, then, two intellectual developments had begun to define a new anthropology of Islam: a politically aware focus on religious inter-pretations and practices, and a historically aware focus on broad spatial patterns and movements. These two developments made possible a bet-ter grasping of the object that is Islam, in which making connections across time and space are intrinsic to its epistemology. They provided new ways for anthropologists to work with scholars in religious studies and history, and for colleagues working in different parts of the world, often in societies once deemed marginal to the field of Islamic Studies, to collaborate. Scholars working in India and the Malay world talked with those working in Africa, and together charted Indian Ocean crossings and communications that also brought in students of Oman and Yemen.[2]

---

[2] For a recent study in history and anthropology across the Indian Ocean, see Ho (2006); a recent collection edited by Simpson and Kresse (2008) provides additional perspectives.

Scholars working in Pakistan and Algeria talked with those working in Britain and France, and charted continuing post-colonial institutional connections.[3] Islam could no longer plausibly be equated with "Middle Eastern Studies" or viewed solely through an Arabic-language lens (or at best an Arabic–Persian–Turkish one) but had to be seen as a set of processes and practices, texts and interpretations, that were constantly in conflict with, and also adapted to, culturally specific ways of living and thinking located around the globe.[4]

In each of the following chapters I approach a set of practices and processes: learning, sacrificing, or mobilizing. In each case I start with shared sets of ideas and methods in order to provide a broad-brush sense of the texts and traditions on which Muslims draw. Then I examine divergent pathways of interpretation and practice in order to exemplify the latitude available within Islam. I often begin with my own work in Southeast Asia and in Europe because doing so allows me to draw on my own engagement with these issues. I then look to colleagues working in other places (or other times), to illustrate both (empirically) the range of possibilities of Islamic interpretation and practice, and (analytically) the broad applicability of the approach outlined here. I try to provide three levels of analysis for readers: an unpacking of the basic features of Islamic religious life, an exposition of the processes that generate diversity across Muslim societies, and an example of the understandings that come from the kind of close-in and comparative perspective characterizing contemporary anthropology.

The scope of this volume seems vast – multiple practices, many societies – but in fact it is quite restricted. It is not an exhaustive survey but an analytical exposition in which I draw on some studies but, regrettably, leave out many others. It is also not about the entire lives of Muslims

---

[3] On Britain–South Asia, see Werbner (2003); on France–Algeria see Silverstein (2004).
[4] This point was made early and elegantly by Richard Bulliet (1994).

but about a certain range of activities, those in which women and men orient themselves toward their sense of a religious tradition. Consequently, I have relatively little to say about certain other important areas of anthropological concern. For example, anthropologists working in the Middle East have, for very good reasons, made tribes and politics central to their work (Abu-Lughod 1989; Caton 2005; Dresch and Haykel 1995; Shryock 1997), but tribal politics is little discussed here. Again, major recent contributions to our understandings of gender and sexuality have come from anthropologists working in Muslim contexts (Abu-Lughod 1986; Boellstorff 2005; Peletz 1996); these issues arise here in discussions of key Islamic practices, such as in Chapter 3 on practices of piety and in Chapter 7 on judging, in full awareness that these discussions fall far short of adequately examining gender and sexuality dimensions of these Muslims' lives. Finally, the very wealth of work in the past decade prevents me from citing all the important studies in what I am calling a new anthropology of Islam, even on the themes discussed here. For all the omissions I beg my colleagues' understanding.

I begin, as do many Muslims in their own lives, with learning.

TWO

Learning

The first revelation came in the form of a presence that overwhelmed a middle-aged man, Muhammad ibn Abdullah, as he sat meditating in a cave near Mecca in 610 CE. The presence was conveyed through sight, sense, and sound; it filled the sky, pressed down upon the man, and ordered him to "Recite!" Refusing, hesitating, he eventually obeyed, reciting what he had heard from God through Gabriel to those who would listen.

I begin with this moment because Muslims do so, by learning to recite and by privileging this point of contact with the divine. From revelation begins learning, and from revelation learning diverges along multiple channels of interpretive discovery. The science of that learning requires following a particular sort of historical discipline, one that charts the chains of transmission that mark those channels.

These chains began with recitation. The most important element of Islamic knowledge, the Qur'an, resulted from men and women collecting the many recitations (*qirâ'a* – notice the relatedness of the two words, from the Arabic root q-r-') given to Muhammad. Muslims today begin to learn their religion – as children, converts, or in a return to the faith – by learning how to speak the Qur'an.[1] For the great majority of Muslims,

---

[1] On the oral character of Islam, explained in a comparative context, see Graham (1987). A capacious approach to the spoken and written Qur'an is offered by Michael Sells (1999).

this process begins with mastering the arts of pronouncing, recognizing, and writing the letters of the Arabic alphabet. Although most Muslims do not have a speaking or reading command of Arabic, most come to acquire a working knowledge of its sounds and shapes and of the meanings of many words; most will learn some of the chapters or *suras* (sing.: *sûra*) that make up the Qur'an. Even native speakers of an Arabic dialect, if they wish to recite verses correctly, must learn the classical form of the language and the acceptable ways of pronouncing Qur'anic forms of Arabic.

Islamic knowledge, even for the most modern of Muslim thinkers, is first (in one's development) and foremost (in one's priorities) a knowing how, rather than a knowing about: knowing how to recite and read scripture, learning how to correctly carry out the many acts of worship and service to God, or *ibadat* (*'ibâdât*), that describe an Islamic life. One may learn about the deeper meanings of verses and of actions, but only once one has taken them on as one's own, embodied them as part of one's repertoire of actions. And here is where our observations of interpretive practices come into play.

Interpretive practice

Let us consider an example, a tiny unit of Islam, the very short chapter of the Qur'an called Surat al-Ikhlas, and see how far we can follow its chains of interpretive practice. This chapter comes toward the end of the Qur'an, bearing the number 112, because of its length. When the revelations were collected they were placed in order from the longest to the shortest, placing this chapter near the end of the Qur'an, even though it was one of the earliest to be revealed. It reads:

> *Qul hu wallâhu ahad*   Say, He is God, one,
> *allâhu s-samad*   God the everlasting refuge,
> *lam yalid wa lam yûlad*   Neither begetting nor begotten,
> *wa lam yakul lahu kufuwan ahad*   and having as an equal none.

The Sura affirms the single most important value of Islam, the unity (*tawhîd*) of God. In a few short lines, it unpacks the dimensions of this unity. God is eternal as well as an indestructible refuge (the word *samad* has both senses), and He is prior to all things, the Creator of all. He created all but is not a father, and here the verse underscores the monotheism of Islam in contrast to Christian ideas of God the Father and of the Trinity. God is without equal. This proposition places Islam in clear opposition to polytheism (*shirk*), which is the act of attributing divine attributes to a being other than God. Polytheism is one of the gravest sins in Islam.

The chapter begins by commanding the reciter: "Say!" (*Qul*). Just as Muhammad began his career as Messenger by hearing the order to "Recite," so the worshipper begins this recitation by quoting God when ordering us to restate the fundamental truths contained in the chapter. The chapter is thus a kind of *da`wa*, a call or outreach to other Muslims, reminding them of the bases of their religion. The title of the chapter, "Sincerity" (*ikhlâs*), adds an additional value to its message, that of sincerity, humility, and authenticity, the appropriate attitude of the worshipper before God.

So far, so textual, but how do Muslims come to appreciate and appropriate this short unit of revelation? Because it is one of the shortest chapters, children will learn to memorize it early in their lives as they begin to assemble their repertoires for worship, or *salat* (*salâh*). They will also hear it explained countless times – by parents, in school, at a lesson held after morning or afternoon prayer, and sometimes they will learn that because it sums up so many key ideas it encapsulates all the Qur'an. Children also hear adults in their community chant it aloud during congregational prayer, on Fridays or on any occasion when two or more people pray together. Usually they will hear it chanted in a straightforward way, with little embellishment. Hearing these repeated chants gives the child a basic idea about the melody, timbre, and rhythm (through paying attention to long and short vowels) that they should use in reciting from the Qur'an.

Children also hear the very different rhythm of the *adhân*, the call to prayer that is performed prior to each prayer time. In singing out the call to prayer, whether in a field, at a mosque, or over a loudspeaker to all in a neighborhood, the reciter typically draws out some vowels to great lengths and pronounces others quickly. He begins with repeated cries of "God is great" (*Allâhu akbar*): twice pronounced very quickly, in a rising intonation, to grab attention (and, in the morning, to wake up those still sleeping), and then twice with the long vowel in Allâh drawn out.

The Surat al-Ikhlas is recited on other occasions as well, for meditation or to achieve a practical end. And here we move from general features of Islam to observations from anthropological fieldwork, beginning with my own. Beginning in the late 1970s, I have worked with Gayo-speaking people living in the central highlands of Aceh province, on the northern tip of Sumatra (Bowen 1993, 2003). The Gayo have been Muslims for centuries, probably since the seventeenth-century reign of the Acehnese Sultan, Iskandar Muda, but written accounts of the area date only from the late nineteenth century. Beginning in the 1930s, reform-minded Gayo religious scholars who adhered to the Indonesia-wide modernist or "young group" (Indonesian *kaum muda*) position have challenged the way that Gayo have performed religious duties. A vigorous debate continues between modernist and traditionalist (*kaum tua*, "old group") scholars over these issues. In their public behavior, residents of the main highlands town of Takèngën tend to follow modernist prescriptions, while in most Gayo villages, men and women carry out ritual practices of long standing and often identify themselves as belonging to the "old group."

When I lived in the Gayo village of Isak, I heard the Surat al-Ikhlas recited repeatedly after Friday worship in the mosque, as a way of meditating that involves repeated chanting or *dhikr*. I also heard it recited at ritual meals held in conjunction with Islamic feast-days, or to help the spirit of a recently deceased woman or man navigate through the trials and tribulations that occur after death.

Indeed, the all-night sessions of chanting verses that follow a death in that community are called *samadiyah*, from the last word in the chapter's second line: *samad*. In the sessions I attended, men and women, seated in the home of the deceased, chanted the chapter forty or sixty times, first quickly and then slowly. (They said it more times if fewer people were present, so that the total amount of merit generated would be about the same for every deceased person.) Many of my acquaintances stated that because the chapter contained so many of the truths in the Qur'an, it had the value of one-third of the entire Qur'an. The assembled villagers chanted many other verses as well, both short, complete chapters, and segments from longer chapters, including portions of Sura al-Baqarah. Verse 255 of this chapter is called the "Throne Verse" for its invocations of God's majesty, reminding us in part that: "His Throne encompasses the heavens and the earth, and their preservation does not burden Him. He is the Most High, the Most Great." Gayo (and Muslims elsewhere) recite the verse to give themselves power. During the late 1940s struggle against the Dutch, some Gayo men would chant both the Throne Verse and the Surat al-Ikhlas as a way of keeping bullets away from them. Today some people recite them as parts of charms or spells.

The average adult in this Sumatran village has at her or his command a great deal of scripture, and knows when and how to recite it. Villagers also argue about which uses are correct and which are not allowable. Many Muslims find the very idea of chanting verses for the dead, a practice found in many Muslim-majority societies in the world, to contradict the reliable report (or *hadîth sahîh*) that the Prophet Muhammad once said that after death one no longer could aid one's relatives:

Three things accompany the deceased [to the grave]: his family, his wealth, and his deeds. Two return and one remains: his family and wealth return; his deeds remain.[2]

---

[2] For a lengthy discussion of the texts and contexts for this example, see Bowen (1993: 251–72).

In other words, after death you only benefit or suffer from what you have done during life; your family cannot help you, and your wealth is for naught. When relatives gather to chant for your benefit, they are at best deceiving themselves, and at worst contravening God's explicit commands, say these Muslims (Bowen 1993: 264–72).

In the Gayo highlands, especially in the 1920s and 1930s, Muslim teachers who wished to alert people to the impropriety of many of their practices wrote and sang poems, including those published in Cairo that I mentioned earlier. These poems often began with a verse from the Qur'an or with a report from the Prophet Muhammad, and then developed the idea in the Gayo language. To discourage people from chanting for the deceased, they would recite the above hadith, and then expand on its meaning, concluding with the message:

If you die and your relatives give alms (*sedekah*), the merit does not reach you.

Did you not hear the words of God, "a person shall have only as s/he has labored?"

By beginning with a statement attributed to the Prophet, and ending with a verse from the Qur'an (the part in quotations, recited in Arabic), these change-oriented teachers secured their message with scriptural proofs (*dalîl*). By singing Gayo-language poetry in between the hadith and the Qur'anic verse, they appealed to ordinary people.

Notice how much ground we have covered by beginning with this small unit of knowledge, the short Qur'anic chapter "Sincerity," and then tracing the diverse ways in which Muslims understand and use it. It functions in everyday life as a unit in worship and rituals, and as a summary of basic Islamic teachings, suitable for expanding for teaching and discussion. Its repeated recitation in the dhikr-chanting sessions (dhikr means "remembrance," here of God) brings men and women to a state of transcendence and nearness to God. Some people believe that the reciting transmits spiritual merit to other people, or that it converts

God's blessings into bodily protection. Others disagree. Its very range of uses gives rise to further citations of verses and hadith in commentary and debate about the proper uses of verses. Knowledge may begin with learning how to recite a small snippet of revelation, but it quickly expands outward and onward to shape a wealth of religious and ritual activities and to incite people to engage in debates about the power and limits of religious acts.

Learning religion begins, then, in mastering the many ways to draw on God's revelations. Revelations tell you how to pray, how to carry out the pilgrimage to Mecca, and how to perform the many ordinary acts of everyday life that could be seen as having a religious dimension: how to enter and leave a mosque, how to greet other people, how to dress and eat properly. This knowledge is practical knowledge. Of course, there are also basic tenets to learn: the five pillars of faith, the required beliefs, and so on, but these are the easier elements of basic knowledge. God's major gift to humans is scripture; humans' major obligation to God is to follow His commands. Humans must thus begin by mastering scripture and learning how to follow those commands, before delving into the subtleties of theology, ethics, or jurisprudence. And indeed, that is how schooling progresses – from knowing how, to, eventually, knowing about.

Islamic history, too, is a history of revelation (or *tanzîl*). Two methodological points follow. First, the facts of where and when God chose to send down a revelation may have theological and thus normative relevance for Muslims. When Muslims turn to the historicity of the Qur'an it is not to debunk it (although some non-Muslim historians have tried that) but to ask whether it makes a difference that, say, the verse permitting men to take more than one wife was revealed after wars had left a number of widows and orphans. Do these circumstances of revelation mean that polygamy is only permitted under such conditions of demographic imbalance? Or do they mean that such was an opportune moment to make believers aware of an option always available to them?

The precise historicity of revelation also gives a high degree of religious value to the exact words used by God, through Gabriel, to speak to Muhammad. Revelation was aural, and transmission has continued to take place in an aural/oral mode. Writing was never absent (a point to which I return below), and Muslims recognize as legitimate a number of slightly differing written forms of the Qur'an. But today, just as centuries ago, Muslims use written scriptural texts in order to learn to recite them. The precise form of recitation continues to refer back to the moment of revelation, the presence of the spoken word (Graham 1987).

The sounds of revelation share in this value of originality. Throughout the world of Muslim-majority societies, many boys and girls, and men and women, learn not only to recite the Qur'an but also to recite it melodically, using certain rules of pronunciation (*tajwîd*). Living far from the Arabic-speaking world, Indonesians enthusiastically enter local, national, and international contests (and do quite well), and they often raise the question: can we not use Indonesian melodies? The authoritative response has been to say no, because the Qur'an was revealed to Arabic speakers – and indeed, some Indonesian reciters will practice sounds from secular Arabic music in order to become habituated to Arabic singing styles (Gade 2004).

This epistemology of revelation – valuing the precise act of aural revelation, repeating the act of oral transmission – derives from the ideology of absolute and unmediated *presence* that founds the religion. Gabriel appeared and spoke directly to Muhammad, and he to others, and so on. Muhammad did not interpret the words, and as an illiterate man he could not have created them; he is a vessel of God's message.

But Muhammad provides guidance to Muslims in a second way as well, through his own statements and actions, which are considered to be inspired by God. If reports, or hadiths (sing.: *hadith*, pl.: *ahâdîth*) of what Muhammad did or said are transmitted reliably over the generations, then they can be taken as a second source of divine guidance. Above, I showed how one of these reports was incorporated into modernist poetry aimed at reforming ritual practice. But these Prophetic reports also provided the basic building blocks of religious practice. Consider the example of worship. The Qur'an does not provide a precise plan for daily worship; Muslims rely on the example of Muhammad. But Muhammad did not leave behind a manual or a complete list of how to worship at each time of the day, how to perform ablutions, what to do on feast days, and so forth. Rather, we have reports of what his Companions saw him do, or the responses he gave to questions about proper worship.

These responses often are quite specific. For example, a reliable report has it that a man once approached him as he stood in his pulpit in the mosque of Medina to pose a question about how to perform the prayer said at the end of the day. He asked: "What is your opinion regarding the night prayer?," to which Muhammad replied: "Two prayer cycles (*raka`a*) at a time, and when one of you knows that the dawn [is near], he should add one more cycle, thereby causing his worship to have an odd number."

This report was transmitted orally from the first hearer to a second one, and so forth. Eventually it was included in the collection of reports gathered and evaluated by the scholar Bukhari, whose collection most Muslims in the Sunni tradition consider to be authoritative (Masud, Messick, and Powers 1996: 6). This report about the night prayer, when combined with other reports about prayer at other times of the day, or other aspects of prayer, yielded a model for worship that is the basis for the prayer manuals of today.

Even when Islamic knowledge takes the form of systematic manuals, however, its validity continues to rest on the reliable transmission of the Prophet's statements and actions to us, today. For this reason, scholars have placed great importance on tracing the chain or *isnad* (*isnâd*) of reliable transmitters in order to evaluate the degree of certainty to be attributed to each report. By the eighth century CE, a Prophetic report was considered complete only when accompanied by its isnad, the list of people who heard and passed along the report, and this coupling of a report with its genealogy continues to this day. Each genealogy begins with the name of a contemporary of the Prophet, who heard or saw an event, followed by the person to whom he or she transmitted the report, and so on, until the point at which the report was committed to writing. The character and reliability of each person in the chain was a matter for serious investigation and debate, for on these qualities rests the strength of the report itself. Hadith scholars distinguish between sound (*sahih*) and weak (*da`if*) reports, with gradations in between.

Although these reports were transmitted orally, in fact they also were written down. Indeed, for most of Islamic history, the study of hadith first and foremost consisted of copying down reports from a teacher, including the genealogy that gave the report its authenticity. Some hadith scholars prepared written compilations of the hadiths that they considered to be sound. By the thirteenth century, most scholars in the Sunni community accepted six such compilations as authoritative. The authority of these compilations gradually superseded the authority of an individual teacher, whose own personal compilation the student would copy.

And yet hearing hadiths remained far more authoritative than merely reading them from a book. Richard Bulliet (1994: 19–20) relates that in the tenth-century city of Nishapur the compilation made by Bukhari was widely available. Nonetheless, fifteen students of hadith made the 200-mile journey from Nishapur to a village in order to hear a man read the text aloud. This man, al-Kushmaihani, was the last living man to have written his copy according to dictation from a teacher who had made his copy in a class taught by Bukhari himself. It was this short and direct isnad, based on the practice of hearing and then copying a text, that had attracted these students.

In other domains, too, a dual approach to knowledge transmission remains: the oral is valued explicitly, but reliance on the written is its sure companion. Brinkley Messick (1993) traces the coexistence of these two epistemologies in legal and commercial affairs from the early days of Islam down to the present. On the one hand, all transactions, from marriages to land sales, must be witnessed. Witnesses may be called on to testify to what they have seen before a judge. On the other hand, written documents always have been relied on, and early in Islamic history, model contracts in written form appeared. In South Yemen, where Messick worked in the 1970s and 1980s, ordinary people highly valued and protected documents attesting to land purchases and inheritance divisions, and these documents carried legal weight, despite the sustained importance of witnessing. Understandably, when they were first introduced, photocopying machines proved very popular.

But what is written on these documents is restricted to matters likely to arise in the future. Marriage contracts, for example, are not intended to be complete records of what is agreed on or paid by one party to another, but are crafted with future disputes in mind. They routinely record the amount of the *mahr*, the gift given by the groom to the bride, because the mahr is a required part of the marriage and because in Yemen it is rarely paid in full (or at all) until divorce, or the death of the husband. At divorce or death, disputes are likely to arise over the amount promised, and that is when one produces a written document. Other payments made at the time of the marriage may well be greater in value than the mahr, but they are not recorded because they are unlikely to be the object of future claims. (I find the same distinction on many Islamic marriage contracts written in the United States and England today: the mahr, but no other gifts, are written down, sometimes creating legal difficulties in civil courts.)

Hearing and writing thus have quite specific values in Islamic knowledge. Muhammad's aural reception of Gabriel's speech began a chain of verbal witnessing, linking hearers across the centuries. As Brinkley Messick argues, the "logocentrism" that Jacques Derrida claimed characterized the Western tradition of knowledge, meaning the privileging of speech over writing, also shapes Islamic knowledge. In Islam, however, that privileging of speech rests on a very explicit foundation: God's acts of speaking. This emphasis on the spoken and heard word then structures other ways of reliably knowing things about the world: you know something because someone has witnessed it, and that person has orally passed on the knowledge to a second, and so forth, down to you. Reliable knowledge involves aural witnessing. And yet writing is always there as well, because it allows one to fix sound in unchangeable form, to link successive events of speaking (as when one copies a spoken text, which then enables another to recite it to a third party), and to resolve future disputes.

But how did we come to understand these dimensions of Islam? Only when anthropologists and historians paid greater attention to the diversity of understandings and practices inside and around what had been taken to be relatively simple religious acts: reciting, hearing, or writing. And only when we began to look at diversities and debates in what had been thought to be relatively simple places: villages or poor urban neighborhoods. Debating hadith and arguing salat turned out to be pastimes of ordinary men and women, as well as of scholars.

Schooling

Traditional Islamic schooling, too, begins with aural ways of learning scripture, and as schools have changed and diversified, they have not abandoned this central component. Messick (1993) chronicles changes in modes of schooling in Yemen, from a traditional method of memorizing to expanded forms of study. In the early years of the twentieth century, boys (and some girls) would spend a few years in daily study of the Qur'an. Gathered around the feet of their master, they would take dictation of a section of scripture on their erasable lesson board, memorize it on their own, and then recite it from memory to the master's satisfaction.

Pupils who succeeded at memorizing a certain portion of the Qur'an would enjoy the celebration of their *khâtam*, the closing of the first part of their schooling, and they would then proceed to study at the madrasa, a word that simply means "school" in Arabic, but that often designates places for religious learning. Quite likely, the madrasa would meet in a part of the local mosque. Madrasa teaching (*darasa* – note the same d-r-s root) involved a text, often memorized by pupils, and a commentary, delivered by the teacher. Students were expected to be able to repeat the text back to the teacher, and this ability was the measure of success. But the students also learned from the commentary and could pose questions to the teacher. Understanding the meaning of the text became part of the curriculum in this way, as pupils learned commentaries on fixed texts.

Throughout the Islamic world, learning in formal settings has combined in different ways these two activities: memorizing texts and learning from commentaries. The Yemeni method stands between the great emphasis on Qur'an memorization (for example in older Moroccan schools; Eickelman 1985) and the focus on abilities to engage in debate (for example in Iranian seminaries; Mottahedeh 1985). Students also made their own manuscript copies of the texts being studied in order to memorize and discuss meanings on their own; as with the transmission of Prophetic traditions, writing acted as a material support to the privileged oral forms of knowing and learning.

New methods of learning entered all these societies at various times in the nineteenth and twentieth centuries, but these methods have augmented, rather than replaced, older ones. The nineteenth-century Ottoman *Tanzimat* reforms were intended to introduce ordering (or *nizâm*) into public life, in part by creating new public schools and courts to compete with, and eventually to replace, the older madrasas and religious courts. The new schools taught Turkish language, sciences, and history as well as religion and Arabic. These projects were realized only slowly, and outlasted the Ottoman Empire. By the mid-1920s, the new Yemeni ruler had opened a school that taught Islam as well as secular subjects in a way that continued to reflect the nizâm reforms. Rather than allowing students to work through a series of texts at their own rhythms, students were assigned to grades, each with its distinct

curriculum. Instruction was in front of a class, with teachers using black-
boards, and students sat in rows, listening.

The general pattern can be found around the world. Elementary
Islamic schools teach pupils to recite and write Arabic, guide them
in memorizing the Qur'an, and perhaps offer basic instruction about
Islamic norms and rituals. There they stop. Some students continue on
to study with an individual teacher or in an advanced school, where they
study the interpretation of Qur'anic verses and perhaps the science of
hadith. But knowing how to recite the Qur'an remains at the heart of
growing up a Muslim – so much so that secularist Turkey, in an effort
to assure the predominance of a Turkish, over an Islamic, identity, pro-
hibits scholars from teaching Qur'an recitation in mosques and schools
to students under the age of twelve.

Written materials play a role in Islamic primary schools, where pupils
might read from small books about Islam under the guidance of a teacher.
Such books treat the topics of tawhîd, the oneness of God, by listing His
names and attributes, and the basic principles of worship. The languages,
scripts, and precise contents of these books vary across Muslim societies
and have changed over time, but such simple books continue to circulate
widely, and for many Muslims, particularly those in rural areas, they
remain the major literary source of religious knowledge. For example,
throughout the Malay-speaking world, pupils in rural Islamic schools in
the 1920s or 1930s read from books organized as sets of questions and
answers, a long-standing Islamic form of transmitting knowledge. The
students read about the proper ways to carry out worship, fasting, and
so forth, in Arabic-script Malay or *Jawi*. Their great-grandchildren in
the twenty-first century might buy similar books in the marketplace, but
these are written in Latin script and are more likely to take one of two
other forms: either a simple list of ritual obligations, or a set of step-
by-step instructions, with diagrams, for correct ablutions and prayer.
Today, however, these books are intended for casual use and study, as
reminders of theology and ritual practice. In most towns and cities in

Muslim-majority countries, reading has become more a private occupation than a collective endeavor.

Qur'anic schools continue to exist in Muslim-majority societies. In southern Morocco, for example, these schools attract many pupils, either to supplement, or to provide an alternative to, their education at the local modern primary school. These students speak a Berber language, and it is through their years in the Qur'anic schools that they learn how to pronounce and write Arabic letters, and to recite verses from the Qur'an (Houtsonen 1994). Students work under a single teacher, and are grouped by their level of mastery of the Qur'an, rather than by age or by number of years of study. Parents may choose to send their children to a Qur'anic school rather than a modern school because of the higher costs and lower evident payoffs of modern education. They also appreciate that children learn how to act in an Islamic way in the older schools. The Qur'anic schools stand for continuity and for village ways vis-à-vis the new, individualistic lives of city folk. Even many of the parents in this region who eventually send their children to modern schools have them begin at the Qur'anic school to acquire a proper moral education, which includes respect for authority, enforced by strict discipline. Teachers at these schools enjoy a general prestige in the community and often work on the side as healers or prayer leaders, or help others to read and write documents.

These schools, with their emphasis on reciting and memorizing scripture, have in some places changed in style but have continued to be important even in formal, modern educational contexts. In Egypt in the 1820s and 1830s, the modernizing Muhammad `Ali made the local private religious school, the *kuttabs* (*kuttâb*), the base of a system for drawing Egyptians into advanced education – though he also used them as recruiting grounds for military service, which action caused their popularity to plummet. Throughout the nineteenth century, the kuttabs "remained the country's only formal source of entrée into the literate tradition" (Starrett 1998: 29), and the British, fearing to tamper with religion, retained the religious elements of the kuttabs into the twentieth century. Although the kuttabs declined in importance, relative to the new type of primary schools, which alone provided entry into advanced "secular" schooling, by the 1980s the Egyptian government had begun to revive the kuttabs (primarily as after-school places for study) as a way of promoting religious education. The state also promoted memorization and recitation of the Qur'an through contests, as do the governments of most Muslim-majority societies.

Today, however, the ways in which most Muslim students learn about Islam go far beyond techniques of recitation and memorization, in their formal schooling and in their use of other forms of knowledge transmission.

Modern madrasas

Although there is no single form of "modern madrasa," roughly comparable ways of teaching and learning spread throughout Asia and Africa beginning in the mid-nineteenth century, in the wake of the colonial implantation of European-style schools (and reflecting the Ottoman school reforms). These new Islamic schools had fixed curricula, separate classes for students of different levels of study, and a set academic year. One received a certificate attesting to the completion of studies at the school, rather than one attesting to one's study with a single teacher. Some schools developed their own distinctive approaches to Islam and produced networks of "daughter" schools that followed similar approaches.

Nowhere have these schools and networks been more forcefully effective in transforming Islamic learning than in South Asia. The "spark" that led to the rapid creation of many new schools was the 1857 Mutiny against British rule, with its violent attacks and counter-attacks. British massacres of Muslims and closings of schools were heaviest in Delhi, and many religious scholars, ulama (`ulamâ') left that city for smaller towns, where they would be able to rebuild centers of learning further away from

British power. These ulama, soured on the possibility of working with the British, preferred to develop spaces in which they and their pupils could live their lives in accord with Islamic social norms and their own desire for spirituality, rather than to enter into government service or engage in political activity.

The most important of these new centers was the Daru'l-'Ulûm school, founded in 1867 in the north-central Indian town of Deoband. The school emulated the organization of British schools, with classrooms, a professional staff, and prizes for top scores at the annual examinations (Metcalf 1982: 87–137). But more importantly, its students learned a fixed curriculum by studying with a number of teachers, rather than seeking out a single individual with whom to work. Students came to the school in Deoband already proficient in Arabic and the Qur'an. In Deoband they studied from a curriculum developed at Lucknow in the late eighteenth century (and still used today) called the Dars-i Nizami, but they spent considerably more time than had been the case elsewhere on the study of hadith and jurisprudence. The language of instruction was Urdu rather than the court language of Persian or the many other vernaculars. The school thus contributed to Urdu's emergence as the shared language of Muslims in northern India.

Some of the early students went on to found new schools, affiliated with the Deobandi Daru'l-'Ulum, in which the same or similar curricula were taught. Within ten years of Deoband's founding, about a dozen daughter schools had been started by its graduates, and by 1900 another dozen or so had appeared across northern India (an area including today's Pakistan and Bangladesh). Adding to the new ties of learning were ties of financial support, due to a new method of financing the schools. Whereas older religious schools depended on the income from long-standing pious trusts (*awqâf,* sing.: *waqf*) or the support of rich patrons, the new Deobandi schools depended on public contributions. Thus were born the international networks of financial support and schools that continue to underwrite much Islamic educational activity.

The major teachers in the Deobandi schools combined the two Islamic roles of the *mufti* and the sheikh: the person so knowledgeable in Islamic legal sciences that he can dispense a legal opinion (*fatwâ*); and the person so adept in the pursuit of mystical knowledge through a Sufi path that he becomes a leader of a local Sufi lodge (Metcalf 1982: 138–97). They thus followed the path of the great scholar al-Ghazzali (d. 1111) in uniting the pursuit of shariah (*sharî`a* – norms or law) and *tarîqa* (the Sufi path).

The Deoband teachers followed, and continue to follow, the *Hanafi* (*Hanafî*) legal school, one of the four major Sunni schools or traditions (*madâhib*, sing.: *madhhab*), and they teach students to follow or conform to (*taqlîd*) that school. Each such school draws on the Qur'ân, the hadith, reasoning by analogy (*qiyâs*) to new situations, and the consensus of scholars (*ijmâ`*). Their position made the Deobandi scholars conservative in their jurisprudence, in that they urged Muslims to follow a single scholar (*`âlim*) or a single set of scholars, ulama, rather than drawing their own conclusions from scripture, or from a variety of opinions. They argued that Muslims needed to find certainty in a time of social disorder (*fitna*) such as that which bedeviled late nineteenth-century British India. This position meant that the Deobandis often did not quote the scriptural sources from which they drew, lest people begin to debate among themselves over the choice of source.

Their approach to learning set the Deobandis apart from the "modernist" scholars led by Sayyid Ahmad Khan, who urged Muslims to base their decisions on Scripture and to not limit their interpretations to the four major legal schools. But Deobandis and modernists shared a number of concerns, and their overlap points to a general trend in modern South Asian Islamic learning. They all exercised *ijtihad* (*ijtihâd*), independent legal reasoning, to arrive at new solutions to problems. They agreed that Muslims should base their religious practices on a proper sense of tawhîd, God's unity, and on that ground strongly opposed the observance of saints' birthdays and making pilgrimages to the graves of holy men. *This* position placed both the Deobandis and the modernists on the same side in their opposition to the Ahl-e Sunnat va Jama'a tradition, better known as "Barelwi" Sufis, from the scholar Ahmad Riza Khan Barelwi (1856–1921). The Barelwis stressed the importance of venerating saints and of seeking intercession from saints for the benefit of the living.

There thus emerged, by the early twentieth century in northern South Asia, a triangle of positions on religious learning and practice that had been generated by distinctions along two dimensions. First, Deobandi scholars urged their followers to rely only on the Hanafi legal school and thereby differed from modernists, who urged Muslims to rely only on Qur'an and hadith. Second, Deobandis and modernists alike opposed those movements and individuals who venerated saints. But as I noted above, opposing saint worship did not mean opposing all forms of Sufi devotion, and a Deobandi teacher could also be an instructor in Sufi meditation and recitation.

This fertile triangle of opposing positions – Deobandis, modernists, and Sufis – has generated a wide array of contemporary movements and organizations, to which we turn in Chapter 8, but here we note that most of the 35,000 madrasas in India today trace their affiliations back to one of these earlier positions and that they grew out of an environment that allowed both mysticism and intellectual pursuits.

The original schools spawned new satellite centers; one being the Nadwat al-`ulama' in Lucknow, India, which produced the proselytizing movement called the Tablighi Jama'at.[3] The Lucknow school and the Tablighi movement emphasized practicing piety and proper Islamic comportment, inspired by Prophetic hadith. The tandem quickly branched out over the region. Mareike Winkelmann (2008) studied a women's madrasa that was established in 1996 in New Delhi and that is located near the city's office of the Tablighi Jama`at. The madrasa continues the Nadwat and Tablighi emphasis on hadith, as well as basic study of Hanafi *fiqh*. In public sessions, to which local women who are not resident at

---

[3] For an insider's view of a day in the life of this school, see Nadwi (2007).

the school are also invited, students comment in Urdu on Arabic texts, notably texts on proper behavior.

Indeed, much of what women learn at the school is how to behave correctly, the proper *adab*. They fashion new ways of being in the world, by being given reminders and examples, very much as do initiates into Catholic schools and orders.[4] Winkelmann tells of a janitor in the school who began to show interest in the teaching sessions and was taught to read and write Urdu and Arabic. She began to modify her clothing, changing from brightly colored garments to white ones, and moved from leaving her head uncovered to wearing a scarf. Men from the Tablighi prepare the meals, inverting the usual gender roles, and both men (at their own school) and the women are taught to marry without a high dowry, an exception to local practice.

Modern madrasas have developed a variety of curricula, in particular regarding the weight to be given to secular subjects versus classical Arabic education.[5] Ronald Lukens-Bull (2005) has explored the range of variation on this dimension in contemporary Java. Some Islamic boarding schools, called *pesantren* on Java, resemble advanced madrasas of the sort described above for Yemen. They make writing central to the learning process. Students come to the An Nur school, for example, equipped with classical texts and fine-tipped pens. The teacher reads several lines of an Arabic text and then delivers a commentary in Javanese. The students copy the commentary between the lines of their individual text, in Arabic-script Javanese. At other times, students gather and discuss the meanings of these commentaries; what might seem to be rote learning can in fact serve as the starting point for further discussions.

In the terminology in use on Java, the An Nur school is considered as a traditional (*salaf*) school, as distinguished from modern (*khalaf*)

---

[4] Compare the study of Catholic nuns by Rebecca Lester (2005).
[5] See the essays on madrasas in Hefner and Zaman (2007) and Noor, Sikand, and van Bruinessen (2008).

alternatives. Traditional schools may also teach learning mystical practices, such as repetitive reciting of verses, as well as forms of Javanese martial arts. "Traditional" in the Javanese context means conserving older ways of learning scripture and shaping the body and self to religious ends. Modern schools alone are (somewhat confusingly) called "madrasah" in Indonesian (and scholars often add the "-h" to distinguish the Indonesian usage from the broader Arabic meaning). Beginning in 1975, the Indonesian government provided incentives for all religious schools to add more secular education to their curricula; many did so, and their graduates are allowed to proceed to university.

Learning Islam as a system

Above, we considered the ways in which modern Islamic schools have brought together classical studies and the pursuit of one's pathway toward God in a format that resembles European schools. As we just saw, this major shift in the way Muslims learn has not done away with the importance of recitation and memorization. Nor have books supplanted the ulama as the source of knowledge: one reads under the direction of scholars and teachers, and one engages in devotional practices under the guidance of a sheikh.

In most of these madrasas, pupils learn about God's commands and jurisprudence, ritual and family life, public law and ways of teaching others. They do not learn about "Islam" as a system of ideas, nor about competing systems of Islamic ideas, "our Islam" versus "theirs." But in the twentieth century, an increasing number of Muslims began to read in newspapers and books about competing ideas of Islam. After World War II, rapidly rising numbers of Muslims attended secondary and post-secondary schools, and some of them wrote about Islam in a way that reflected their education in other, secular systems of learning, from engineering to politics.

A number of scholars have pointed to the importance of mass higher education in changing how Islam looks to Muslims: less as a series of fixed texts controlled by scholars, and more as a set of propositions and institutions, understandable by anyone with a general education. Increasingly available printed materials and electronic forms of communication have altered the character of learning by altering the nature of authority. I do not agree with the blanket claim that religious knowledge has been radically democratized, that anyone can make claims regardless of the opinions of ulama, nor that the technology of printing has been the major cause of this shift in epistemology. Rather, a number of associated developments, especially during the last half of the twentieth century, have reshaped both the way some Muslims come to know Islam and the ways they can transmit their ideas and emotions to others.

We will encounter many of these modes of apprehending Islam in later chapters. Here I wish simply to underscore the novelty of print and electronic media that seek to explain the "meaning of Islam": the beliefs, the acts of worship, and the nature of shariah. These books and other materials are ubiquitous not only in the new territories of Islam such as Western Europe, North America, and Japan, but also in the old territories, such as Pakistan, Indonesia, and Egypt. For young men and women growing up in a social environment where Islam was more or less taken for granted, such books would not have had the prominent place they now do. But we all live in a "secular age," in the sense that even devout believers know that in the next country, if not next door, live people who believe with equal devotion in a different religion or believe in no religion at all (Taylor 2007). Learning thus becomes a matter of persuasion – convincing someone to join Islam, or reminding oneself that Islam is the true religion, a task unnecessary in a world of taken-for-granted religion.

Let me underscore two features of this epistemological shift. The first is a style of writing about Islam in universalistic and systematic terms, as a "system" (*nizâm*). The widely read works of Abul A`lâ Maudûdî (Maududi) and Sayyid Qutb have traveled across languages and social contexts so well because they present Islam in this way: as a complete and self-sufficient system of principles and norms that does not depend on the expertise of judges and ulama, but can be understood and applied by any reader.

Take for example Maududi's short book *Towards Understanding Islam* (Maududi n.d.). In 2004, I purchased a copy in English at a bookstore in Denver. It had been edited and printed in Malaysia. In it, Maududi sets out the basic concepts of Islam: the nature of prophecy, the required beliefs and forms of worship of God, the distinction between faith and Divine Law, and so forth. The reader could be anyone, Muslim or not, living in any country. The book is a universalistic exposition of "Islam," not within a specific legal tradition, not for a particular people, and not with respect to any period.

This book has been translated into a number of languages, and is used in basic classes on Islam throughout the world. In France, I saw it used as a text at a school whose students are people of Muslim background who were not brought up conversant in their religion. I also saw it on the desk of the official in the French Ministry of Interior charged with regulating religion. Although Maududi is also known for his idea that contemporary societies exist in a state of ignorance (*jâhilîya*), religiously equivalent to pre-Islamic Arabia, and for his (conceptually related) activities founding Pakistan's Jama`at-i Islami party, in this book he does not discuss these ideas. Instead, Maududi presents Islam in a neutral, descriptive, scientific tone: Islam as a system.

The second major development, less well appreciated, has to do with the new presentations of religion vis-à-vis science. If the project of European modernity required differentiating science from religion, the various projects of counter-modernity nourished by religious visions have taken as one of their priorities the task of fusing science with religion. Many Muslim children (and adults) learn this fusion from two directions:

they encounter a version of science that is portrayed as requiring God, and they encounter a presentation of Islam that has already incorporated science.

Let me return to my copy of Maududi. The Malaysian editors have added a series of footnotes that show the scientific value of Islam. When Maududi describes the benefits of daily worship for the Muslim's attitude toward God, the editors (Maududi n.d.: 97) add that "salat is a systematic exercise program" and describe in detail the ways it contributes to the flow of blood and the tone of the ligaments. They also describe the medical virtues of ablutions for cleaning the nostrils and preventing disease.

The incorporation of science into Islam lies at the base of a number of important school texts. The successful glossy series of books, written by a Turkish author with the pen name of Harun Yahya, skillfully quote leading scientists in ways that support an Islamic vision of science. (These texts are used in some Islamic private schools in Europe and North America and are translated into many languages.)

Egyptian schools pick up this double movement between Islam and science (Starrett 1998: 139–41). Indeed, Egypt provides particularly good examples of ways in which the major public institutions, including the schools, are the battlegrounds for competing visions of national or religious ideologies. Egyptian science texts emphasize the evidence for intelligent design that they say comes from mainstream science. Starrett describes an Egyptian children's magazine associated with the Muslim Brotherhood that presents an EKG chart and then points out that the images showing the heart beat spell out the name of God; in other words, every heartbeat writes on the machine "Allah, Allah, Allah." In each grade, Egyptian schoolchildren explore different hygienic benefits of the ablutions. These texts also link the personal cleanliness spread by Islam to the early advancement of Islam as a civilization, sending the message that "Islam is a religion of cleanliness, and therefore it's a religion of advancement and civilization."

Boundaries and song

How have these new styles of learning and debates about correct ideas of Islam reshaped everyday "lived Islam," if at all? Recent anthropological work traces conflicts and innovations concerning learning and legitimacy, and highlights the importance of debates over Islam even in rural settings.

In the towns and villages in Pakistan's North-West Frontier, close to Afghanistan, Sunni Muslims long have lived side by side with Shi'ites of different streams, including Isma'ilis, and have participated in the South Asian practices of venerating saints and celebrating love through Persian Sufi poetry (Marsden 2005). But in recent years these relationships across different traditions have come under fire. The network of Deobandi-related schools has attracted young men who have learned interpretations of Islam that condemn Sufism, Shi'ism, and the Isma'ilis. Their views have been reinforced by the nearby presence of the Taliban in Afghanistan.

What have these changes in the region done to everyday life in these towns and villages? Things have changed, as relations have become more fragile between Sunnis and others, and contrasting styles of schooling lie at the heart of these divergences.

All the young boys and girls in the village where Magnus Marsden lived and worked used to sit together to learn about Islam. Now, however, they attend different schools from the beginning of their religious education, studying in the afternoons after their secular schools. In this village, the main dividing line is between Sunnis and Isma'ilis; in other towns and villages other Shi'ite groups play larger roles. Here, Sunni children study the Qur'an in the mosque school (the Dar-ul Ulûm, from the name of the first Deobandi school) while Isma'ili children go to the Isma'ili equivalent, the Jama'at Khanas.

Sunni and Isma'ili patterns of religious learning differ in what is learned, in who acts as an authority, and in how pupils embody the act of learning. Teaching in the Sunni mosque resembles the memorizing

35

and reciting I described above for Yemen and Java. At a certain point, the pupils move from simple memorizing to studying the meanings of texts, but in the form of a standardized meaning (*ma`nâ*) that is not to be further interpreted. When they are about to recite, the children adopt the postures they would for prayer, with their trousers adjusted, caps firmly in place, and hands folded across their stomachs. Sometimes they precede a recitation with a call to prayer. Their teachers are all men who have done advanced study in Islamic subjects at a school affiliated either with the Deobandi network or with the Jamaat-e-Islami (the Pakistani Islamic political party and social movement).

By contrast, the Isma'ili children learn from recently written textbooks provided by the Isma'ili central office in Paris, distributed by the regional center. The books stress the history of Islam, highlighting the key moments when the Shi'ites branched off from Sunnis, the establishment of the Imamate, and the history of the Isma'ili Shi'ites. The books contain many pictures. They also stress the importance of women's roles in education. Indeed, their teachers are young women with lay education. They embody their roles in a way that suggests less of a sacralizing of education than in the other schools. "Veils are loosely draped on heads, prayer caps are rarely worn, and hands not washed before instruction begins" (Marsden 2005: 166).

After the elementary level, a few Sunni village boys take the sixteen-hour bus ride to Peshawar to study at a higher-level Deobandi school. Their departure is experienced as a trial for the affective ties between the boy and his mother. They return on visits dressed in "down country" clothing consistent with the stricter approach to Islam, which may include the black turbans associated with the Afghan Talibans. The Ismai'lis perceive the turbans as a threatening signal, given their own persecution by Taliban. Some of the returning students carry mishwaks, wooden sticks used to brush the teeth in imitation of the implement used by the Prophet. They are now "learned men" (*dashmanan*), with certificates of study (*sanad*). They often try to correct household practices they see as un-Islamic – and sometimes are mocked by other villagers for their overly pious and unthinking attitudes.

These students say that they become full of religious emotion from their study. Some, however, retain their youthful desire to hear love songs. Some of these "learned men" even make love amulets for other villagers. Marsden gives the example of Arkhon Sahib, who attended a Deobandi school, studying fiqh and theology, and joined the Deobandi-originated Tablighi Jama'at. He traveled with the Tablighi to preach a return to a purer form of Islam in the region. The Deobandis and Tablighi condemn practices such as amulet-making. But the amulets made by this learned man are scraps of paper with Qur'anic verses written on them, onto which he has blown other verses. And even though Arkhon declares that Isma'ilis are non-Muslims, he is called on to make amulets by Sunnis and Isma'ilis alike. For Arkhon and his clients, what is at stake here is a particular task and a set of means for accessing power, not a matter of debating doctrine. But this apparent balance or cross-cutting practical linkage is far from taken for granted: Arkhon makes considerable efforts to justify what he does, saying that because he does not sell the amulets he commits no sin, and that in any case it is the Qur'an that does the work, not the pieces of paper.

Here is the contribution of anthropology: to look into the ways in which different men and women living at the heart of the "Islamic revival," and studying in madrasas said to brainwash otherwise intelligent people, in fact lead multidimensional lives and may even make amulets and invite the singing of love songs. At the same time that some proclaim a narrow doctrine that considers Isma'ilis to be non-Muslims, they can engage in everyday relationships with them. Doctrinal debates, on the one hand, and everyday concerns, on the other, give rise to different forms of boundary making and boundary maintaining. We should not infer from one any particular forms of the other.

We can find the same phenomena for the arts. Throughout South Asia, debates erupt over whether Muslims should sing or listen to devotional songs and poems. In the towns and cities of northern Pakistan, in areas where many Muslims are harsh critics of Sufi practices of saint-worship and the Afghan Taliban occupy political offices, many Muslims listen to and perform love songs that come precisely from the Persian-language Sufi heritage. They consider that heritage to be an important way to develop moral character, even as they condemn other Sufi practices.

Marsden (2005: 122–56) reports on the travels and performances of one musical group, the Nobles, in the town of Markaz. Muslims in the town are Sunni and tend to be from Deobandi backgrounds. No cults of saints are to be found, and learned men in the market routinely denounce signs of illegitimate innovation (*bid`a*) and polytheism among the townspeople. With the rise of the Taliban in neighboring Afghanistan, increasing numbers of these scholars denounce all music and performance as anti-Islamic. But even in this Deobandi town, musical groups stage performances in private homes that are attended by hundreds, and their cassettes or CDs are in great demand. In organizing the evenings, the groups follow regional norms of politeness and add to the performance time for collective prayers, meals, and parodies of overly pious local men. They also, however, feature songs that draw on the words and images of Persian Sufi poetry, especially the images of love and devotion. (Songs are in the *ghazal* genre and sung in the local Khowar language.)

That prayer and song are performed in the same room sends a message that all these practices are considered to be within the range of what is permitted in Islam. Singers deliver a commentary on those who come from outside the region when they mimic ironically the tones and themes of singers in the *qawwali*, who come from Pakistan's Punjab region. Now, the singers and the poets include members of the Tablighi Jama'at and of Pakistan's Jamaat-e-Islami party, both associated with rigorous conceptions of Islam. One such poet compares his beloved to the angels, and in performances mocks the stricter learned men of the town. Precisely because he is also educated in Islam, he can respond to his critics – some learned men sought to take him to court for blasphemy because of his comparisons of women to angels – by quoting the Qur'an back at them. Even close to, if not really inside, the heart of these relatively strict views of Islam, Muslim men and women continue to foster alternative ways of learning and of celebrating spirituality.

At the other end of the Urdu-speaking Muslim belt, on the island of Mauritius, debates arise over similar issues. There, the Urdu-speaking Sunni Muslims who call themselves Ahl-e Sunnat va Jama'at, whose tradition is better known globally as that of the Barelwi Sufis, routinely perform and listen to devotional songs called *na`t*, sung in praise of the Prophet Muhammad but also for renowned saints, and in particular for `Abd al-Qadir al-Jilani, to whose order (the Qadariyya) these Sunnis maintain a close relationship. The other major Islamic groups in Mauritius – Deobandis, Jama`t-e Islami members, and the local Tablighi Jama`at (all three of whom trace their origins back to the Deobandi school) – oppose these songs as instances of polytheism.

Patrick Eisenlohr (2006) describes how people frequently listen to recordings of na`t songs in everyday life and engage in public devotional celebrations, usually at the time of the birthday of the Prophet, or that of a saint. Those who organize such celebrations transcribe the songs onto sheets to be photocopied and distributed to all those attending as aids for their participation in the singing. These Muslims consider that, through their singing, they improve their morals and predispositions, their adab. The recording media have been crucial for expanding the access of local Muslims to the songs, because many Mauritius Muslims understand spoken, but not written, Urdu.

Given that both the distribution and use of these songs *and* the attacks on them by Deobandis are increasing, local na`t performers have had to seek ways of justifying their use. The extensive use of electronic media have given them doctrinal ammunition: because the recordings come from India, acknowledged by all sides as the center of their Islamic learning, they retain a degree of religious authenticity and legitimacy. Furthermore, performers have developed a set of criteria for correct performance, including pronouncing Urdu correctly and not sounding too much like Bollywood film actors. Just as Indonesian reciters of the Qur'an are told to mimic Arabic voice styles to capture the presence of the word as revealed in Arabic (and may listen to Egyptian pop songs to pronounce "better"), so too, here, the performer practices an Urdu that will sound "authentic." In Eisenlohr's analysis, the very existence of such criteria for unvarying reproduction of an original spoken or sung genre increases that genre's legitimacy, invoking as it does the broader Islamic notion of the genealogy or isnad.

The normative effect is twofold. First, electronic recording reduces the distance between an authentic performance somewhere in India and a re-performance in Mauritius because the aural word is directly "present," as was Gabriel's to Muhammad, Muhammad's to his first listeners, and so on. The isnad is foreshortened or telescoped, and the likelihood of error is proportionally reduced. Second, retaining unvarying vocal techniques (principally in the manner of pronouncing Urdu) provides additional assurances that the singers will faithfully reproduce the original per-formance. To the extent that their insistence on faithful reproduction resembles the insistence of a scholar on following an attested genealogy, their practices are more likely to be accepted by others. The na`t seem less outside Islam, and thus less subject to charges of shirk, if the manner of learning and performing them *seem* to be Islamic.

This example suggests that in today's context of a relatively democratic access to religious texts, available to anyone through a variety of print and electronic channels, Muslims will develop new techniques to sustain legitimacy. But the tropes for legitimacy remain the same: the isnad, or attested transmission through a series of reliable persons, was, and is, at the heart of learning, whether in reciting the Qur'an, selecting hadiths, or attesting the authenticity of song styles. Anthropology returns us to the heart of Islamic thinking, and shows how Muslim men and women fashion new criteria and new practices in terms central to that thinking.

Few practices are more central to Muslims' religious lives than the regular worship of God; its centrality makes it an ideal object for studying how in their daily lives Muslims both focus inward on thoughts and emotions, and open outward toward broad social and political movements.

THREE

Perfecting piety through worship

Although Islam means "submission," Muslims do more than simply carry out what God has ordered them to do. In daily prayers or worship, in special observances on feast days, and in ways of dressing and speaking, Muslims develop a variety of ways to relate to the divine. They do so, however, on the basis of a widely shared set of ritual templates. Here is the apparent paradox that we encounter time and again in the study of Islam: that even as Muslims align globally around their major obligations – to pray, to sacrifice, to carry out the pilgrimage to Mecca – they also exercise choice and creativity in how they understand and carry out those rituals. From these opportunities for selection and creativity comes the observable diversity of religious lives within and across Muslim social worlds. In choosing how to formulate prayers, how to venerate saints, and how to dress for everyday life, Muslims are engaged in religious creativity, and in ways that challenge some conventional Western theoretical understandings of freedom, agency, and choice.

Submission through salat

Even if you do not know the word, you are already familiar with salat (*salâh*), the basic act of worship in Islam. Several times daily, and particularly at midday on Friday, Muslims will recite, kneel, bow, and bend toward Mecca to fulfill one of their obligations to God. In the United States, newspaper editors seeking an illustration for a story about the Middle East routinely pull from their files a photograph of large numbers of Muslims prostrating themselves. (Often these photographs are irrelevant to the accompanying story, perhaps added to make Muslims seem exotic or threatening.)

Worship, often referred to as "prayer," is one of the central acts of worship and service to God (*ibadat*: *'ibâdât*, from the root `-b-d, "servant," here, of God). It is one of the "five pillars" of Islam, along with testifying to one's faith, giving alms, fasting during Ramadan, and making the pilgrimage to Mecca. Muslims often distinguish between two kinds of duties in the world, the acts that they perform for the sake of God, the ibadat, and the acts that are for the welfare of other humans, the *mu`amalat* (*mu'âmalât*). Although this distinction is important, its meaning is hotly contested. Many Muslims would deny that it separates religious acts from secular or mundane ones, because even such everyday activities as running a business, greeting a neighbor, or eating lunch also should be guided by the principles given by God – and they can cite verses of the Qur'an and statements of the Prophet Muhammad that bear on each of these activities. Many of these Muslims, indeed, would extend the meaning of ibadat to take in all activities that may be carried out with God in mind. Other Muslims cite a hadith from the Prophet to the effect that Muslims should follow him with regard to worship and service to God, and follow their own learning in the pursuit of their other affairs. This major disagreement – actually a whole nest of debates about the various ways one should or should not draw lines between "religion" and the rest of life – runs throughout the topics we discuss here, and concerns the very nature of a modern Muslim society and individual.[1]

---

[1] On the role of tradition and the Prophet's life in modern Islamic thinking, see Brown (1999). For a concise view of the distinction between "modernism" and "reformism" in terms of the discussion here, see Lapidus (1988: 557–70).

In this chapter, I focus on salat because it illustrates some of the key features of the religious rituals performed by Muslims. Above, I claimed that it was central to the religion, because on a doctrinal level, that is, in writings and discussions by learned people about the duties of Muslims, it appears as such. Most Muslims, furthermore, will accept the primacy of the five pillars, at least in theory, relative to other religious acts, such as devotions to a saint or the choice of dress. But in everyday life, other religious rituals may be socially or culturally more important than salat. For example, in places as different from each other as northern Iran and northern Paris, Muslims are more likely to celebrate their religiosity through fasting than through worship. In a number of societies, celebrations of the Prophet's birth or the death of his grandsons provide key moments for creating social ties, or for giving voice to strongly felt sentiments of sorrow and hope. In these places, more social and emotional work is carried out through those rituals than through worship or through any other of the "five pillars."[2]

However, precisely because salat is doctrinally central, it provides an excellent starting point for investigating the different ways, across societies, that Muslims interpret a religious practice. Here is where the anthropological approach provides specific insights. Salat differs from "prayer," *do'a* (*du'â'*), which is the requests and supplications to God that an individual might make at any time (and which we consider in the next chapter). A Muslim may carry out salat either individually or collectively, in a mosque, a house, or in the open. Collective salat perhaps may be most usefully compared to the regular collective worship services of other religions, such as a Catholic mass or a Jewish temple service, in that it is highly scripted, both in the order of events and in the recitations. In salat, the worshipper carries out two, three, or four ritual units or cycles, the number depending on the time of day, all while facing Mecca. In each

[2] On these issues for Turkey and central Asia, see Tapper (1984); Tapper and Tapper (1987); for Paris see Bowen (2009).

cycle, the worshipper executes a sequence of movements – standing, bowing, prostrating, kneeling, sitting – while reciting, in Arabic, phrases that praise God, affirm his oneness, and ask for guidance. In addition, at the beginning of each cycle the worshipper recites the opening sura of the Qur'an, al-Fatihah, and then another short sura, or part of a longer one, as he or she chooses. Beginners usually recite one of the final, short sura such as "Sincerity" that we considered in the previous chapter; more highly trained worshippers are able to select from a wide range of verses, sometimes with a particular message or mood in mind. At the end of the last cycle, the worshipper turns to the right and then to the left, saying a greeting each time. He or she then may choose to say prayers to God.

Muslims mention two important additional conditions for the ritual to be effective – what we may call "felicity conditions," following the philosopher J. L. Austin (1975). First, the worshipper must be in a state of ritual cleanliness, which usually means performing ablutions just prior to worship. He or she washes the head, face, arms, and legs, passing water over each part of the body three times, while uttering words that indicate an intention to worship. One may remain in a ritually clean state after worshipping, so in theory one could perform salat at several moments during the day without having to re-wash, but this is difficult. The second condition is more often the topic of commentary: having the right frame of mind during the worship itself. What elements make up the "right frame of mind" are, of course, up for debate. Most widely mentioned is having the right intention (niyya). On a number of occasions, Muhammad is reported to have emphasized the importance of intention. I think most Muslims would agree that for the salat to be accepted, the worshipper must be intending it, that is, having it in mind that "this is now worship." For example, if one were to sleepwalk through the cycles, one would not have worshipped. But what about the daydreamer? How much can your mind wander without canceling the merit of the worship itself?

Such matters might seem trivial, but in fact they get to the heart of what it is to worship. Is it simply running through the mechanics, or communicating with God? (One could compare the debates between Augustine and the Donatists in the early Christian Church over whether a priest's character and behavior could invalidate the mass.) For the women of Cairo interviewed by Saba Mahmood (2005), the mental state of the worshipper is critical. These women are part of a broad movement of Islamic revival (*al-Sahwa al-Islâmiyya*) in Egypt. In nearly all the neighborhoods of Cairo, women gather in houses or mosques to hear lessons about worship, and about how they can and should draw on the Qur'an and hadith to shape their everyday lives. Their focus on *ibadat* is itself a critique of the secularization and westernization of contemporary Egyptian society. They do not see their actions as a feminist rethinking of the principles of Islam – as do other women in Egypt and elsewhere – but as an effort to cultivate their individual capacities to feel, think, and practice their religion within the established interpretive traditions of Sunni Islam. They stress both the obligation (*farâ'id*) to worship God and the attitude with which they carry out that worship, an attitude characterized by such virtues as humility (*khushû'*), sincerity (ikhlâs), and *taqwâ*, an orientation toward God that one may translate as piety, or as fear of God.[3]

These women were less remarkable in the consistency with which they worshipped than in the degree to which they worked to attain that consistency. Many of them consulted manuals guiding them in techniques to bring up the right attitudes in prayer. They told Mahmood that piety in everyday life helped them to cultivate the proper attitudes for worship, and, conversely, that praying five times a day helped them in organizing their daily lives. In one discussion in a mosque (Mahmood

---

[3] Mahmood's work has led to a number of new studies on women's piety, many creating what I see as a productive tension with her thesis; among others see Haniffa (2008) on Sri Lanka and Jones (2010) on Indonesia, as well as Deeb's work mentioned below.

2005: 122–34), a young woman recounts to another, Mona, that she has difficulty arising early for her morning prayer. Mona tells her that her failure indicates that in her daily routines she is negligent, her mind not thinking of God, and that this state of mind results in her being unable to arise for the prayer. Learning that the young woman often argues with her sister, Mona instructs her to focus on God and on his revealed command that we control our anger.

Dwelling on the power of God may develop a worshipper's attitude of *taqwa* (piety/fear). Some of the Cairo women were drawn to the lessons of a woman named Hajja Samia precisely because she evoked fear of God in her weekly lessons (*dars* – recall the root d-r-s for learning) in the mosques. *Taqwa* requires keeping in mind the torments and threat of hell that will be the reward for one's misdeeds, but also, and more importantly, one's awareness that God is all-powerful, and that we, by contrast, are prone to commit sins. This attitude can keep us from sinning, and worship can help strengthen it. Specifically, some women learned to develop it by weeping for fear of God during worship, particularly toward the end, when one addresses communications to God.

In my own conversations with Gayo Muslims in Sumatra, the same themes emerged, particularly the importance of the attitudes of humility, sincerity, and intention during worship. In the 1930s and 1940s, some Gayo religious teachers tried to develop a stronger consciousness of correct worship attitudes by creating an entirely new genre of poetry, mentioned above. Some of these poems taunted the man or woman who went through the motions of worship while their minds were elsewhere. For example, a poem entitled "On How to Worship" begins by reciting a verse from Sura 17 of the Qur'an on the importance of correct intention in worship, and then features a long dialogue between a speaker who (correctly, from the author's reform-oriented position) understands the import of the Qur'anic verse, and an unenlightened person who merely "follows my grandfather's instructions" when at worship, without bothering either to understand the meaning of what he recites, or to focus

on God during the worship. This casual worshipper recites only the shortest of verses, the verse "Sincerity" that we have previously encountered,
and which begins, as you may recall, with the words *qul huwa*, here
rendered as *qul hu* (Daudy 1950: 1):

> As for the worship prayers, I make them short,
> Make them brief, not too long.
> Up and down, I recite the Fatihah;
> Once that's over, I add a bit of "Qul hu."
> If it's accepted, so be it;
> If not, what can I say?

As the "right-minded" interlocutor (with whom the reader is supposed to
identify) then explains, such worship will not be accepted. Other Muslims
go beyond describing the minimal acceptable mental state for the salat,
and instead discuss its role in bringing them closer to God by inducing
a heightened awareness of submission to, and intimacy with, the divine.
The Sufi poet Rûmî (d. 1273) echoed the sentiments of many when he
wrote, "the prostration of the body is the proximity of the soul," and the
poet al-Farîd (d. 1235) wrote that during the worship he approached God
such that "both of us are a single worshipper" (Schimmel 1975: 154).

For some worshippers, entering into worship provides a way to put
one's thoughts together. Many Gayo spoke to me of moments in their lives
when, confused or disoriented in a new surrounding or by unexpected
turns of events, they turned to salat as a way of strengthening self-
control and, thereby, control over their environments. This "ordering
force" of orderly worship may be harnessed by officials, as described by
Gregory Starrett (1998: 150–3) for contemporary Egypt. Modern Egyptian
textbooks and government documents make the salat a virtuous practice
for the individual and for the nation. As we saw above, readers learn
that the regular practice of salat brings the benefits of exercise to the
individual. For the nation, the benefits are more in the moral domain.
In one privately produced children's book, a clerk lectures unruly clients

on the practical lessons they are supposed to draw from the Muslim worshipper's attentiveness to maintaining straight, unbroken rows before beginning congregational worship, and states that, "Islam is a religion of order and discipline." The advantages of such rhetoric may be obvious to a government constantly preoccupied with the problem of how to co-opt Islamic institutions without being dominated by them.

Leaders of social movements have also from time to time drawn on images of order in worship to motivate their followers to work in unison. James Siegel (1969: 263–9) describes the address given in 1964 to six thousand worshippers gathered for the Id al-Adha worship, on the Feast of Sacrifice, by the former governor of Aceh, Daud Beureuéh. Beureuéh was the leader of a movement that sought to unite all residents of Aceh province. He identified as the major enemies of such unity not external forces, but the passions and interests of individuals. He saw collective worship as a means to overcome these passions and interests as well as an embodiment of that unity. As he proclaimed that day to the worshippers:

The entire community must, five times a day, face toward Mecca and, at the proper time, engage in worship. So, too, for the whole Islamic community, we must come together. We are with God, we face toward Mecca. When we pray in assembly (berjama'ah), we are face to face with each other after prayer. The poor face the rich, the evil the learned, the weak the firm, and the humble face the proud. (Siegel 1969: 263–6)

The sense that worship is first and foremost submission to God, and that it is modeled after the Prophet's example, applies to the pilgrimage and to other activities of worship and service to God. However, in carrying out the pilgrimage the Muslim also has a sense of commemorating specific events in the Prophet's life and in the long chain of sacred events stretching back to Abraham (or even back to Adam) and his son Ishmael. The pilgrim is directed in manuals and by his teachers and group leaders to recall Hagar's search for water for her son Isma'il, and the miraculous appearance of the Zamzam well in the midst of the desert. In tracing

Hagar's hurried steps, the pilgrim is imitating her frantic search for water. Pilgrims commemorate the Prophet Abraham's willingness to sacrifice Isma'il when they sacrifice an animal during the pilgrimage, as do Muslims everywhere in the world on the same day, and generally in the same way. Pilgrims also commemorate the Prophet Muhammad's own performance of the pilgrimage as they move from one step to another.

By contrast, one does not commemorate a specific historical event when one worships, one does what Muhammad eventually put together as a set of rules for worshipping, as we saw in the previous chapter through the example of the night prayer. Muslims everywhere share this sense that worship is done as it is because we are all commanded to do it in that way. Groups that differ on the details of worship – how to hold the hands, what is said aloud and what in silence – justify their particular choices in terms of the Prophet's example. But to stress the primacy of "getting it right" over other kinds of meaning is not to deny additional meanings carried out by worship. Muslims may be inspired by the meanings contained in the Qur'anic verses they utter, as in the case of "Sincerity." Many have found that worship involves drawing closer to God, or helps them order their thoughts and feelings, and others have made of the congregational worship an icon of the orderliness, equality, or unity that people should bring to their everyday lives.

Social performatives

The example of salat also returns us to the key anthropological issue of how the central rituals of a number of religions are meaningful socially and spiritually, and, in particular, to the several ways in which they are *performative*. First, they nearly always are said to *accomplish* something: communion or commemoration, transfer or receipt of merit, communication with a deity, marriage or divorce, or simply one more act of obedience to a rule: pray five times daily, cleanse yourself of pollution. Usually there are rules – Austin's "felicity conditions" for a successful performance – to let you know when you have been successful at accomplishing this goal. You perform the hajj if, and only if, you have done this and that, and avoided doing these other things; your Islamic marriage is dissolved (*faskh*) if, and only if, a duly constituted Islamic authority proclaims it so, and so on. This is the sense in which in Islam you can speak of a *hukm* (generally "law") as the legal consequences of an action: the hukm of pronouncing a *talaq* is a divorce, for example. (This sense of performance as accomplishing an explicit goal – doing what it is supposed to do – was the central insight of early speech act theory.)

But actions do more than that. Some religious acts also *diagram* a central orientation of the religion, as when the spatial separation of the priest behind a rood screen once stood for the unique power of the Church to perform sacraments – you were not summoning Christ's body and blood, the priest was doing that – or when the coming together of diverse faithful at Mecca, or in a *jema'ah* prayer, stands for Islam's qualities of egalitarian universalism. With respect to such cases we may speak of "iconic" relations of meaning, referring to a picture or a diagram. Relationships diagrammed may be spiritual ones, as well, as when the bodily positions assumed during salat are thought to indicate relationships of the worshipper to God. Rites of passage also diagram, by making actions on the ground stand for a passage from one spiritual or normative state to another: we find these aplenty in Islam, from the steps of ablutions to the stages of the hajj. You don't just obey God; you change your state. Here was a major addition to speech act theory, coming in part from the work of C. S. Peirce and brought into recent work in linguistic anthropology (Silverstein 1977).

Third, and also drawing from Peirce, acts may *index* particular socio-religious statuses. To "index" here refers to a relationship of co-presence, as when a vestment indicates the priestly status of the wearer, or a particular placement of the hands at salat can indicate the legal tradition or the religious movement with which the worshipper identifies. Much of the communicating we do in life is of this order, as when we indicate

our refinement and social capacities through speech registers and knowing asides, or our willingness to carry out a threat by speech tone and
gestures, without "saying" anything, but by sending the right signals.

A gesture forming part of a religious event can do all these things,
as I already have suggested by reference to the salat: through worship, I
may accomplish my obligation to God, diagram my submission to His
will, and index many things, including: showing my status in the set of
regular worshippers when I stand in the first row, showing my status
as a hajj by my choice of garments, and my affiliation to a particular
socio-religious movement by whether I hold my hands crossed or by my
side, and "saying something" about my piety by remaining afterwards to
perform dhikr recitations – which, depending on how I perform them,
may also indicate my membership in a particular Sufi order. I will come
back to these several meanings below.

Now, all this indexing and diagramming and accomplishing can also
make key religious actions (the mass, baptism, salat) into loci of social
conflict. Why would this be the case? First, because people agree no more
on the key theological issues than they do on the manners of practice, and
so much of what is disputed theologically concerns performance: what
you should do, how you should do it, and what the consequences will be.
Should Jews or Hindus sacrifice animals? How does transubstantiation
work? What invalidates the salat? Here is where theology is made flesh,
or word, depending on how you come out on these issues; here is where
it generates a set of specific practical imperatives, about how to do things
in your religion.

Second, people may fight over religious practices because much dispute about actions also concerns the legitimacy of the authority involved
in them. Who is it who makes Christian communion "work"? Who is
it who annuls an Islamic marriage? The legitimacy of one's marriage,
one's worship, or one's salvation, may depend on the answers to these
questions. And because it is greatly important to religious authorities

that they be able to control access to the goods of salvation, disagreements about the right way to accomplish these ends is likely to lead to conflict.

Finally, because these practices are so salient and central, they become excellent theatres for *social* performance, for commentary on other matters, less narrowly religious than social, political, and cultural. The taking of communion becomes more than a way to salvation, it also becomes a text for commenting on the ideal relations that hold among communicants and through the Church. And as we shall see, the precise form of Islamic worship becomes a basis for commentary on communication, or on society, or on God.

Because the form of the salat is so clearly prescribed, one may choose to recite different verses and thereby convey different meanings, but one may not add or subtract formal elements – adding a prostration, hastening the proper time of worship – without incurring charges of illegitimate innovation, *bid`a.* Because the focus of normative scrutiny is this set of formal elements, "orthopraxy" becomes a minutely observed metric of certain convictions about hadith or about other ritual traditions, or about social affiliations.

Some of these convictions or stances have to do with the theory of correct ritual performance itself. In certain times and places, for example, some worshippers choose to say the opening phrase, the "Bismillah," silently rather than aloud, because they insist on only doing what the Prophet Muhammad did, and they believe that he was not known with certainty to have pronounced the Bismillah aloud. Furthermore, this particular choice of speech style within the worship ritual indexes the general orientation of the worshipper on the question of how to carry out Islamic rituals. Numerous reform movements within the broad family of Sunni Muslims have tried to realign Muslims' everyday behavior around a commitment to follow Muhammad's example as attested in reliable or sound hadith, rather than relying on the legal schools. So the mere fact of not saying the Bismillah aloud signals one's likely position on a range of ritual-related issues.[4]

In the Dutch East Indies of the 1930s and 1940s, this question – silent or audible Bismillah – led both sides to marshal their arguments in widely distributed Malay-language books. Those who argued for the quiet Bismillah lambasted the refusal of most Muslims to follow the Prophet. Those who championed the audible Bismillah argued that following a legal school, in this case the Shafi'i (*Shâfiʿî*) school, was the best way to keep useless and divisive disputation to a minimum. Other considerations sometimes entered as well. For example, Gayo villagers argued that they always must pronounce the words of worship clearly and audibly so that God could hear them. In their minds, ritual was mainly about communicating with God. For them, this view also explained why one should engage in chanting after someone's death, and why one could speak to the souls of the dead at graves, or on other occasions. For them, the audible Bismillah indexed a belief that ritual practices were *mainly* about communication, rather than *mainly* a mimesis of Muhammad's acts (Bowen 1993: 289–314).

In these cases, the debates turned on the rules for correctly performing the salat – in other words, the felicity conditions – whether the right rules were the out-loud ones or the silent ones. But the messages were far broader, about your whole attitude to the traditions of Islam. This sort of indexical sign we can call "diacritic," for the ways in which it serves to set off a particular position on an issue or a particular social group vis-à-vis another.

Some of these diacritic indexicals regard social affiliations. How you hold your hands, or move your fingers, for example, does not have intrinsic social meanings, but they can become easily visible diacritics, ways of telling who among a body of worshippers belongs to one or

---

[4] For a range of these social messages signaled through *salat*, see the essays in Parkin and Headley (2000).

another social group. Arbitrary with respect to doctrine, such minute differences index social affiliations and thus, once imbued with this meaning, become perceived as highly motivated signs.

For example, in northern Nigeria in the late nineteenth and early twentieth centuries, if you crossed your arms during worship, rather than letting them hang at your sides, you marked yourself off as a member of a specific Islamic movement. Which movement depended on where in Nigeria you were worshipping: if you were in Kano, you were proclaiming yourself a member of a Sufi reform movement; if you were in nearby Sokoto, you were "saying" that you were aligned with the Mahdiyya messianic movement. Later on, in the city of Ibadan, this same distinction in arm placement became a signal of ethnic identity; you would identify yourself as either Hausa or Yoruba ethnic identity in the way you held your arms. The same physical gesture and same kind of meaningfulness (diacritic indexing) yielded completely different social contents in these two different Nigerian settings (Paden 1973; Cohen 1969).

Ways of organizing worshippers for the congregational salat also can send social messages about Islam. In 1950s Aceh, as noted above, attracting large numbers of worshippers was intended to highlight Islam's universal character and thus its suitability as the basis for a new Acehnese society. By contrast, in a Jakarta worship group practicing in the 1970s, only Muslims deemed to be very pure were allowed to take part in the congregational salat. This restriction was intended to signal Islam's capacity to create a pure community and, eventually, a purer society (Bowen 1989).

The ways in which specific arrangements of salat can be taken to convey social meaning are almost endless. Often rather strong debates arise about what precisely the social meanings are. For example, what is signified by the separation of men and women in the mosque during worship? When women are behind men, does it diagram their subordinate status, does it reflect a theory about the unequal distribution of sexual desire (how men and women respond upon seeing the other prostrate), or is this theory simply one more way to promote an idea of women's inferiority? If, by contrast, mosque rules are such that men and women worship on different sides of the mosque, is the message different or the same?

In these cases, choices about how to worship can signal certain broader stances about ritual or about social affiliations. But Muslims sometimes develop ways to avoid doing so, that is, to hold distinct positions on a ritual but to avoid indexing that position. I noted earlier that in the Gayo highlands relatives of a deceased person will gather to chant verses of the Qur'an seven, and again, forty-four, days after someone's death. In the village of Isak, people with very different ideas about the nature of this chanting came together on these occasions and chanted in identical fashion. But these men and women held a range of distinct ideas about what it was they were doing, and these quite different theories of efficacy, if made public, would have led to heated arguments. For some people, recitations automatically relieved the torment inflicted on the deceased, a theory akin to the theory that accompanied the chanting performed after a death in pre-Reformation Europe (most notably the Gregorian chants). Others thought that the chanting did please God, but that He then could exercise discretion in relieving the deceased's suffering or not doing so. Still others thought that God would do nothing in favor of the deceased simply because people were chanting. (These "modernists" also recited the Bismillah silently.)

Now, on other occasions, people would debate this issue and put forth verses or hadith to support their positions. But on these post-mortem occasions, no commentary was provided and no reason emerged to have to defend one position or another. And nothing about the form or content of the chanting indexed one or another position. There are powerful social and emotional incentives to leave things this way, of course: most people would have found it in very bad taste to engage in open arguments at a funeral.

In recent work in France I have found a quite different example of indexing a position through commentary about the salat. I have been struck by the force of the position that one should uphold the idea of a legal school or *madhhab*, in this case the Maliki (Mâlikî) school prevalent in North Africa. One should do so, say some religious teachers, in order to provide a sort of bulwark against "Salafi" teachings that they see as based on simplistic readings of scripture, rather than on the deeper scholarly traditions. In one Islamic institute I have attended near Paris, students learn Maliki teachings on how to perform salat in minute details, for example concerning how many degrees in space a person in prayer may turn to avoid another person without invalidating the prayer. No one in the school argues that following these rules for salat gives the worshipper the moral upper hand compared to people who follow other Sunni schools, nor do they say that God has any preference in the matter. Indeed, the position of the institute is that you should learn one legal school well and then you can choose intelligently among different schools' opinions. But the broader message that these teachers hope to send is that true Islamic learning is rooted in traditional scholarship even if it innovates on the basis of that scholarship. The teacher is indeed "performing the worth of tradition" as he teaches intricacies of worship (Bowen 2009a: 96–105).

These examples illustrate the social indexical ways in which salat – and even teaching about salat – can be meaningful, but, as we discussed above, salat and "meta-salat discourse" also can be primarily about one's dispositions, internal states, and bodily habitudes. To return to the example of intention: having the right intention can be taken to be a felicity condition for God's accepting the worship, but, inversely, it may also be seen as itself the *outcome* of regular performance of salat (as in Saba Mahmood's examples from Cairene prayer circles). And for that reason, the performance of salat and other prayer actions also may be taken as an index of the worshipper's piety – or perhaps more precisely, of the importance the worshipper places on refining her piety. Here is a case where the theory of efficacy then makes possible an additional social-indexical function: you pray often to raise your piety, and your frequent prayer indicates that your piety is probably increasing.

The general point is hardly specific to Islam, of course, and we can think about a broad range of ways in which Christian exegetes and ordinary people put forward doctrines of signs of salvation, from the successful ascetic Protestant businessmen described by Max Weber, whose work in the world was proof that God must be smiling on them, to the snake-handlers of West Virginia, who, taking a cue from the Gospel of Mark, find injury-free snake-handling to be a sign of possession by the Holy Ghost.

In all these cases, successful performance indexes the appropriate inner state or even the presence of grace in the performer. If successful, these indexing events can then become the basis for making certain social claims – to be a proper imam or worship leader for a congregational *salât jamâ`ah*, for example, or to be a member of a Puritan church.

Beyond prayer

That many Muslims regularly perform salat does not mean that all Muslims do so, nor does it mean that even regular worshippers do so in the intensely self-reflexive way described above. Some are torn between conflicting ideals; others might try out an intensely religious life and then abandon it; others shape their lives in different fashion. No more than we would take life in a Catholic convent as indicative of Catholic piety as a whole would we infer from the intense worship practices of some the biographies of all.[5]

---

[5] Although Mahmood (2005) has been criticized for doing precisely this, I read her book not as an overall account of Muslim women's religious lives in Cairo,

To say this is not to say that the ideas and ideals of a pious life are absent from the consciousness of other Muslims in their everyday lives, but that they recognize several different moral registers, and that these differences can introduce a sense of ambivalence or even fragmentation into their life experiences. Working in Egypt, Samuli Schielke (2009) takes as his point of departure not the salat, but afternoon soccer games played during the fasting month of Ramadan. As they play, these young men are experiencing both the sociability that is itself seen as a virtue, and a sense of religious appropriateness. Soccer replaces activities they wish to avoid during this month of heightened piety, activities such as chasing girls or drinking beer. Playing soccer is both fun and an ascetic discipline; it both replaces forms of fun inconsistent with pious living and, "by virtue of its temporally limited nature indirectly legitimizes less consistent approaches to religion and morality for the rest of the year" (Schielke 2009: 25).

Elsewhere, pious women emphasize other dimensions of their lives, such as those Shi'ite women in Beirut who underscore public piety or "commitment" (*iltizâm*), of which worship was only one strand, along with political activism and social welfare work (Deeb 2006). These women see visibility as a key element in personal piety and public participation as essential to showing Muslim women as modern in an international context (Deeb 2009). Public piety returns us to the importance of religious performance: one performs one's personal piety in part by doing it in public. But these public behavioral signs are often contested. For example, many pious Beirut men and women refuse to shake hands with someone of the opposite sex, as a matter of piety. Someone shakes or does not shake, and this behavior indexes his or her degree of observance of this religious norm. However, just because a norm is observed in many settings does not mean that everyone agrees that it should exist as a social

but as an attempt to introduce into Western feminist thinking a different way of exercising agency, with her Cairene cases as examples.

norm. Many men and women (including religious scholars) consider the norm of not shaking hands to be "silly" – even as they observe it (Deeb 2006: 106–11).

Preacher and congregation

Congregational worship involves new possibilities for performance and interpretation, in that an imam selects verses to recite as he leads the prayer, and the sermon-giver or *khatib* (*khatîb*) chooses a set of texts for his homily.[6]

According to Charles Hirschkind (2009), Cairene sermon-givers emphasize the importance both of arousing the proper emotions in listeners through their words and of orienting them toward appropriate conduct in their daily lives. They mentioned three important elements of a sermon that would produce the proper responses in listeners. First, a sermon must wake people from their states of lassitude, so that they will pay attention to the message. Second, it must instruct listeners in Islamic beliefs – what happens to the soul at death, for example. Third, it must link the narratives of the Qur'an to the everyday lives of listeners. Sermon-givers see their task as allowing God's revealed words to be apprehended by listeners, not as skillfully conveying those words, because the words emerged already perfect with no need for elaboration. Skill would be superfluous, perhaps morally presumptuous. The onus is on the Muslim who listens to a sermon or to Qur'anic verses to adequately prepare his or her heart to take in the full meaning of the words.

Young men in Cairo who listen to sermons on cassettes told Hirschkind that listening brought tranquility, humility, and regret, emotions that should be seen as ethical responses to the sermons. These emotional/ethical dispositions are indeed the ones mentioned by Islamic

---

[6] In addition to the works cited here, see the important study by Richard Antoun (1989).

moralists as essential to instilling a propensity for right conduct in a person. In sermons such as those delivered by the popular Shaykh Kishk (d. 1996), the khatib would ask his listeners to repeat word by word the invocations he uttered in his sermons.

Listening to religious words is supposed to, and often does, call forth audible responses from listeners. Muslims will audibly pronounce the Arabic for "God bless him and grant him salvation" or the English "peace be upon him" when hearing the Prophet Muhammad's name invoked. Listeners are often cued up for this response, but can be confused if the wrong reference is uttered. At a lecture I attended in a Paris mosque in 2001, one Muslim speaker would frequently refer to "Muhammad," clearly intending the Prophet, but his failure to say "the Prophet" led his listeners to stumble or fail entirely to supply the requisite response. People in the audience began to grumble among themselves. Hearing this happen several times, the moderator turned to the speaker and asked that he say "the Prophet" or "the Prophet Muhammad." Not only would this form of reference be more respectful, but it would, and did, restore the appropriate response pattern.

Let me turn again to my own Indonesian fieldwork to illustrate how the preacher and the imam may respond one to the other in order to relate the choice of verses for worship to the sermon. In the village of Isak, during the 1980s, the weekly sermon was given in Indonesian, with the requisite recitations in Arabic. On a Friday in 1989, the khatib was a man who, although born in the village, had lived elsewhere for several years – and so was in an ideal position to deliver the kind of social critique that preachers sometimes wish to provide. He had learned that several villagers, known to everyone for their relative wealth, had not paid their tithe, *zakat* (*zakâh*), in recent years. He made them the target of the sermon: although he did not mention them by name, all present knew of whom he was speaking.

He began with two Qur'anic verses: one that blames those who think of God only when they are in difficulty, and another that targets those "who have eyes but do not see, ears but do not hear." He proceeded to illustrate God's meaning by telling the story of clove growers in West Aceh who had refused to pay the zakat on their cloves, on grounds that their wealth came from their labor and not from the fertility of the land. Theirs was not an entirely frivolous claim, in that they found some support among religious scholars. However, nature did not look kindly on their efforts, in that disease and storms devastated their crops and reduced many to poverty. The khatib left the worshippers to draw their own conclusions.

As the khatib was delivering his sermon, the imam for the day, a different man who also was native to the village and also had spent years away, was mulling over the verses he would recite for the prayer. Because this was a Friday congregational prayer, there would be two verses, one for each of the two cycles. He settled on verses from Sura 87, al-A`la and Sura 88, al-Ghashiya. As he later described his choices to me, the first warns people to think of the torments of Hell that await them, and not to focus only on the things of this world. The second elaborates on this idea, reminding listeners of what awaits those who go to Heaven and what awaits others in Hell. By choosing these verses, he could add to the point made in the sermon (to which he wholeheartedly subscribed) without repeating the choice of verses.

Thus a dance of Qur'an and homily, across the two major moments of the worship service, managed to link outside events to scripture while leaving implicit the precise targets of the two men's shared ire, the villagers who had refused to pay zakat. Worshippers got the point, however; several talked about who had been the intended target. Moreover, they tended to subscribe to the idea that failure to pay zakat could lead to financial disaster. When one of my neighbors had two successive years of poor harvest, several others in the village imputed his problem to a failure to pay his tithe.

The compass of this example was relatively small, if the artistry elegant; sometimes sermon-givers address national or international events. Patrick Gaffney (1994) studied sermons in Upper Egypt in the late 1970s, during the period of great political turmoil following Anwar Sadat's peace initiative with Israel. They include those delivered at a mosque in the city of Minya by Shaykh Uthman, who had inherited local charisma from his distinguished father, was imprisoned as a member of the Muslim Brotherhood, and continued to argue for interpretive pluralism against those who believed there was only one correct Islamic view.

In a sermon delivered in late 1978, Shaykh Uthman told the story of Khubayb, a man who was sent by the Prophet Muhammad on a mission of predication (da`wa). Shaykh Uthman hung a number of messages, mainly concerning events of the day, onto this story. He stated that one should bear the weapons that best fit the times and place, as did Khubayb, and in today's times this means persuading, not killing – "and I hope that our brothers will understand this in its broadest meaning." He noted that Khubayb was an exemplary young man, unlike those young men and women, "hippies of some kind," who hang around the local railway station. One of Khubayb's companions killed himself, but the Prophet said those who kill themselves burn in Hell forever and "only fools and crazy people" ever commit suicide (Gaffney 1994: 208–37, 279–93).

Many of the references in this sermon can only be discerned by some-one (such as Gaffney) who knows the local debates. Shaykh Uthman opens the sermon by speaking of differences: God "made nations out of many customs that they would be different," and then quotes the Quran: "Oh you who believe, if you should quarrel on anything, refer it to God and the Messenger" (Qur'an 4:59). The verse is one quoted by a radical Islamic group active in Minya and elsewhere in Egypt, al-Jam`iya al-Islâmîya, "The Islamic Association," to bolster their argument that they know God's true will and that all who do not agree with them are outside the right path. Shaykh Uthman surrounds his quotation of the same verse with reminders that God allowed for pluralism by creating different customs, thus turning this verse back on the radical group. And he juxtaposes through the sermon the activity of da`wa, "call" or predi-cation, with the use of reason (`aql). Listeners would know that Da`wa was the name of the Muslim Brotherhood's publication. They also would understand the emphasis on reason as aimed at extremists and thus as bolstering the Shaykh's call for tolerant pursuit of the path. Shaykh Uthman was able to remain within the genre conventions associated with sermons – at least those followed in this part of Egypt at this time – and make a multifaceted case for pursuing the Brotherhood's "Middle Way" between westernization and radicalism.

Now let me turn to the poor outer cities of Paris, where in the housing projects Muslims have created worship spaces by knocking down the walls between apartments. The Tunisian scholar Dhaou Meskine presides over Friday worship at one of these mosques, in Clichy-sous-Bois, where the French riots of November 2005 began. I visited the mosque with Dhaou in April 2006, during the period of celebration of the Prophet Muhammad's birth (*maulid*). In a housing project, residents in one building had refashioned three apartments to form a collective prayer space. In the main room, the seat from where the sermon is delivered, the *minbar*, of simple plywood construction, is placed so as to show the direction of Mecca.

At the proper moment, Dhaou rose and grasped the staff lying next to the minbar and delivered a fifteen-minute sermon in Arabic on the Prophet Muhammad and his life. He then sat, rose, and, after delivering a benediction in Arabic, added a very short French version. In both, he stressed that they should all look for the middle way, between those who condemn the celebration of the Prophet's life and those who would treat it as a religious feast day, an *Id* (`*Îd*). It is simply a time for recalling Muhammad's life, he explained. "This year has been a particularly difficult one for Muslims, and we can profit from recalling the conditions Muhammad faced, and by consulting his biography." He then gave examples of how Muhammad had kept calm in the face of threats, and offered solutions to racism by uniting peoples from all different origins. "Anyone who does not love any one of God's prophets is not a Muslim, according to the Prophet." He explained that we should not humiliate others but that the economy and politics of the world do so: "When we push poor countries into debt by charging interest on loans, they cannot then build schools or mosques or wells, so they have famine and war. Muhammad offered the solution to this problem by abolishing interest and this revelation is appropriate for the entire world today."

Now, although speaking against interest could happen anywhere and at any time, this particular instance responded to a debate then current in France and elsewhere in Europe. In the late 1990s, the matter of interest-bearing mortgages was taken up by the European Council for Fatwa and Research, a collection of jurists of various nationalities who mostly now reside in Europe and who are led by the Qatar resident Yûsuf al-Qaradâwî.[7] At its 1999 meeting in Dublin, the Council issued an opinion in response to questions about borrowing from banks to buy a home. Their opinion affirmed the prohibition on usury and urged Muslims everywhere to avoid borrowing at interest, but it also said that if Muslims in Europe could not find alternatives then they could take out a bank mortgage for a first house. The Council argued that renting a house placed Muslims in a state of financial insecurity, a conclusion reinforced by a report from the European Union on immigrants and housing. Owning a house also allows a Muslim to settle in close proximity to a mosque, added the Council.

But some local scholars disagreed with this opinion, and Dhaou Meskine was among them. "There are too many families in France who live in debt," he told me after the sermon, "and 4,000,000 who have been unable to repay their debts." He went on to explain that there were other, creative ways of obtaining money, such as repaying the seller of the house gradually, perhaps at a higher price, and that he had successfully experimented with such arrangements himself. Meskine also objected to the very idea of different laws for different places: "Sheikh Qaradâwî says that

---

[7] On the European Council see Caeiro (2006); on al-Qaradâwî's roles in multiple contemporary networks, see the essays in Gräf and Skovgaard-Petersen (2009).

interest in Europe is acceptable because Europe is not a Muslim land. But laws must be universal: if it is forbidden to steal, or lie, or falsify papers, or to make illegal marriages in Muslim lands, then such is true for all Muslims, including those living in Europe, in the 'land of treaty.' That is the nature of religion; it is intended to apply everywhere" (Bowen 2009a: 137–43).

Wearing Islamic dress on three continents

Few words or images better capture current strong feelings about Islam than "veiled women," but by juxtaposing Islamic dress with prayer I wish to highlight the close ties between a sense of piety and a way of dressing.

For many Muslims, adopting modest or Islamic dress is a step toward constructing a life around piety and accountability to God. For others, and probably for most non-Muslims living in Europe and North America, seeing Muslim women with their heads covered sums up the problem of Islam's practices of patriarchal oppression. But if we seek to understand the meanings of Islamic practices to Muslims, we must begin with the diversity of ways in which Muslims have interpreted and carried out commands to dress modestly.

In many societies in the Mediterranean world and further eastward, adult women (Christian and Muslim) long have favored head coverings and long dresses. Men also have chosen long, flowing garments and different kinds of head covering, to protect themselves from the heat. But within Islam, donning or removing a particular form of head covering has been one way to mark a particular change in status, or the adoption of a particular political or social position. For example, after the Prophet Muhammad's death, his widow Aisha (`Â'ishah) assumed a prominent political role. When Muhammad's third successor Uthman was killed, she appeared on the very place at the Mecca mosque where Abraham is said to have laid its original foundation, ceremonially took on a head covering, and addressed the crowd. Her act of covering her face publicly constituted a claim to have the authority to speak to the community, and one commentator (El Guindi 1999: 112) compares her act to the Prophet's act of covering his head and much of his face with a black cloth on his triumphal return to Mecca.

This action contrasts with that taken by the modern political leader Huda Sha'rawi in 1923, when she arrived home in Cairo from an international women's conference held in Rome. At the Cairo train station she and others publicly removed the veils that had covered their faces (although they did not uncover their hair). This act spoke for the upper class of Egyptian women, for whom advancement meant the adoption of European cultural practices in speech, clothing, and style of life, although not European domination of Egypt. Others were more cautious about imitating Europeans, but through the war years and thereafter, the cause of women was linked to a rejection of veiling (Ahmed 1992).

Since the 1960s and 1970s, women and men in many societies have turned to head coverings as a sign or instrument of a revival of piety and accountability to God. In many places they have intended this turn to be seen as a rejection of the fashions and norms of the moment. The markedly Islamic dress of many Muslim women today is part of a recently and explicitly adopted way of living, and not a continuation of past ways of dressing. (The same can be said of men's appearances.)

One feature of these recent turns toward Islamic dress is a justification of dress by reference to scripture. The Qur'an contains no specific dress code, but in two places it directs women to cover themselves. In one sura (24: 30–1), God directs all female believers to "draw their head coverings (khimâr) over their bosoms and not display their beauty except to their husbands" and close relatives. In a second verse (33: 59), God tells Muhammad: "Tell your wives and daughters and the believing women that they should cast their outer garments over their persons; that is most convenient, that they should be known and not molested." The command in the second verse seems to be intended to protect Muslim women when they are abroad. The first verse is more general. A hadith supplements it, reporting that when Asma (Asmâ') (the daughter of Abu Bakr and sister of the Prophet's wife Aisha) appeared before him in transparent clothes, the Prophet turned away and said that "when a woman begins to menstruate, nothing should be seen of her except this and this," pointing to his hands. Although more specific, this report could of course be taken to be a reaction to the extremely revealing garments of Asma, or as a way of speaking about modesty.

Trends toward adopting Islamic dress appear in many different societies, but they have no single, uniform meaning. We can gain some idea of the variation in interpretations by considering several examples, from Egypt, Java, and France. The Islamic Revival movement that developed in Cairo and elsewhere in the 1960s and 1970s promoted Islamic ways of dressing and Islamic ways of living. Students and other activists often made the new items of dress in their homes. They made loose, flowing garments for men (trousers) and women (gowns). Women wore head coverings; men grew short beards.

Researchers working with different groups of women and men in Cairo have developed differing interpretations of what these new dress styles have meant for their wearers. Leila Ahmed (1992: 222–5) worked mainly with middle-class women and especially students, and argues that women who adopted Islamic dress did so in order to combine their heightened religious sense with their desire to pursue careers in school and workplace. This argument has a social and a psychological dimension. Socially, adopting conservative dress may have made it easier for some women to engage in careers while preserving their relationships with conservative family members. Some stated that this dress also protected them from male harassment. Psychologically, wearing Islamic dress made these women part of a community of religious-minded people in a larger social environment that lacked clear moral signposts.

Studies of working-class women in Cairo give a somewhat different picture of the role and significance of Islamic dress. Arlene MacLeod (1991) also finds women putting on Islamic dress as part of their move into the world of work, but emphasizes the contradictory pulls they face between home and work. If Ahmed argues that these modes of dress can secure autonomy, MacLeod suggests that the women she worked with dressed as they did in an "accommodating protest" against the strains of their lives.

The Cairene women studied by Mahmood (2005) gathered together in mosques to learn more about Islam. These women spoke of their dress as part of the process of improving their piety and trust in God, and their attitude of patience and perseverance (*sabr*) in the face of life's struggles. They rejected the notion that these forms of dress constituted forms of protection or badges of identity, or the very different idea that dressing in this way is the result of a fully formed inner piety. Rather, dressing in a certain way is, for them, part of a package of practices that fashion the self in the direction demanded by God.

The sharp differences in these analysts' interpretations reflect differences in the projects and situations of the women with whom they spoke. Islamic dress appears in all these conversations, however, as part of a process, of a movement toward a goal, and not as the continuation of the past. This same characteristic of new Islamic dress appears even more starkly in our next two examples, from Java and France, because many of the reasons given for wearing Islamic dress in Cairo do not apply. Javanese women do not have the same past memories of Islamic dress to refer to, nor is there the same degree of a (real or imagined) need for protection in public against male harassment. Women in Indonesia generally, and Java specifically, own businesses, work in fields and factories, and buy and sell in public markets. Suzanne Brenner (1996) argues that Javanese women who put on Islamic dress do so in a sharp break with the past and that in this respect their actions are part of the construction of modernity.

For most of the twentieth century, many women in Java and elsewhere in Indonesia did wear dress that was associated with Islam in one way or another. Women returning from the pilgrimage to Mecca wore a scarf or cap, often white. Women who became part of the modernist Muhammadiyah movement often wore the combination of a tight-fitting blouse (*kebaya*) and tightly wrapped batik sarong, perhaps with a brightly colored head scarf. To the extent that these clothes signaled a relationship to Islam, it was presented as a relationship within Indonesian traditions of dress.

The loose, long "Islamic clothing" that became popular in the late 1980s is perceived by wearers and non-wearers alike as referring to universal Islam, or perhaps even to its Arab origins. Because few of the strategic effects of dressing in this way that are invoked elsewhere (protection, career, public mobility) apply in Java, the religious meanings are paramount. As in Cairo, university students who decided to dress Islamically did so in a social context of increasing wealth disparities between rich and poor, and a search for religious support and direction among university students. They formed university study groups and recitation circles.

Those Javanese women who decided to wear Islamic head coverings, *jilbab*, sometimes came into conflict with the state and frequently did so with their own families. The Suharto regime, in power until the late 1990s, promoted an ideology of religious toleration, which in practice often meant the suppression of religious expression. In the 1980s the government for a time banned wearing head covering in state-supported schools, and disallowed wearing any head covering for identification cards. One woman refused to remove her scarf for a high school graduation photograph and was denied her diploma, and then thrown out of the house by her father (Brenner 1996: 679). Brenner writes that her parents might have felt that a daughter who wore a jilbab was implicitly rejecting her parents' values and their religious practices. "Javanese believe that children shouldn't try to be teachers to their parents" said one woman whose parents had ordered her not to wear a jilbab. Furthermore, these "children" find that the new, better understanding of Islam came from outside Indonesia. They stressed their own "awareness" (*kesadaran*), that came only after they had attended study sessions, heard sermons, or read books that explained the meaning of Islam and the Qur'an.

Once they adopted the jilbab these women emphasized their new sense of the discipline required of them: to cover appropriately, not to go to movies or gossip, ride on the back of a motorcycle behind a man, or even shake hands with men. This sense of discipline also was a sense of self-control, of performing religious obedience and devotion, and thus of *ibadat.* The choice of dress at times has taken on considerable public significance, as when, during the 2009 Indonesian Presidential elections, some candidates' wives were criticized for not wearing jilbab.

Brenner's analysis converges with Mahmood's in stressing the individual self-fashioning that is at the heart of these women's adoption of Islamic dress. We hear more in Brenner's account than in Mahmood's about the changes in personal behavior that accompany this adoption; this difference may reflect different possibilities for social interaction in Java, compared with Cairo. Other ethnographies of Cairo women remind us that the social contexts for their decisions contrast sharply with those on Java.

In France, recent studies reveal a wide array of practical reasons for taking a headscarf, often linked to family dynamics. Often the decision to wear a scarf was part of identifying with "religion" as opposed to mere "tradition," where "religion" was marked by more conscientious religious practices or the study of Islam through books and classes. One woman (Venel 1999) said: "Evenings I talked with my father: 'Don't do this or that.' But you couldn't say it was very religious; it was 'Don't steal' and never 'You must carry out your prayers.'" In this instance, the distinction drawn was between a rule-based morality and a more self-conscious carrying out of a broader set of religious obligations. Other women reported that their families observed the fast during the month of Ramadan and ate only halal (*halâl*) meat, but that they neglected prayer; in these cases the distinction was between "tradition" (eating and fasting) and "religion" (again, marked by regular prayer). The way a woman wore a headscarf could place her on one side or the other of the tradition/religion opposition: either "as in the old country," which allows hair to show, or with an appropriate understanding of the scarf's meaning, i.e., in a religious manner (Venel 1999: 52–5). About half of the younger women who did wear headscarves had begun to do so at a moment of transition from middle to high school or from high school to university. Disputes about headscarves seem to take place among sisters at home as frequently as they do in the workplace or at school. One young woman wearing the headscarf at home was accused by her sister of "introducing politics into private space" (Souilamas 2000: 192–4). Some see the decision to wear the headscarf as coming after a certain maturity and also a degree of formal religious knowledge.

In the more outwardly pluralistic setting of London, England, some women are fashioning their own Muslim "looks" against the background of Muslim-majority neighborhoods. Emma Tarlo (2010) provides the case of Fatima, who comes from a close-knit Bengali neighborhood in England. When she is at home, Fatima favors the South Asian *shalwar kamiz* (long tunic over trousers), so as to fit in culturally. But in London, where she works, she adopts a style that she considers to be "more British on the one hand and more Islamic on the other" (Tarlo 2010: 95): long skirts and fitted tops, combined with brightly colored headscarves (worn to conceal the hair and neck) and large earrings. She finds this style to be more covering than the Bengali one, and so more Islamic, but it also reflects a fashion sense acquired on Oxford Street and not in her Bengali neighborhood.

English Muslims engage just as much in bricolage as does everyone else. Performance artists Sukina and Muneera come from Bristol and a Jamaican background. On stage, their clothing choices become part of their Poetic Pilgrimage performance, and they might combine long skirts and floral headscarves with hooded tops and denim jackets to present themselves as urban, black, British, and Muslim. Muneera uses bright eye shadow to convey a bold look and counter assumptions that scarves mean submissiveness.

These choices are not made outside of politics, however. In the long-running Shabina Begum court case, a schoolgirl claimed that wearing a *shalwar kamiz*, already allowed by her public school, was insufficiently Islamic; she demanded to wear a longer jilbab. Tarlo argues that Begum's claims were from the beginning part of a campaign led by the group Hizb ut-Tahrir to radicalize British Muslims.

Against this religious-political background, the hijab can become a threat on a more personal level, affecting even the most liberal and multicultural-minded of Londoners. Jane had fled her Catholic upbringing to embrace pluralism and choice, but her friend Loraine's conversion to Islam and her decision to wear the full-length jilbab led her to reassess her own life choices. She began attending her local Catholic church in order to secure a place for her son in the church school and pull him out of his current multi-religious school, lest he be drawn toward a similar, and in her eyes, dangerous, religious and personal transformation.

In London, increasingly Muslim men, too, dress in visibly Islamic ways, wearing beards and long tunics. The issues are not symmetrical: whereas Fatima and others are dressing so as to be both more Islamic and more British, men's choices echo distant cultural preferences: either South Asian style long beards or Arabic style short ones, together with the tunics and robes that refer to dress patterns of specific Muslim-majority societies. If some women are trying to look less foreign through their Islamic dress choices, men are doing something quite different. Gendered dress preferences are not symmetric: men are less likely to be pressured to "dress Muslim" than are women, and the messages sent by men's clothing have much more to do with identities, piety, and authority than with modesty.

On Java, in Cairo, and in France and England, dressing oneself in Islamic fashion has become a way to mark out an identity, always with respect to some alternative fashion; it is "diacritic" in that it opposes one sign to another in order to convey a meaning. For some people it involves signaling or facilitating a transition toward a more independent or a more pious life; for others it involves signaling a particular kind of religious orientation. Contrasting these cases makes clear the anthropological point we already saw with respect to prayer: that there is nothing necessary about the meaning of an item of bodily decoration. People attribute meanings to objects against the background of earlier or broader meanings. It makes little sense anthropologically to ask what "the meaning of the veil" is, as is so often done in Europe and North America today, but more sense to ask "what do different actors think has been communicated" by choosing a particular way of presenting oneself.

 This same stricture applies to worship more broadly: in choosing ways to approach God, Muslims choose among an array of states of mind, modes of dress, and physical movements. These choices have to do with both working on the self and engaging in social performance. This double orientation makes worship a key locus for debates about piety and sociability.

FOUR

Reshaping sacrifice

In the last two chapters we have considered two perspectives that characterize modern forms of Islam. In studying worship we learned that some
Muslims have engaged in a social and moral critique of the ways in which
others carried out their ritual obligations. Their objections developed as
part of a broad movement for Islamic reform in the late nineteenth
century. "Modernist" scholars emphasized the importance of returning
to the scriptural texts to rediscover the proper approaches to worship,
and of rejecting those practices that did not have a clear scriptural base.
They also emphasized holding proper intentions and attitudes when at
worship, an emphasis that has led some to hinge Islamic revival on the
subjectivity and bodily attitudes of Muslims.

This moral critique of traditional practices sometimes joins with an
epistemological shift that casts Islam as a system of propositions rather
than as an accumulated body of ideas and practices. This perspective on
Islam can support a modernist position but it need not do so. One may
render Islamic "systematic" in ways that support older ways of thinking
about Islam as a set of accumulated norms and practices. Nonetheless, there are what we may think of as meta-textual "elective affinities"
between the two ideas, to the extent that both – the modernist moral
critique and the Islam-as-system epistemological shift – privilege the
immediate relation of the Muslim to sources of scriptural proof.

Both the modernist critique and the new epistemologies have led to debates concerning how to correctly carry out one's obligations to God. These debates have occurred across a wide geographic canvas, however, on which is traced a history of Muslim adaptations of the Islamic tradition to local cultural and social forms. As Islam spread across Asia and Africa, Muslims developed new and divergent ways of worshipping, sacrificing, treating birth and death, and resolving conflicts.

Studying Islamic practice comparatively thus becomes rather complex, as we encounter different positions on what have become worldwide debates about scripture and tradition, and at the same time situate these debates in historically deep local traditions of understanding and practice. Doctrinal position-taking cuts across cultural variation, then, even as it picks up certain elements of local traditions.

In this chapter I will focus on one ritual, the Feast of Sacrifice, to try and unpack these complex interactions of doctrinal debates and cultural differences. Once again, I begin with a shared set of textual references, and then draw on anthropological accounts of diverse local interpretations and local versions of these broader doctrinal disputes.

Across the world, many Muslims sacrifice an animal on the Feast of Sacrifice, the Id al-Adha (`Îd al-Adhâ), which occurs on the tenth day of the last month of the Islamic calendar. This day falls in the middle of the pilgrimage period, and pilgrims perform the act in the city of Mina near Mecca, while other Muslims carry out the sacrifice wherever they reside.

The explicit command to sacrifice at this moment has a clear scriptural base, but how Muslims interpret it brings in varying and changing ideas about how best to carry it out. We saw a similar combination of a basic requirement and local variation regarding worship, but sacrifice brings up additional patterns and ideas, including the absolute submission to God instantiated by the Prophet Abraham when he prepared to kill his own son; heightened attention to the importance of maintaining distinctions among things forbidden and things permitted (harâm and halal), for food and for other matters; and the importance of transmitting benefits from the living to the dead. Rituals of sacrifice also may become vehicles for emphasizing gender distinctions, a way of creating an independent being from a newborn child, and an instrument for propitiating spirits and creatures of many sorts.

Muslims across the globe associate sacrifice with feasting and sociability. This association explains its continued cultural importance for Muslims who have newly moved to lands where they are religious minorities. Although sacrifice is often difficult to carry out in lands of new settlement, many Muslims in Europe and North America, even if they seldom worship or visit a mosque, try to carry it out. For an anthropologist, the continued importance of eating together is hardly surprising, for rules about what one eats and does not eat, and occasions to eat gloriously with friends and neighbors, are central to many religious traditions.

When Muslims sacrifice at the time of the pilgrimage, they follow a model set out by Muhammad. Despite its importance to Muslims, the obligation to perform this sacrifice is not one of the five pillars of religious practice, nor is it described in the Qur'an. The Qur'an does refer to sacrifice in general in several places. In one of the last, short, and therefore frequently recited chapters, God commands Muslims to sacrifice to him and to him alone: "pray to your Lord and sacrifice" (108: 2). Muhammad carried out sacrifice as part of his own pilgrimage to Mecca, and thereby established the model for today's hajj. In his statements, accepted as reliably transmitted, he underscored the value in God's eyes of sacrificing on the appointed day, mentioned the value God places on the blood flowing from the animal, and stated that on Resurrection Day the animal will come to the sacrifice (Muslim n.d.). The Qur'an distinguishes this sacrifice from other, older practices, which it represents as giving the blood of the sacrificial animal to God: "Not their flesh, nor their blood, reaches God, but it is the piety from you that reaches Him" (22: 37).

Muhammad also reminded his followers on numerous occasions that by sacrificing they were following the example of the ancestor Muslims share with Jews and Christians, the Prophet Abraham. In the Qur'an (37: 100–10), Abraham tells his son (whose name is not given) that "I have seen in a dream that I must sacrifice you." His son agrees, and "when they had both surrendered to God, and he had flung him down upon his face," God spoke to Abraham and said that he has passed this test. Then God "ransomed" the son with a victim. Qur'anic commentators elaborated the story of Abraham and his son and specified that the son was Isma'il (*Ismâ`îl*). When little, he and his mother, Hagar (Hâjar), traveled to Mecca, where they searched for water and eventually found the well of Zamzam. Father and son were then reunited and together built the Ka`ba.[1]

Abraham's story is about submission and about the substitution of an animal for a human. The animal to be sacrificed has taken the place of a human. This idea of substitution shapes the ways Muslims prepare animals for everyday eating as well as for the annual sacrifice. Anyone killing an animal for food must make it clear that the killing is done in the name of God. For the annual sacrifice, some might add a dedication, in which they make explicit that the victim represents the person sacrificing the animal: its flesh stands for his flesh and so forth. In some societies a family accords special consideration to the animal destined for the knife, treating it as one of the family. Muslim commentators have emphasized the importance of sparing the victim undue anguish, and that the sacrificer must keep the knife out of the animal's sight and speak to it in a calming way.

In the ideal sacrifice, the animal submits willingly to its fate, as did Abraham and his son. For that reason, some Muslims emphasize whenever an animal is killed, it must be aware of the act itself, and that the person killing the animal must recite a blessing and quickly cut the conscious animal's throat. (This rule applies for all killing in order for the

---

[1] See Bonte (1999) for the basic references subtending Muslim sacrifice and the other essays in his volume for additional case studies.

food to be halal.) Although Muslims see these strictures as evidence for the humane approach of Islam to the unpleasant necessity of killing animals for food, in some countries laws regulating food preparation stipulate that animals must be rendered unconscious before they are killed – here lie the roots of ongoing disagreements among Muslims in Europe.

Less prominent but practiced by many Muslims are other forms of sacrifice that accomplish a very different goal, namely, separating elements that ought to be separated. Muhammad told his followers to offer a sacrifice for the birth of a child, and many Muslims practice this distinct rite of sacrifice, called the `aqîqa in classical Arabic. The word `aqîqa is derived from the verb `aqqa which means "to separate," and the basic sense of the sacrifice is to separate the child from its mother, and introduce it into the social world, usually seven days after birth. Two basic elements often are included in the ritual (along with the animal sacrifice): cutting some of the infant's hair, and giving him or her a name. In some societies additional steps are taken to protect the infant from danger coming from the natural world.

Moroccan models

In the 1980s, the anthropologist Abdellah Hammoudi (1993) studied sacrificial rituals in a village of Berber-speaking Muslims in southern Morocco, near Marrakech. The sacrifice performed during the pilgrimage month was similar to that performed elsewhere, but it was accompanied by a masquerade. For days beforehand, men and women prepared special foods and chose the sacrificial victim with care. Those who could afford it killed a sheep. The animal had to be without defect (ideally a non-castrated male) to be a suitably complete offering to God.

On the morning of the feast day, the men proceeded to a spot marked off for the prayer, an outdoor area indicated only by a pile of whitewashed stones. As they assembled they chanted praises to God, and, when all the village men had arrived, an imam led them in two cycles of salat. (Unlike the ordinary Friday worship, the sermon comes after the salat.) In the first part of the sermon, the imam reminded his listeners of the perils of the grave, the tests to which they would be put after death, and their only hope: adhering to the rules of Islam. After a brief rest, he then celebrated the feast day and described its rules at length: the victim must be an edible domestic animal in good condition, and the killing must take place during the next three days. Sermons delivered in other years placed more stress on Abraham's exemplary willingness to sacrifice his son as the feast day's central message.

From the place of worship the men proceeded to the mosque, where they held a meeting about the mosque's finances and auctioned off that year's walnut crop to pay for the mosque's upkeep. Each man then returned home, where he slaughtered the victim or had it done by some-one else. Women prepared the animal, sometimes outlining its eyes in black (underscoring the role of the animal as a substitute for humans). Men laid the animal on its side, facing Mecca, and one man, dedicating the animal to God, quickly cut its throat with a large knife. The women caught the spurting blood and preserved it for use in warding off harm and curing illness. The meat was prepared for eating, then or later, and the skin was dried to be sold, given away, or used in the masquerade to follow, days later, when an unmarried man would don the skin of a victim, prepared in such a way that "everything on him is topsy turvy," with the animal's testicles hanging over the player's rear. Other young men played the roles of Jews, workers, or women in the carnivalesque procession that flaunted sexuality and reversed social hierarchies.

The separation of men and women, their complementary roles, and the carnival-like masquerade are characteristic of this part of North Africa. As we shall see later, in other societies the Feast of Sacrifice appears quite different. But in many respects – the sermon, the choice of victim, the method of killing – this rural Moroccan sacrifice resembles those in Indonesia, Iran, or Los Angeles.

In urban Morocco, other political messages are layered onto the social and religious one. Elaine Combs-Schilling (1989) describes how the rulers of Morocco use the sacrificial ritual to publicly reaffirm their claims to be the direct descendants of the Prophet Muhammad. Each year on the day of sacrifice, the king publicly plunges a dagger into a ram's throat, re-enacting his ascendant Muhammad's own commemorative sacrifice in the seventh century. In Combs-Schilling's account, the sacrifice also reaffirms patriarchal power in the family and embodies a notion of male fertility. In many urban households, the patriarch follows the ruler's lead by publicly killing a ram. The size and virility of the ram is taken as a measure of the man's own virility. The men of the household stand erect to witness the sacrifice; women and children are either absent or in the background, seated. Women play only the role of passive observers to the sacrifice; after the killing they may dab some of the victim's blood on their faces to "share in the power of sacrifice" (Combs-Schilling 1989: 231).

Already we can see that men and women play different roles in different Moroccan contexts. Hammoudi's account from the Berber village shows how the public role of the married men is complemented by the ritually crucial activities of women in preparing the victim for slaughter. Women purify the victim with henna, thereby transforming it from ordinary animal to sacrificially appropriate victim, and they gather the victim's blood for use in guarding the home and in combating illnesses. Other anthropologists working in Morocco add to the picture of variation by noting that often the head of household has someone else kill the victim, and that the victim may be a sheep or goat. Moreover, it is not clear that most Moroccans think of the ritual as linking their sacrifice to that performed by the ruler (Munson 1993: 122–4).

Even looking at one country, then, we quickly realize that with the ritual of sacrifice we have both a core set of practices and ideas, and a good deal of room for variation. Below, I ask what some of those Moroccans do when they and others from North Africa move elsewhere: what do they preserve and what do they leave behind? We will not be surprised if there are vigorous debates among Muslim migrants over these questions.

Indonesian contrasts

If we move to Indonesia we can see, first, distinctions among Indonesian Muslims that stem from their broader theological debates and, second, an overarching Indonesia-wide pattern that contrasts with the overall Moroccan one and that has to do with broad cultural contrasts between the two regions.

As I mentioned earlier, for years I lived in the largely traditionalist village community of Isak in the Gayo highlands of Aceh. There, households sacrificed various kinds of animals: chickens, ducks, sheep, goats, or water buffalo (Bowen 1993: 273–88). Nearly all Isak households performed a sacrifice on the feast day. At the very least, a household would kill one of its chickens or ducks, or buy a chicken or duck from another household. If times were very bad, two households might jointly hold a feast and share a duck. As long as the throat can be cut and the meat eaten, I was told, the sacrifice meets the demands of God. (In principle, said some, half-jokingly, even a grasshopper would do as a sacrifice.)

Just prior to cutting the victim's throat, the sacrificer dedicated the animal to one or more living or deceased relatives. In 1978, my neighbor Abang Das sacrificed a buffalo for the benefit of his parents and grandparents. Just prior to cutting the animal's throat he pronounced the Bismillah ("In the name of God, the Merciful, the Compassionate") and the confession of faith ("I attest that there is no deity but God and that Muhammad is his Messenger"), and then dedicated the buffalo to his father, mother, and their families, followed by his own name.

In contrast to the Moroccan case, most of these sacrificial events were carried out in the back of the house, with no more ceremony than the quiet utterance of the dedication. Who actually cut the throat was not of great importance; a man might delegate the job to someone else. In their social practice, Gayo thus distinguished between the knife-wielder (Hubert and Mauss's [1964: 9–28] "sacrificer") and the person in whose name it is performed (the "sacrifier"). Nor was the event interpreted in patriarchal terms. The sacrifice was carried out for the household as a unit: women as well as men spoke of "their" sacrifice, and couples decided jointly on a list of people who would receive its spiritual benefit. In the case of a buffalo, the beneficiaries usually included parents of the husband and the wife, and daughters as well as sons. Widows also carried out sacrifice (without being socially redefined as men), and when a wealthy female trader in Isak sacrificed a buffalo everyone spoke of it as her sacrifice, not as her husband's (who was also part of the household). This set of features alone makes the Gayo case markedly different from Moroccan public forms, where, as we saw, the physical act of throat-cutting iconically signifies the virility, power, and self-sufficiency of the male, as opposed to the female.

In Isak, the throat-cutting is not the most publicly salient moment of the ritual, nor are the Moroccan patriarchal messages communicated. The focus of social attention is instead on transmitting benefit to one's relatives by means of the sacrifice and, especially, at the ritual meals (*kenduri*) held afterwards. The kenduris held on the Feast of Sacrifice varied considerably in their size and form. If a family killed just a chicken or duck then they would eat it with little fuss. At most, the household head or a learned relative recited a short prayer. If they sacrificed a sheep then they would be likely to invite neighbors and relatives to share the feast. If a buffalo was killed, then everyone in the village was invited to eat together. Guests brought raw foods (milled rice, coconuts, and sugar), which the hosting household and their close relatives prepared for eating, and they could then take home a bit of the raw meat from the sacrificed animal.[2]

---

[2] See the parallel processes of embodied ritual and Islamic challenges in highland Java, as analyzed in the work of Robert Hefner (1985, 1990).

At feasts where a buffalo or sheep was eaten a religiously learned man would lead a group recitation of short Qur'anic verses, recite a long petitionary prayer (punctuated by choruses of "*âmîn*"), and, for good measure, repeat, for God's hearing, the names of the beneficiaries of the just-completed sacrifice. These recitations play an instrumental role in securing the benefit of the sacrifice; they also reaffirm relations of sociability among the participants (see Robertson Smith 1894).

Some ritual meals were attended by upwards of one hundred people. These large meals featured the same night-long recitation sessions (the *samadiyah*) as in the funeral commemorations mentioned in Chapter 2. The learned man who led the guests in chanting would have been given a list of the people to whom the merit should be transmitted; he then embedded these names in a long prayer (sometimes saying the names very softly), thereby directing the evening's merit to the intended beneficiaries.

In Isak, for each of the four years when I was present for the Feast of Sacrifice, three or four households each sacrificed a buffalo, sponsored a village-wide feast, and held an all-night recitation session. They held the feasts at different times so that men or women with ties to more than one village would be able to satisfy their multiple obligations. These major feasts were occasions for relatives who had moved away from Isak to return and join in transmitting merit to those who had died before them. The sponsors whom I knew well spoke to me about the dead who were to benefit from the night's sessions; these days were times for reflection and remembrance as well as for contributing to the welfare of relatives and neighbors.

These events of transmission (at the moment of killing, the after-noon kenduris, and the nighttime samadiyah) are central to most Isak villagers' ideas about sacrifice. Indeed, they generally reserve the Gayo phrase "to sacrifice" (*gelé qurbën*, literally, to cut the throat of a sacrificial animal) for occasions when a goat or buffalo is killed and served at a kenduri. Kenduris are a general framework for ritual in Gayo society (and elsewhere in the Malay-Indonesian archipelago). Most kenduris combine the recitation of prayers with the burning of incense and the offering of special foods; both incense and foodstuffs help to transmit the message of the meal to the intended spiritual recipient. Kenduris are held on Muslim calendrical holidays and for a wide variety of practical purposes: to fulfill a vow, to request help from ancestors in healing a sick person, or to call on God to ensure the safe passage of a deceased person's spirit into the next world. By making the Feast of Sacrifice into a kind of kenduri, Isak Gayo have configured it as an event of transaction and communication.

The sacrifice also provides a specific, future material benefit, for on Judgment Day the persons named as sacrificial beneficiaries will be able to ride on the animal to the place of judgment. Only one person can ride a goat or sheep, but seven can ride on a buffalo. A buffalo sacrifice thus provides the opportunity to bring together parents, children, and grandchildren on the back of the afterlife vehicle, and if they had the resources, most Isak households would stage a buffalo feast sometime during their lives.

Isak couples shaped their sacrificial strategies with afterlife sociability in mind. Each couple tried to provide a vehicle for themselves, their children, and, if possible, their parents and grandparents. Parents felt a particularly strong obligation to provide a vehicle for a child who died young, as did children for those parents and grandparents who did not have the resources to make a sacrifice in their own name. I heard stories about children who would not acknowledge their parents on Judgment Day, because they had not bothered to sacrifice for them. "Without a sacrifice there is no tie between parents and children," said one woman. The prospect of future abandonment by one's children horrified most people and provided further encouragement to perform the sacrifice. It also led people to include in their dedications even those parents or children who already had a vehicle provided for them, in order to ensure that family ties would be preserved during the harsh times of judgment. I was told that in the past, just before a sheep was sacrificed all the close relatives of the beneficiary would grasp its tether rope, thereby strengthening their ties in the afterlife.

Isak transactions and images contrast sharply with the centralized dynastic meanings and father–son pairs of Morocco. Gayo and Moroccans conceive of the sacrifice in Islamic terms. Both views are articulated through the performance of the Feast of Sacrifice and through the rich imagery of the past (Abraham's sacrifice) and the future (Judgment Day). Isak Gayo project that imagery out from the ritual event to the family's fate in the afterlife; Moroccans concentrate that imagery on the immediate structure of domination in the kingdom, the community, and the family.

Modernist critiques

Islamic ritual form is differentially shaped by theological positioning as well as by cultural molding. The Gayo modernists living in the town of Takèngën developed new ways of carrying out the sacrifice in contradistinction to village practices. In other words, they did not simply read a script from scripture, but developed their religious practices in a dialogue with pre-existing ritual observances. Precisely because most Gayo historically came to understand the Feast of Sacrifice in terms of feasting and transaction, modernists have worked to rid the feast day of those two elements. They do not hold kenduris on the Feast of Sacrifice (although they do on other occasions), and they emphasize the sharp distinction between the living and the dead.

In 1989 I observed the celebration of the Feast of Sacrifice in the Baléatu neighborhood of Takèngën. Baléatu residents are strongly associated with the modernist Muslim organization Muhammadiyah, whose school is located next to the neighborhood prayer house. When asked about the purpose of the ritual, Baléatu residents invariably referred to God's command in the Qur'an to follow the example of Abraham. (Isak residents, when asked the same question, usually mentioned the importance of providing a vehicle for the afterlife.) For these modernists, to follow the example of Abraham means to adopt his attitude of selfless and sincere devotion, or *ikhlas* (recall the importance of this attitude for salat worship). One scholar explained that one receives merit from the sacrifice only if it is done with the proper intent, "for the sake of God and not for a worldly reason." He called the notion that the sacrifice becomes a vehicle for the afterlife "amusing."

In recounting the story of Abraham, Baléatu narrators emphasized his prior decision to give something away in devotion to God, not the moment of sacrifice itself (precisely the moment emphasized by Moroccan narrators). "Prophets had always sacrificed," explained one scholar, by which he meant they had always been willing to surrender something, "but the prophet Abraham said that he would sacrifice his child if one were born to him; the idea came to him in a dream." The subtle difference between Abraham offering to give up a child if he receives one, on the one hand, and being commanded to slay his existing child, on the other, is indicative of the difference in cultural emphasis between the attitude of abnegation in Indonesia and the act of killing in Morocco.

The general town sequence of the Feast of Sacrifice resembles that followed in Isak: public worship, followed by the killing of the sacrificial animal, followed by meals. But the form and meanings of each stage are quite different. In Isak, each household approaches the event as an opportunity to transmit spiritual and material benefits to their relatives and themselves. The key events are the act of dedicating the victim and the several kenduris which one might attend during the the day and at night. For Baléatu residents, the congregational worship was the most important element in the ritual; the killing of the victim was strongly played down, and the meals consisted of casual home meals and the communal enjoyment of food in a non-ritualized setting. Greater religious importance was paid to events taking place in the streets, at the open-air site for congregational worship, and in the neighborhood prayer house. The spatial contrast indicated a shift in the social focus of the key ritual event, from the private, if shared, interests of the household, to the general interests of the community as a whole.

As it happens, this shift in turn made it possible for the Takèngën ritual to be more closely integrated into the ideology and control apparatus of the Indonesian state. The congregational worship service held on the morning of the feast day (the only religiously required component of the sacrifice), was socially relatively unimportant in Isak, but was the culmination of several days of activity in Baléatu. Although many Baléatu people did take time to obtain a goat for sacrifice, they were more concerned with their preparations for the morning worship service (for which some purchased new clothes) and the visiting of neighbors and graveyards that would occur afterward. The feast day was preceded by a night of takbir (takbîr – proclaiming God's greatness with cries of "Allahu Akbar"). A convoy of cars drove around and around the town, led by a loudspeaker car from which the takbir was called out over and over again. The evening's amplified proclamations, following a day of recommended fasting, built up a sense of expectancy for the next morning's worship activities.

By about six o'clock on the following morning, several of the best Qur'an reciters had arrived at the site for the congregational worship, a broad field next to the Takèngën town mosque with a stage at one end. The reciters began to chant the takbir over loudspeakers, and continued to do so for over an hour, while men, women, and children gradually filled up the worship space in front of the stage. The district finals of the national Qur'an recitation contest had just ended and had created a particularly receptive atmosphere for this part of the service. The reciters on the stage were all winners in past years' contests, and the crowd of worshippers clearly enjoyed their skills. Men and boys filled the space closest to the stage; women and girls were in an area behind them. Men, women, and children were dressed in their finest: men in fancy sarongs, some in sport coats; women in brightly colored blouses and sarongs. The worship service was preceded by a welcoming address from the district military commander, setting the event in its governmental frame. The sermon, which follows worship, generally takes as its topic the willingness of the Prophet Abraham to sacrifice his son to God. On this particular occasion, the sermon-giver talked about the importance of sacrifice in all areas of life, and specifically for the success of the development of the country. He stressed the value of ikhlas, sincere devotion, in such sacrifices, likening our efforts in infrastructural development to the obedience displayed by the Prophet Abraham.

The clearly state-saturated nature of this public worship event brings us back to the larger dimensions of Combs-Schilling's argument about the Feast of Sacrifice in Morocco: that the Moroccan ritual has developed in support of the monarchy as well as of the patriarchal household. Indonesian modernism has different political implications, in terms of what one might call the intransitive quality of its discourse. Modernist speeches and sermons emphasize proper piety: one should sacrifice, be devoted, worship – to God, of course, but, more importantly, as an intrinsically valued set of actions (value-rational rather than ends-rational in Max Weber's terms). This form of discourse is easily claimed by the state as its own, because a request for everyone to sacrifice can sound vaguely religious even when the goals are clearly secular.[3]

Isak and Baléatu celebrants differ in how they kill the victim and consume its meat. Residents of Baléatu wish to clearly distinguish their practices from the Isak-type forms that they find un-Islamic. For this reason they have played down the instrumental religious significance of the killing and the meals, emphasizing instead the general values of family and community. Whereas in Isak the morning worship was followed by sacrifice and ritual meals, Baléatu residents returned home to express the depth of family ties. In one such family, children and

---

[3] My observations occurred during the New Order regime, but little has changed structurally since Suharto's downfall: intransitive sacrifice continues to fit onto state discourses about sacrifice for the nation.

close friends took turns kneeling in front of the two parents, crying out apologies for misdeeds over the previous year and receiving their blessings and admonitions: "you have to learn to behave better"; "you are the youngest and so you always catch it; do not take it to heart, little one." Everyone in the neighborhood then moved to the prayer house and adjacent Muhammadiyah school to hear speeches, chant the takbir, and eat together. The prayer house leaders began organizing these meals in 1974 to dislodge the celebration from its village context of feasting and transaction, and residents called the meals "eating together" and never "kenduris." They underlined the importance of giving away food without hope of a return as truly selfless sacrifice, and mentioned the invitations given to orphans as proof of the event's real character.

The ethic of avoiding self-interest also shaped the way that individuals carried out their obligation to sacrifice. The elder brother in my household enjoyed spending much of the day before the sacrifice buying two goats, one for his own household's sacrifice and one for the meal at the prayer house. Once he had purchased the goats, he turned them over to a family friend, who prepared them for their joint meal, at which no prayers were said. By virtue of its purchase, the meat had already been consecrated to God.

Baléatu religious modernists see sacrifice as proof of our sincere and selfless willingness to obey God. The prominence of the takbirs, the morning worship, and the historical sacrifice by Abraham all support this central theme. But town modernists also characterize what they do in explicit contrast to village ways of celebrating. Baléatu people emphasize the sharp divide between the world of the living and the world of the dead, and recognize only a thin strand of communication across it, mainly through prayer to God. Practices that, in Isak, involved transactions with spiritual agents are, in Baléatu, located firmly among the living only. (Isak-born town modernists often remember such spirit transactions with a shudder, and pretend that they belong to the pre-Islamic past of the highlands.) Celebrating the relations among family members is done in the home through cathartic obeisance and not by way of the sacrificial victim. Eating together (lexically distinguished from holding a ritual meal) is purely and simply that, with no suggestion that the meal or accompanying prayers are directed toward a spirit. Food is given away to orphans as a social demonstration of the sincere devotion to God that should be the sole animating force of religious actions taken during the holiday.

The possibility for women to carry out a sacrifice on the Feast of Sacrifice is explicitly defended in Indonesian religious scholarship. The influential scholar Hasbi ash-Shiddieqy, in a work on the Feast of Sacrifice (1950), underscores the legitimacy and indeed, the importance, of allowing women to carry out a sacrifice. The author interprets the words of earlier Muslim scholars as indicating that a woman who owns an animal to be sacrificed ought to kill it herself, or at least act as formal witness to the killing. He also makes the case that sacrifice generates merit for the sacrifiers. He argues that, because the Prophet Muhammad stated that the sacrifice was from him, his relatives, and his followers, we receive benefit (*pahla*) from the sacrifice. Although this interpretation does not sanction the idea of transmitting benefit to others, it does introduce into respectable religious discourse the notion that the sacrifice confers a spiritual benefit. The general emphasis in the two Gayo cases thus points toward a more general, regional religious culture that transforms the shape and understanding of its Muslim rituals.

The Gayo examples provided the opportunity for a fuller demonstration of the multivocal nature of religious practice. The *dominant* forms found in any one community (Isak or Baléatu) represent only the current state of play in an ongoing dialogue over ritual propriety. In similar fashion, the Moroccan domestic rituals stand in a dialogic relation with the public, patriarchal forms. But these two internal dialogues differ in their nature, largely because they grow out of two very different concatenations of religion and power. In Morocco, the highly public ritual of patriarchy and kingship is a mainstay of the regime's legitimacy; alternative forms are very much offstage. The Indonesia state, by contrast, does not derive its legitimacy from religious claims, and the local-level differences in ritual understanding derive largely from religious debates and divisions. Here, in contrast to Morocco, it is the more public and state-supported forms practiced by town modernists that have developed as a response to alternative ritual forms.

Of course, many other permutations of the Feast of Sacrifice are possible: for example, the Iranian displacements of the moral and political message of the sacrifice onto the martyrdom of Husain at Karbala (Fischer and Abedi 1990: 166–8). But even these two cases, Morocco and Indonesia, show how Muslims have shaped a particular set of ritual duties in sharply contrasting ways, with cultural foci that do not derive in any direct way from Islamic scripture, but rather are the products of adapting, elaborating, and transforming scriptural and other elements in directions that make sense locally.

Adapting sacrifice to France

As Muslims have moved into new lands of settlement, they have faced new constraints, and have wondered whether they should change how they respond to the command to sacrifice. Since the 1960s, considerable numbers of Muslims have immigrated to countries in Western Europe. Most of these Muslims have come from the countries of northern and western Africa, Turkey, and southern Asia. During the 1950s and 1960s, European governments encouraged the immigration of workers to serve the expanding industrial sector as inexpensive laborers. Many of these early immigrants were single men, or married men whose families remained behind. Both the immigrants and the host countries thought that the stay was temporary. Some governments built large housing projects, both in city suburbs and in relatively isolated areas, to encourage the eventual repatriation of the immigrant workers and, indeed, to encourage their isolation from the cultural mainstream. France offered instruction in languages of origin for immigrant children in order to facilitate their "return."

But things did not go as planned, both because economic recession in the 1970s led to hostility toward these immigrants, and because, rather than going "home," they stayed, and brought their families or created ones in Europe. The children were Europeans in culture and language, whether or not they were granted citizenship. They began to demand rights of citizenship, including their right to practice their religion unimpeded. This economic, cultural, and political conflict was increasing in intensity in the late 1970s and 1980s, at the moment when "political Islam," as it was misleadingly called, took world center stage. The Islamic Revolution in Iran and the rise and repression of Islamic parties in North Africa and Turkey led to a worldwide excitement among younger Muslims about the possibilities for constructing new kinds of nations, ones in which Islam would play an important public role. The aftermath of September 11, 2001, raised tensions still further.

Less noticed have been the creative efforts by European Muslims to adapt religious practices to new social surroundings. Sacrifice has been one focus of those efforts for a number of reasons: it offers possibilities for creating new kinds of social relations, and it raises all sorts of questions and problems, from the very practical issues of hygiene and transport, to cultural debates about how to treat animals.[4]

We already saw that Moroccans generally carry out their sacrifice within the family, with the father often killing the animal, at or near home, before the family proceeds to join in collective worship. The same is true of other North Africans, Algerians, and Tunisians. But French law, and indeed European law, forbids the slaughter of animals anywhere but in an abattoir, and then only by someone who has been certified by the state. Therefore, it is illegal to carry out a sacrifice in a house,

---

[4] For a parallel analysis of the Pakistani adaptations to British social life see Werbner (1990).

farm, garage, or even in a municipal space designated for that purpose. Those families who own their own house might be able to kill their animal at home without being troubled by the long arm of the law, but most Muslim families live in urban environments and often in housing projects. The degree to which families have been able to sacrifice at home despite the Europe-wide ban on such practices depends on the attitudes of each country's (and each locale's) authorities, and also on the spatial dynamics of immigration. For example, in Belgium many immigrants live in pavilions, where it is easier to carry out the killing in private, and local authorities have felt the pressure from Belgian ranchers to allow this lucrative trade in sacrificial animals to continue. In Britain, certain urban areas are mainly Pakistani, and thus few non-Muslims witness the sacrifices.

Nothing in principle prevents people from arranging for sacrifice at an abattoir, as the law requires. But practical problems arise: the majority of Muslims live near, or in, large cities, far from abattoirs, and when many properly sacrificed animals are required on the same day, the demand becomes difficult to meet. Since 2008, French supermarket chains have tried to provide properly prepared meat, and these efforts have begun to meet the demand. French law did require animals to be stunned before slaughter; a 1981 law made an exception for religious slaughter, but annual human-rights campaigns protested this "loophole."

Even in the 2000s, the majority of Muslim household heads living in France were born elsewhere. Their thoughts about whether and how to sacrifice frequently refer back to practices in their countries of origin. One Algerian worker told ethnographers about the poverty his family suffered when he was growing up. His father would manage to buy a chicken to sacrifice, but this did not count for them, as he later said, "As God is my witness, with the best of intentions we could not sacrifice. Today, I would not be forgiven if I did not sacrifice" (Brisebarre 1998: 64–5). To sacrifice means to kill a ram or sheep, and to do so at home: "There are those who do so at the farm, but normally it should be done at home." The memory of what his father wished to do but could not shapes this worker's sense of what must be done.

A Moroccan worker living near Paris stated more forcefully that he never would go to the abattoir – he would stop sacrificing first. "It is `âda, custom, because the Prophet himself sacrificed at home. If you kill anywhere else, it is not the `Îd; you might as well just buy the meat directly from the butcher!" (Brisebarre 1998: 68). And yet things may change; this man's eldest son rejects the practice entirely, even as, respecting his religious obligation, he intends, when he becomes the head of his own household, to give the value of a sheep to a poor person.

If in North Africa some men and women were able to fashion a close tie to the sacrificial animal, taking it into their houses, and speaking to it at the moment of sacrifice, an industrial production of sacrifice, even if it meets the scriptural tests, breaks that sense of personal tie, the identification of the person and the sacrificed animal, that is at the base of a logic of sacrifice. In 2004, I followed one of the new experiments in sacrifice near Paris. A mobile slaughter unit had been set up by a private enterprise working with the regional authorities. The day before the feast day, I went to talk with the young man herding the sheep and taking orders from area Muslims for the sacrifice, which was to be carried out the next day. Abdel explained that Islam requires the sheep to be at least six months old, and goats one year old, to be eligible for sacrifice. They expected to slaughter one thousand sheep.

JRB: So it is going well, you are selling lots of sheep?

ABDEL: No, people don't want to do it this way, they would rather cut the sheep's throat themselves.

JRB: Is this a matter of religion?

ABDEL: Yes, religion; it is not about the meat but about having your children and wife there, and cutting the sheep's throat in the name of your mother and other relatives. Now how could we keep track of who each person wants the animal sacrificed for? So people would rather do it themselves, but that is forbidden; you may not take the animal out, and there are

95

barriers so you cannot do that. Years ago people could go to places west of Paris and buy an animal and sacrifice right there, and that is what I did, and then there were abattoirs set up near here, that Muslims ran. But the government did away with them. This abattoir: the French run it with a veterinarian, and there is a woman there now guarding it, that is why it is permitted.

I myself do not sacrifice, because I would rather send money to Palestine; if you send 200 or 300 Euros they can buy five sheep. Here we do not need meat, we eat it every day, but there they do need it.

JRB: If you were allowed to do it yourself, as in past years, would you sacrifice or still send money?

ABDEL: I would still send the money but I don't know about others. After all, you cannot eat all the meat yourself and indeed you are supposed to share it with poor people but who is poor in France? There aren't any poor people. So better to send it where there are poor people.

Abdel had thoughts that went far beyond the sheep to the broader issue of Muslims' sacrifice for France:

People are not happy with this slaughterhouse. Why cannot France let us carry out the sacrifice? France does not want to do anything for us, but it was the Muslims who built France, the metro, the trains, the buildings. My father and mother came here just after the war, he built France, but now they do nothing for us; they treat us as people who should leave, put us together with terrorists.

On the next day, some families were waiting for their sheep to be processed and the meat to be handed to them. Each purchaser had been given a ticket with a number on it and told when to return for the sheep. The chain was about two hours behind schedule; it was, after all, the first time. Others were congregating at the slaughtering end, including those whose sheep was currently being slaughtered. After approaching a woman in charge, I was allowed to walk around the back near the point where the sheep entered the processing unit. A man in his forties stood there with his two children. In previous years they had sacrificed by taking their "camping car" into the country and finding a farm where they could sacrifice. He stopped doing that because he was concerned about the health of the animals, with all the diseases. Somehow he, too, had talked his way to the entry-point to the assembly line, and with his sons by his side could look at their sheep as it was about to be killed and say the Bismillah out loud to the sheep.

Others managed to go back and pet and speak to their sheep at some point well upstream from the entry-point but were kept from the sacrifice place and could only watch through the windows in the mobile buildings. "Many people are disappointed," explained a woman in charge, "because they would like to read out a list of names for the sacrifice and say the Bismillah, but it would slow down the chain if we let them do that." At one point, too many people had managed to get back to where the sheep were, and she made an announcement over the loudspeaker telling everyone to stay out of the area of sacrifice and wait where the sheep were being delivered, because it was slowing down the assembly line.

Trust and timing

The ordinary Parisian Muslim who goes to a butcher shop the afternoon of the Id's first day has no way of telling whether the meat offered him was slaughtered after the morning prayer, as is required in Islam. Abattoirs are tempted to cheat, to kill some animals early in the morning so as to get the jump on the Id supply. The Id presents such a difficult challenge to Muslims in France that the services that certify that meat has been slaughtered according to rules of halal generally avoid getting involved. Some supermarkets sold meat "for the Id" in the early 2000s, but were found to have killed the animals the day before the prayer. In December 2007, some stores in the Carrefour supermarket chain entered into alliances with local Muslims to act much as halal butchers had, and took orders for Id meat for delivery on the evening of the first day of Id. The store at Gennevilliers, with a large Muslim clientele, worked with an Islamic association, Ennour, and it was the latter that took orders inside the store. A Muslim woman in hijab assured clients that this time there would be no trickery. Here was a solution to the problem of trust: the visible piety of Ennour's representative worked together with the logistical powers of the large chain.[5]

Now, the state saw an opening here, because there is no obligation to sacrifice on the first day; you can wait until the second or third day. Tunisian imam Dhaou Meskine explained in 2004: "The sacrifice must take place after the prayer and theologically speaking it can be on any of three successive days, but that would be like saying that you must wait for your Christmas present; all the children want to celebrate Id on the first day."

Just before the Feast of Sacrifice in February 2003, the *sous-préfet* of Mantes-la-Jolie, the site of one of the large "cathedral mosques," issued a statement "reminding" officials (including official Muslims), that "the Muslim religion authorizes sacrifice over the three days" and that instead of sacrificing, Muslims were permitted to send money to "their countries of origin," implying that all Muslims were immigrants. Many Muslim leaders objected to the Interior Ministry that this statement was out of order (Dhaou Meskine commented: "As if he were a mufti!"), and the Minister, at the time Nicolas Sarkozy, denied that any state officers would usurp the prerogatives of religious authorities. And yet Sarkozy had written to Muslim leaders a week earlier asking them to "remind the faithful that that ritual sacrifice is part of tradition and not among the obligations pronounced by your religion" (*Le Monde*, February 11, 2003).

Now, at the same time, another prominent teacher, Hichem El Arafa, had issued a fatwa which, too, reminded Muslims of what was possible within Islamic norms (*Oumma.com*, February 10, 2003). Indeed, his position was much more radical: because most butchers cheat and kill

---

[5] *SaphirNews.net*, December 22, 2006. Quotations from Paris-region scholars are from my interviews.

sheep the day before the prayer or early that morning, he said, it would be better to order a sheep for the second or third day rather than risk making an invalid sacrifice; or one could fast for one day, an act that, according to a hadith, absolves the Muslim from the need to sacrifice for one year prior to, and one year following, the fast.

With the lack of slaughterhouses and the problem of trust in butchers, many Muslims returned to old ways. Dhaou Meskine: "The result is that the sacrifice takes place in bathtubs, whatever else people say." Indeed, many Muslims either worked out unofficial – and technically illegal – arrangements, or they sent money home to their countries of origin. At some of the vast housing complexes, some officials turned a blind eye if a family sacrificed in the courtyard. Larbi Kechat of the Adda'wa mosque (with the largest number of worshippers on this feast day) asked the butcher next door to where he lived to kill a sheep for him. "Everyone just fends for himself; they go to the country or find another way; nothing is organized." Fouad Alaoui, then secretary-general of the Union des Organisations Islamiques de France (UOIF), the largest French–Muslim organization, was in the habit of going to a farm, together with friends, where they chose some sheep and had them slaughtered: "One of us is a doctor and can make sure that the slaughter did not harm the animal in such a way as to make it unfit for the sacrifice, the internal organs were not punctured, and so forth."

In 2002, I asked students at one large Islamic institute what they did on this day. One young man sent money back to Senegal and asked someone there to sacrifice in his name. Another did the same with his relatives in Mali. One had a friend in the suburbs who bought a sheep and kept it there and they killed it together for the Id. One was on the pilgrimage and so sacrificed there. Another man, who has an Algerian father and a mother from Martinique, had gone to Normandy and found a farmer and divided the sheep with the owner of a nearby abattoir. An Algerian man who lived in a suburb asked their regular butcher to set a sheep aside for him.

In 2003, the teacher Hichem El Arafa himself said he had not sacrificed that year and had not for several years:

For one thing the children do not like meat very much. One year we had a lot of meat left over and put in the freezer and it stayed there a year and we had to throw it out. There are two main reasons for the feast day. One is to bring the children around you and kill the animal and put away meat to eat, dry it in the sun and it lasts awhile. The second is to distribute it to others, especially to people who need it. But here we have enough meat anyway, and it is not clear to whom one could give it. Oh, sometimes I ask among the family to see if there is a relative in Tunisia who needs it and then I send enough to buy a sheep, about 100 Euros now. That makes more sense because they need it.

Increasingly, there are calls to think of the day as a time to make donations to needy Muslims elsewhere in the world. At least since 2004, Islamic Aid (Secours Islamique) places spots on Beur FM radio asking Muslims to send Id money for the poor in other regions (in that year it was Chechnya and Palestine), and they provide their address and phone number. This is what the Centre Tawhid bookstore manager, Abdelkadir, does. In 2004 he said, "I don't sacrifice. It's better to send money to Palestine or Chechen, where people have a greater need. Here we eat meat all the time, so it does not mean anything, but there they don't." He had a Secours Islamique can at the end of the counter for customers' donations.

These examples indicate a continuing pull between two notions of what to do in a new place. One is to try and replicate as closely as possible past practices, in order to secure a genealogical tie to a homeland through embodied practices of family-based sacrifice. The family can continue to gather around and say the Bismillah to the sheep, even if someone else cuts its throat. But doing so is only intermittently possible – the mobile abattoir I saw in 2004 lost money and did not appear the following year. The alternative is to highlight the ethnic component of sacrifice, taking the Baléatu modernists' emphasis on self-abnegation one step further.

Sharp though the split with tradition might seem in this case, "ethicizing" sacrifice would be one more instance of changing ritual practice by giving new weight to one of its elements, as have worshippers when they stress the ethical element of prayer.

By focusing on a single command to sacrifice on one day a year, we have been able to tease out two sources of variation. One is the set of local differences, such as the broad cultural contrasts between Morocco and Indonesia, or the practical challenges that stem from differences between urban Europe and rural Morocco. The other is the set of doctrinal positions taken with regard to the propriety of ritual actions, a contrast we saw most clearly in the Indonesian case, where the nature of humans' relationship to God was itself at stake: do we give in order to receive (the older village logic), or give in a selfless manner (the logic at the heart of the modernist critique)? Many specific elements of Muslims' lives diverge and flourish across these two axes, as we shall see for other domains in the following chapters.

FIVE

Healing and praying

In the last three chapters we worked from central, scripturally enjoined elements of Islam – revelation, worship, sacrifice – to diverse local interpretations and practices. This direction of analysis highlights the importance of referring to, and drawing from, a tradition, but it only includes those elements that are part of that common tradition. It leaves out local, culturally specific practices that some Muslims, but not others, might consider to be part of their Islam. This kind of omission is a weakness of classical approaches in religious studies, which only admitted to the canon of Islam that which could be seen as part of a single tradition.

This methodological concern leads me here to take the opposite route, and start from ways in which some people seek to heal or otherwise change the world through spells and prayer, and only then ask whether in doing so they draw on Islamic frameworks. Some Muslims develop specific ways of healing (or for that matter harming) that involve appeals to Islamic spirits or to God. Sometimes outsiders (including other Muslims, critical of these practices) might refer to these appeals in terms like "sorcery," "magic," or *bid`a* (illegitimate innovation), or shirk (polytheism). But for the practitioners, to heal in a religious fashion is to draw on God's benevolence. Even harming others might be understood as merely returning a malicious spirit to its original sender.

Prayer and spells

Across Muslim societies, men and women draw on the power of the Qur'an to ensure the health of their families or crops, the welfare of their dead, or to counter the illness-causing work of a malevolent spirit. They also may recite spells in their local language, or entreat the spirits to leave the afflicted. They may address their pleas to God, to Muslim spirits (jinn), or to other spirits. They might add biomedical remedies or consult an agricultural extension officer. In short, people try to cover their bases.

Usually people refer to these utterances with a term cognate with the Arabic *du`â'* (prayer) in the sense of a plea or request, and as such different from salat (the act of worship). These do'a, as I shall call them, are the key to how people draw on the Islamic tradition to act on the world by way of unseen elements: objects, spirits, or God.

On Mayotte, an island off Madagascar, Michael Lambek found in the 1970s that men and women said do'a to God in a number of ways, from structured mosque sessions to collective meals to individual actions. People would hold a ritual meal at which guests recited from the Qur'an on the host's behalf. They saw their recitations as a moral act, reasoning that one has done what one can, and now simply has to wait to see if, and how, God will respond. Going a bit further, slaughtering a cow for a feast, for example, created a moral obligation on the part of the recipient(s) to help in transmitting the request. The sacrifice, a *swadaka* (from Arabic *sadaqa*, "voluntary offering"), transferred responsibility up the chain, from the initial person, to his or her neighbors, to God – who, of course, has perfect freedom to do what he wishes. Sometimes, individuals made use of other material and spiritual intermediaries (Lambek 1993: 103–33). They could place leaves on a stump and pray to spirits known to hang about to take their request (for health, or good crops, or someone else's misfortune) to God. Alternatively, they could visit the tomb of a spiritually powerful person and, in the past, give money to the tomb attendant so that he would ask the spirit of the deceased to carry the plea to God.

This structure of recitation, sacrifice, and obligation underlies a range of events. In Mayotte, as in many other Muslim societies, ritual meals are held at certain times of the life cycle, particularly shortly after birth and shortly after death, as well as on the two major religious feast days, the Feast of Sacrifice and the Id al-Fitr held at the end of the fasting month. Mayotte villagers also held such meals annually to commemorate famous religious teachers (*fundi*), and on those occasions an entire village contributed to the feast.

A further expansion of this ritual logic came at successive moments following a death, when sacred music was performed as well. Moreover, before the Feast of Sacrifice people would hold an additional ritual meal (the *kuitimia*) for deceased ancestors, and first and foremost for one's deceased parents. Those who gathered sent the merit generated by their Qur'anic recitations and chanting (and the essence of the food itself) to ancestors, to the former religious teachers of the village, and (in a chain of religious ancestry) to the four caliphs and the Prophet Muhammad. Siblings and in-laws might pool their resources, and honor all their deceased parents at one meal, especially if they lived close to each other.

Lambek emphasizes that these rituals underscore the structure of Mayotte village society: equality among siblings and among villagers, and obligations toward one's kin and to a lesser extent toward one's village. The living and the dead each intercede on the other's behalf with God. Holding the rituals, especially the kuitimia, is religiously optional (*sunna*) but practically, as well as morally, obligatory, because if you fail to do so, your ancestors won't get their special "packages from God" and may then cause you trouble.

The conceptual structure underpinning Mayotte do'a*s* gives God the key role, as he must agree to transmit them to their intended destination. Of course, some people might send do'a designed to do others harm, and then one has to explain why God would be a part of such things. The answer partially lies in notions of His just and fair character, that those who suffer must have merited their suffering. But in practice, one utters do'a that seek out the party who has caused an illness, a theft, or another bad thing and that then takes vengeance on that person. One can recite a do'a that simply asks that the malefactor receive the punishment that he had intended to send to the victim. This practice minimizes social disruption, because you need not openly accuse anyone else, and anyone who might think that he or she had suffered from such a "return to sender" do'a is unlikely to find a sympathetic hearing if he or she complains. After all, it is the do'as that seek out the responsible person on their own.

Mayotte recitations and spells thus accomplish a number of socially important goals. They send blessings to the dead, benefit the living through a reciprocal economy of prayer, and punish those who commit misdeeds. These villagers thought of the causality involved in a double way. Do'as have certain effects – they seek out the evil-doer, and benefit your parents – but in the end nothing happens unless God wills it. The only certain thing is that a person who sends a do'a, for good or ill, will be held accountable by God for his actions.

Across the Indian Ocean, in the Gayo highlands of Sumatra, I found a very similar set of practices and beliefs at about the same time that Michael Lambek was working on Mayotte. The Gayo employed do'a for a range of purposes, believed that you can return an evil spell to its sender by way of God, and held collective meals on many of the same occasions as did the Mayotte villagers (Bowen 1993: 77–172).

If we look a bit deeper into the uses Gayo make of do'a, we can also see how they have drawn on older Malay-world figures and on broadly distributed Islamic ideas about creation and powers. In many societies across the Malay Archipelago, people think of the soul and spirit as connected to the material world through the placenta. The placenta is buried, or in some places hung from a tree, and serves as a continuing tie to the natural world, and in particular to a spirit called the "Old Hunter," who lives in the hills and can be appealed to in hunting (and who, as the brother of humans, sometimes is identified with Cain). He is also called on to protect a newborn child when he or she is first presented to the natural world. These Malay-world ideas provide one foundation for spells, by explaining why humans have a tie to the natural world, and how specialists might shape that tie to protect people and ensure their welfare.

But Gayo healers and teachers also set out a second set of ideas that link human souls and spirits to God through the process of creation. In a narrative of creation that derives from widespread Sufi theories of being, human souls are the individuations of a pan-human spiritual element, the Light of Muhammad (*Nur Muhammad*). Creation moved from the Light of God, through the Light of Muhammad, to the formation of individual souls. By powerfully summoning one's powers of concentration and imagination, humans can work back up through that chain of creation to harness the Light of Muhammad and the Light of God. The energy required to do so is called *maripët*, from the Arabic term *ma`rifa* or gnosis, which means approximately "powerful depictive imagination." Gayo esoteric specialists have in effect drawn on long-standing Sufi ideas about gnosis, that behind visible reality there is a spiritual reality and that one can gain access to that deeper reality through meditation, to explain how human healers can draw on God to heal the sick. A theory of knowledge becomes a theory of power.

In contrast to the Mayotte healer, Gayo healers sent back a malevolent spirit not only by reciting do'a but also by evoking the tight tie between the outer and inner layers of reality. My favorite healer, Aman Kena, would force the problematic spirit to locate itself inside a certain kind of citrus fruit, and then he would send the spirit back to its originator, saying: "Hey citrus, it is not you whom I strike but devils and Satan who connive and hate. It is not I who strike you but your own conduct that strikes you."

This declaration recalls the sixteenth-century Acehnese Sufi writer Hamzah Fansuri's account of God's immanence in the world, in which he rendered a Qur'anic verse (8: 17) concerning Muhammad's forces battling against those of Mecca as: "It was not you who slew them, but God who slew them." In this disavowal of uniquely human agency, the healer makes explicit that he has harnessed God's powers to expel the spirit.

Healing Muslims – and Hindus?

Now we travel part-way back across the Indian Ocean to Hyderabad in southern India, where Muslim healers treat Muslim, Hindu, and sometimes Christian patients. We move from a world where a few specialists draw on ideas that today we associate with Sufism, to a world where Sufi brotherhoods are important structuring forces in Muslim society, and indeed in public life. Joyce Flueckiger (2006) worked with one female healer, Amma, who, from her "healing room," treated patients with physical complaints or marital difficulties with a broad array of spiritual instruments. The most common among them were divination using the Arabic letter-value of a patient's name followed by provision of an amulet, to be worn or to be immersed in drinking water.

The techniques concern us less here than the social structure of the healing theory used by Amma. Both Amma and her husband, Abba, saw themselves as participating in two Sufi orders, the Chisti and the Qadiriyya. Abba was considered to be a *pir* (*pîr*). This word means "teacher," but also "saint," and designates someone who had received knowledge from his own teacher and permission to pass this knowledge on to his students. As a woman, Amma could not be a pir, but dispensed practical knowledge that she associated with the Sufi orders. They both saw themselves as Sunni Muslims, but also as close to `Ali, the Prophet Muhammad's son-in-law, his fourth successor, and the first Shi'ite imam. Indeed, they adorned their walls with pictures of `Ali, whom they associated with their Sufi lineages. When Abba died,

Amma put up on her wall a picture of a saintly figure dressed in green, holding a sword and on horseback, and thus identified as ʿAli, but with a picture of Abba's face pasted in. (Here, starting from a particular case helps us see how "Sunni" and "Shiʾite" categories can interweave in daily life even as they provide the raw material for social and political boundaries in some public settings.)

Amma worked equally frequently with Hindu and Muslim patients, speaking in Telugu with the former and Urdu (her first language) with the latter. (A close friend often helped in her Telugu conversations.) She used the same remedies with both groups, usually drawing on the power of Arabic letters. Her close Hindu friend ritualized a brother–sister relationship with Abba by performing the Hindu ritual of Raksha Bandhan with him, tying a string on his wrist. The friend's Hinduism prevented her only from becoming his disciple. Some treatments were called "Hindu" because they did not involve the use of written Arabic. Other treatments involved reading from the Qurʾan, but these were as likely to be used to cure a Hindu patient as a Muslim one. The efficacy of treatments draws on powers of spirits and God, and is universal, applicable to anyone.

Amma said that her power came entirely from the Qurʾan. Intriguingly, Abba emphasized that power came less from the spoken than from the written word of God: *kalam*, the pen. This idea returns us not to revelation (which was oral), but to the creation of the world by God through writing on the Eternal Tablet. Underneath Abba's and Amma's practices is a conception of the world in which God alone is the creator of all things, but the Hindu deities, too, exist, as do all manner of spirits (jinn). Muslims acknowledge the existence of jinn, and this recognition provides a channel for recognizing spirits of many kinds. During conversations with Flueckiger, Amma and Abba constructed different translations across the boundaries of Hinduism and Islam. In one conversation where the topic was the Hindu goddess, Amma remarked that the Prophet Muhammad was an avatar (the worldly form of a deity), just as were Krishna and Ram. At another moment, translating in the other direction across these boundaries, she assimilated Ram and Krishna into the list of the many prophets who preceded Muhammad. For his part, Abba argued that whereas God has no offspring, Ram and Krishna did, just as did Muhammad, and therefore those figures were not gods at all.

In these efforts to work out these ontological issues, Abba and Amma were constructing relations of equivalence across Hindu and Islamic notions of spiritual beings that would allow them to treat both Hindus and Muslims for their illnesses, acknowledge the work of spirits, the existence of avatars, and the reality of jinn, and yet also reaffirm the absolute distinction between God the creator and all else, creation. For all their apparent blending of ideas and traditions, they did retain that distinction.

Amma and Abba created a duo to harness her healing power in a way that would accord with dominant ideas about the transmission of power. On the one hand, Amma's role depended on Abba, as only men can inherit the status of a pir. His collaboration with her provided legitimacy to her activities in terms of the Islamic understandings shared by ordinary people in Hyderabad. Conversely, her healing powers led people to seek discipleship with him.

Across South Asia, women can gain different sorts of legitimacy from those available to men. Alyson Callan (2008) studied this dynamic in her work with female saint-healers in the Sylhet district of Bangladesh. She found asymmetry: although male healers draw on spirits and embody the power to heal, female saints must work through possession by spirits. This possession gives them certain socially unusual powers. Ideas about gender and power have been changing; Sylhet sends the greatest numbers of Bangladeshis to England, and return migrants bring new ideas about Islam with them that include critical observations on these possession practices.

Claiming to be a saint is a bit daring for a woman in Bangladesh, but if her power comes from the outside, in this case from spirits, rather than from a stable and internal power, that situation makes her claims more acceptable to the male scholars who set the tone and the conditions for public discourse concerning Islam. This interpretation of women's healing powers leads some scholars (and others) to acknowledge the healing power of these female saints, or *firani* (from pir). But the complementary relationship retains a sharp inequality. Men who are recognized as pirs have a permanent relation with spirits, due to their mastery of the power the spirits offer. This power gives a pir an embodied, stable status as a saint. Women, by contrast, have a temporary relationship with spirits. They negotiate with the spirit and act as intermediaries for it. Although women may aspire to higher degrees of autonomy and agency by developing a possession relationship, their ties to spirits lie in a field marked by locally specific forms of male/female asymmetry. Spirits may provide new channels for women, but they also mark the social asymmetry of male and female actors.

Let us say more here about the figure of the pir. He is a *wali*, a "friend of God." He is a master of a spiritual discipline and someone very close to God – in short, a holy man. He is worthy of respect but also of awe for the powers that his divine favor grants him. Living, he is to be consulted and obeyed; in the grave, he continues to provide aid and guidance. The saint is a part of Islamic ideas and practices across cultures, but that which makes one a saint is inflected by local ideas about power and authority.[1]

In subsequent chapters we will trace networks of Sufi teaching and preaching that extend across continents. In Pakistan and India, the pir or sheikh, and his students or *murids*, make up the basic unit of the chain of learning that guarantees authenticity of spiritual knowledge (recall the "isnad paradigm" from Chapter 2). These chains usually extend nominally upward to `Ali, the son-in-law of the Prophet Muhammad

---

[1] One by now classic demonstration of this cultural shaping of a shared idea was carried out by Clifford Geertz in his *Islam Observed* (1968), a study of holy men as central figures of Islamic politics in Morocco and Java.

(and in this extension lies the overlap of Sufi and Shi'ite histories and ideas), but they also pick out a particular teacher whose practices, and usually whose name, lend the chain of teaching its specific character. For example, the Qadiriyya order of spiritual practices is centered on a genealogy (*silsila*) of teaching that reaches from a current teacher back to ʿAbd al-Qadir al-Jilani (1077–1166 CE). These chains of transmission are inevitably recited during sessions of meditation and recitation, and they are thus both constitutive of an order and salient in its practices. The founders of orders also may figure in local stories about powerful people.

However, ordinary people generally choose to consult one pir rather than another because of his reputation rather than because of the particular Sufi order with which he is associated. Pirs may diagnose a problem as resulting from the actions of spirits or from other causes, such as the application of a magical poison. The remedies include exorcisms and amulets.

The same practical logic applies to *ziyarah* (*ziyâra*), visits made to the shrines of past pirs. Peter Van der Veer (1988) has shown that in certain regions of India the power of such shrines has been generally acknowledged by at least some Muslims, Hindus, and Sikhs. These powers often are quite specific: one shrine may be known for the pir's success in combating blindness, another for his efficacy against floods, and so forth.

The focus of pir devotion on resolving practical difficulties makes it easy to see how many South Asians would wish to continue to rely on their pirs if they moved overseas, where they would be at least as likely to have a need for practical help, thrown as they are into a new, and sometimes hostile, social environment, with a wide array of practical difficulties – illness, betrothals, employment – to overcome, and a local bureaucracy that would make pirs seem like the most easily accessible of remedies. We will return to this story of transnational resituating of pir power in Chapter 8.

So far, we have paid little attention to social movements and state actors in our discussion of South Asian healing. In Pakistan, particularly, various public actors have launched critiques of "improper" Sufism and of insufficient attention to the Hindu–Muslim boundary, and these critiques restrict what people may do and how they may talk about what they do. Katherine Ewing (1997) studied the transformations of shrines in Pakistan during the 1970s and 1980s. Pakistan had tried to construct a version of Islam that would both find favor with a large portion of the citizenry and fit into the project of state modernity, with religion remaining in its own proper domain and oriented toward encouraging proper social and economic behavior.

Sufism of a certain sort fit that bill, the reform-oriented kind that one shrine administrator characterized (positively) as "Calvinist" (1997: 81–8). Most of the pirs in Lahore (where Ewing worked) claimed to be "reformist" and to support shariah and denigrate polytheism (shirk), but different Muslims could mean quite different things by these terms. Some ordinary people denounced all that pirs did as shirk, whereas others saw writing amulets and healing the sick as perfectly proper, condemning only other forms of Sufism – much as Marsden found for the north-west region of Pakistan.

Those Sufis who best fit contemporary Pakistani state policies are those who emerged from the group calling themselves "Ahl-e Sunnat va Jama'a" but are often known as Barelwis (and discussed in Chapter 2). This movement emerged in the late nineteenth century in the Punjab as a way of both affirming the legitimacy of the pirs as mediators between people and God, and emphasizing the importance of normative practices in everyday life, converging in this respect with Deobandi teachings.

But in everyday life, pirs are accused of practicing polytheism, by which their accusers mean that they attend to spiritual beings other than God. Ewing (1997: 99–103) recounts a conversation between a pir she was interviewing and a neighbor of more strongly reformist leanings. The discussion turned on the very different interpretive frames that the pir and the neighbor held for understanding the term *sadaqa*, or gift. The pir described a way to expel a malicious spirit who was causing someone to be ill: slaughter a sheep in the jungle, he said, and leave it there as a sadaqa to the "thing" causing the problems. The neighbor then posed a question, intending to challenge the pir by shifting the frame of the discussion. He asked whether one sometimes gave sadaqa to the poor. Such is of course the standard meaning of sadaqa, and the question implied that such was the only acceptable meaning of the word and thus of the action.

The pir answered the question in a way that highlighted Islamic rules for purity but retained elements of his original interpretive frame: "You slaughter it by yourself. You must dump all the blood down the drain to make it halal. Not a single drop of blood should remain in the house." All the meat then should be cut up and distributed to others; "you cannot eat the meat of that goat." He then described another form of sadaqa where a live animal is let loose in the street: "they take it out of the house, away from themselves, and leave it." As Ewing insightfully explains, in both cases the pir was describing an act that could be taken at face value as a gift to the poor – or in the second case as a gift to whoever then catches the animal and takes it home – but his manner of speaking disclosed that he was also thinking of the direct, curative effects of the acts. The person who slaughters the animal must ensure that not one drop of blood remains in the house. If one lets a live animal loose, then the critical matter is to make sure that it leaves the house. In both cases, the malady afflicting the house is expelled along with the animal.

But as Ewing explains, the pir was careful to craft his answers in such a way that they could be taken to fit an interpretive framework consistent with reformist ideas about Islam – unlike Amma and Abba, or the healers in the Gayo highlands, who explicitly acknowledged theories of causality that conflict with reformist ideas because they imply direct relations of causality between the healing practices and the desired results. In the Lahore discussion, the neighbor held a position that any theory of spiritual efficacy without God's direct intervention was a form of poly-theism, and the pir tried to avoid explicitly contradicting that position.

This discursive situation – healing practices that must be given reformist justifications – generates profoundly ambivalent attitudes on the part of some who seek healing from the pirs.[2] Let me give two of the examples provided by Ewing. Ilmaz (Ewing 1997: 110–21) considered all living saints to be fakes, and she loudly and roundly denounced their fakery. But her house sat on the grave of a deceased saint, and her prac-tices implied a very different idea regarding the deceased saint's powers. She attributed all that happened to her when she was at home, for good or for ill, to her relationship to the saint. In her account, the saint acted to shape the fortunes of the living, as indeed did all the dead, only he had much more power because of his saintly status. If people did not accord his grave proper respect, she explained, he might cause them or others in the house to fall ill. Indeed, she classified her own illness as an instance of ta`wîz (magic) that had been initiated by a living person but that reached her by way of the saint.

Her reaction to her illness was not to react against the saint but to try and show him proper respect. She kept a shrine to him in her house, burning oil lamps to him every Thursday, as people would do at a public shrine. In her interpretation of things, it was his relationship to her that served as the general explanation of domestic conflicts: when cousins moved disruptively into her house and her husband seemed to be showing untoward affection toward one of these cousins, she inferred that the two of them were showing insufficient respect to the saint and bringing on these unwelcome events.

A second case concerns a resident of Lahore, Zabida, who maintained an active relationship with a public neighborhood shrine, which was dedicated to a deceased saint (Ewing 1997: 121–5). When Zabida's husband asked to have his place of work transferred nearer to home, and the request

---

[2] On these ambiguities and ambivalence see also Simpson (2007).

was granted, she attributed the welcome news to the saint's intervention. She told her husband to take some money to the shrine. But because these events took place in an urban context, where people of many different religious opinions monitored public comings and goings, Zabida had to take steps to prevent accusations of shirk. She did so in part by contrasting her relationship to the saint with those maintained by other people, including Muslims who did not understand Islam correctly, and non-Muslims. She spoke of those who "do *pûjâ*" to the saint, using the word used to describe Hindu prayer before a deity's image. By contrast, she described herself as going to the shrine to "offer du`â," or Islamic prayer. She explained that when she prayed, the saint interceded with God on her behalf, and that of her family, because he was closer to God. She elucidated this closeness by likening it to that within the anthropologist's own family. She might ask Ewing's daughter to get her mother to do something because the daughter is closer to her mother than anyone else is. The saint does not grant requests, she explained, but passes them along to God. But nonetheless, at times she was reluctant to admit that she visited the shrine, so strong was the sense that such visits came perilously close to shirk.

Negotiating religious boundaries

In these examples, healers consider themselves to be Muslims who work within an Islamic context, although they might also treat non-Muslims. Islam provides the "dominant discourse" (Baumann 1996) for healing practices, and healers and clients take care to justify what they do in terms that would satisfy reform-minded Muslims, suspicious of deviations from the true path in the direction of polytheism.

But in other societies, Islam itself is placed in question. Let us turn to examples in Africa, which also will underscore multiple potential modalities of healing through spirit possession. Beginning in the 1960s, anthropologists working in north-eastern Africa found that women sometimes were possessed by spirits, and that their events of possession stood in contrast to the Islamic ritual practices of men. Possession was seen as a means for women to compensate for their inferior social status in the public sphere.

By the 1980s, Janice Boddy (1989), Michael Lambek (1981), and others were reframing studies of possession, in order to emphasize the cultural forms and lived experiences associated with events of possession. In the society Boddy studied in the northern Sudan, men controlled public Islamic rituals, including worship associated with two Sufi orders. Women were barred from participation in the Sufi chanting sessions (*zikr*). Their role was to embody both femininity and the responsibility of reproducing society (in part by undergoing "pharaonic circumcision"), while men bore the responsibility of protecting and nurturing the women.

Women could be possessed by "red jinn" (*zairan*, sing.: *zar*), identified with blood and fertility. Red spirits are powerful, and can make the possessed person ill, or strengthen her fertility. They are morally ambiguous, as are sources of unseen power in much of Africa and Asia. Islamic leaders exhorted women to resist spirits' efforts to possess them, but women could only be cured of the mild illnesses brought by possession by entering into a life-long contractual relationship with them. The possession provided a new scope for women, placed them in a new position vis-à-vis the outside world. The spirits always came from outside the society, and indeed sometimes came from Europe, Turkey, Ethiopia, or China, allowing the possessed woman-plus-*zar* to experience her life from a broader perspective.

In a similar vein, in her work in Niger, Adeline Masquelier (2001) traced the complex tensions between possession involving *bori* spirits and the recent adoption of Islam. Women have to negotiate their continued practice of *bori* possession vis-à-vis their recently converted Muslim husbands. As elsewhere, possession can both mark gender asymmetries and highlight contrasts between modalities of practicing Islam which are locally considered to be more or less orthodox. Michael Lambek, working on Mayotte, found a similarly marked contrast between women's spirit possession and men's stricter observance of core Islamic practices – although women did also pray and men did also participate in possession. The contrast at times was sensually striking: As he watched a procession of possessed women pass by a mosque, "the warm, boisterous, unruly, and sensual spirits, dressed in their colorful garb, marched out of the forest as the men soberly, individually, and with measured dignity prepared to prostrate themselves before the single, unquestionably ethical, and all-powerful God" (Lambek 1993: 367).

Across these works of the 1980s and early 1990s, spirit possession in certain African societies appeared to give women powers to speak, control, and heal in sites that stood in contrast to mainstream Islamic rituals. Possession became a key site for theoretical and comparative studies in anthropology (Ortner 2005), in part because it brought together issues of gender separation and dominance, the possibilities and difficulties of interpreting acts as "resistance," and, in these African cases, the boundaries between Islamic and other forms of orientation toward the unseen world.

Working in the quite different context on the Kenyan coast, Janet McIntosh (2004) describes the role of possession in reinforcing boundaries between those who practice Islam and those who do not. Islamic spirits may possess Giriama women and, to a lesser extent, men, and attempt to induce them to convert to Islam. Some of them do so. The spirits compel the possessed people to develop patterns of avoiding foods that mimic the food avoidance patterns followed by Muslims. They lose their appetites during the day in Ramadan, and they vomit if they eat foods avoided by Muslims, such as the palm-wine and bush rats that Giriama generally do eat and that stand for the Giriama contrast with the Muslim Swahili. (Indeed, Swahili may refer to Giriama as "dogs" and "rats.") For McIntosh, possession embodies ideas about their own impurity in contrast to the purity of Muslims and points toward Islamization as the answer. She argues that the tensions experienced and articulated in these terms stem from contests over the control of land between Swahili and Giriama peoples, and that the Swahili racialized the Muslim/non-Muslim contrast in order to justify their own superior economic position. Giriama, in turn, have "somatized" it, meaning that they have come to sense a struggle within their own bodies between their impure Giriama selves and the Islamic road to purity.

Anthropology long has taken as one of its key concerns the role of boundaries in everyday life. Inspired by Durkheim but nourished by ethnographies of prohibitions, marriages, and gender, anthropologists have explored the ways in which people employ sacred and spiritual forces to create and transform social boundaries. Here we see the added value of studying the social situations of Islam; by asking how people imagine and govern their relationships with the sacred, we can see where Islam does and does not enter into the equation, how it can provide a repertoire of ideas and justifications for social projects that have their origins elsewhere, in conflicts over resources or power, or in efforts to maintain social distinctiveness.

Throughout this chapter, we started not with Islamic texts but with locally specific practices by which women and men engage with the spirit world. Then we examined in what ways they understood these practices in Islamic terms. This methodological reversal from the previous chapters allows us to discern zones of Islamic analysis that would otherwise go unnoticed, exterior as they are to canonical ideas about proper Islam. Herein lies another important mode of an anthropological approach, one that allows us to accompany local actors as they work from locally defined ways of life to broader Islamic frameworks.

SIX

ॐ

Pious organizing

In examining healing and spiritual power we encountered references to Sufism, but this category includes a far broader range of phenomena than those we discussed. When scholars of Islam mention Sufism, they might mean one of two things. Many Muslims throughout the world practice one or more ways of praying and praising God, drawing on the mystical tradition of Islam called *tasawwuf*. They invoke God's name in recitations often called dhikr, literally "remembrance." In this sense, Sufism refers to a set of practices based on widely accepted ideas about communication and devotion available to most Muslims.

But a Muslim might also belong to an organized Sufi group or order (*tarîqa*), which traces its particular set of practices back to a founder and highlights this genealogy as its grounds for sanctity. An order has a leader – a sheikh or pir – and rules about how their members worship. Some orders also structure political or economic life. Some of the larger orders (Naqshbandiyya, Qadariyya, Tijaniyyah) have spread across continents and indeed may have been one of the major vehicles for the coming of Islam to parts of Asia and Africa. Today, membership in these or other orders links some Muslims living in Muslim-majority societies with those living in Europe and North America.

The word "Sufi" might, then, be used to refer to widely available practices, or also to membership in a religious order. Although some in Europe and North America might be surprised to learn that Sufism is a dimension of Islam and not only a literary or philosophical domain, in fact most members of a Sufi order are not otherwise different from other Muslims. Most carry out the ordinary obligations of Muslims to pray, fast, and so forth. Many other Muslims share the basic ideas that undergird Sufism. God bestows blessings on humans, and in particular on those who are closest to him, his "friends" or *auliyâ'* (sing.: *walîy*), one of the terms often translated as "saint." Some saints are higher than others; at the highest level, a saint serves as a "pole" (*qutb*) and provides particularly powerful blessings during his life and after his death.[1]

The pursuit of tasawwuf may lead a Muslim down multiple paths. A Sufi pathway includes both a set of practices – reciting a particular phrase, moving in a particular rhythm – and a genealogy (silsila) of authority that links the practitioner through the person who created the practices and then to a Companion of the Prophet, usually `Ali, the Prophet's son-in-law. Many of these pathways take on the name of the founder and sometimes become institutionalized as Sufi orders. As we saw in the last chapter, the Qadiriyya order is attributed to `Abd al-Qadir al-Jilani. Each of these orders developed its own characteristics. For example, the Naqshbandi order followed by many at the South Asian Deobandi school (and elsewhere throughout the world) emphasizes the relationship of the order's leader, the sheikh, to the individual disciple, and teaches silent and immobile recitation. Those who follow the Qadiriyya order practice their recitations with loud speech and strong movements.

We should resist the temptation to speak of "Sufis" as if they were, or are, a class of people, apart from the Sunni or Shi'ite mainstreams. At least since the great flowering of Sufi thought and practice in the twelfth and thirteenth centuries, many Muslim jurists and teachers also have been initiates in Sufi orders. Institutions were developed to support devotional activities (called *khanqah* or *ribat*) but the institutions were part of mainstream religious institutions to the extent that a single institution

---

[1] On early Sufism see Karamustafa (2007).

might give lessons in jurisprudence, support Sufi devotions, and serve as a public mosque. Indeed, the historian Jonathan Berkey (2002: 240–1) writes that by the late fifteenth century, "the terms *madrasa*, khanqah, and 'mosque' were often used interchangeably."

So widely have devotional practices and teachings been accepted by Muslims that many of those who are claimed as relatively "hard-line" advocates of rigor and opponents of deviations in Islam in fact were members of Sufi orders. Let me give just two examples. Ibn Taymiyya (d. 1328) is claimed by the Wahhabis as their theological ancestor and fiercely attacked many forms of Sufism, but he was himself a member of a Qaridiyya order. In 1928, Hassan al-Banna founded the Muslim Brotherhood in Egypt, the organization that has devoted itself to developing private and public Islamic institutions based on Islamic law. He was also a member of a Sufi order and wrote on the importance of developing personal discipline through Sufism, as well as on building a better Islamic social order based on law.

The Sufi path leads toward a kind of knowledge that is distinct from knowledge about things, or `ilm*; the Sufi path leads toward gnosis, apprehension of divine reality, ma`rifa. The seeker on the path toward this knowledge must lose him- or herself, and the acts of chanting, meditating, or even whirling are intended to move one on the path toward that self-loss. But the student's teacher, sheikh, or pir aids the ordinary person by being a channel of God's grace.

Shrines and sheikhs

New work in anthropology has examined how Sufis pass through successive states in pursuit of this goal. Pnina Werbner (2003) studied the Naqshbandi Sufi "regional cult" centered on the shrine of Zindapir in Pakistan and extending to Britain. She describes the chanting of dhikr engaged in here, as elsewhere, but when she asked leaders of the cult, "deputies" or *khalifas* (*khalífa*s) of Zindapir, to describe their path toward knowledge, they responded by presenting the odes or *qasida* (*qasîda*) they had written in praise of the sheikh. These poems (Werbner 2003: 171–5) praise the sheikh as the pole (qutb) of all those who are close to God, as the feeder of the poor through whom God's grace flows, and as the source of an intense gaze that conveys God's blessings *barkat* [*barakât*]. The poet portrays his own experience as being caught in a whirlpool from which the sheikh saves him. Here the poet is expressing the tenet emphasized within the Naqshbandi order, that one must return from these esoteric experiences to a life within the shariah.

Similar stages or steps were described by Julian Johansen (1996) for the Muhammadiyya Shadhiliyya order in Cairo, which holds twice-weekly sessions of chanting and questions-and-answers called the *hadra*, "presence." Sessions are held after the night prayer, and anyone may attend. After the congregationally performed prayer there begins a fixed sequence of recitations; these are the vehicles for drawing nearer to God, and so bear repeating here, as similar sequences are found in other orders. First, the man who called the congregation to prayer "seals" it by reciting the Throne Verse (Qur'an 2: 255) mentioned earlier. Worshippers then chant three common phrases, thirty-three times each: *subhân Allâh* ("God glorified"), *al-hamdu lillâh* ("thanks be to God"), and *Allâh Akbar* ("God is great"). They are then free to carry out individual silent prayers. Books are passed out containing the twenty-ninth of the thirty sections into which the Qur'an is usually divided, and everyone reads (or recites by heart) the first chapter in this section, al-Mulk (no. 67). After this, the order's leader, Sheikh Muhammad, becomes the chant leader, calling for one phrase after another to be repeated by all present, each thirty-three times, followed by multiple recitations of the Fatihah, the short opening to the Qur'an, each time dedicating it to a specific beneficiary, beginning with the Prophet, his family, and his Companions, and then allowing anyone present to suggest that a recitation be dedicated to a particular ill or needy individual. The main activity then follows: the formal session of dhikr, including repetitions of the Sura al-Ikhlas and of other chapters and prayers. Johansen points out that one series of recitations includes different names of God, in the precise order in which they appear in the Throne Verse. After the long dhikr, the sheikh accepts written questions and delivers his answers.

In both the Zirpindi order in Pakistan and the Shadhiliyya order in Cairo, seekers or students sit literally or figuratively at the feet of a sheikh, who himself once learned from his own sheikh, and so on upwards, at least in theory, to a Companion of the Prophet. They engage in chanting as an exercise to approach closer to God, but they do so under the guidance of their leader, from whom they receive additional blessings. They also combine a search for knowledge of God through recitations with a search for knowledge of what God has commanded, by asking the sheikh for guidance, or by studying at a school.

We will return to these and other examples of Sufi institutions for other purposes; here what is critical is that many Muslims pursue two goals simultaneously: living in accord with God's norms or path in the outer world (shariah) and seeking a mystical path (tariqa) toward God.

Sufi orders were among the earliest topics for anthropological study, probably because they provided socially well-demarcated objects of study: orders that held meetings, visited sacred graves, had healing practices and explicit histories, and sometimes included strong political and economic dimensions. Early British anthropology focused on Africa, which meant that Africa provided the first anthropologies of Sufi orders: the icon of anthropology at Oxford, E. E. Evans-Pritchard, studied the Sanusiyya Sufi order in Libya (1949), and Ernest Gellner, at the London School of Economics and at Cambridge, studied saints in the Atlas Mountains of Morocco (1969). The next generation of anthropologists in Britain and the United States continued this line of research; notable among them were studies on Sufi orders by Michael Gilsenan in Egypt (1973) and Dale Eickelman in Morocco (1976).

So central did Sufi studies become for the anthropology of African Islam that for many readers it is likely that Sufi orders, and one in particular, came to stand for African Islam. The order in question was that of the Mourides in Senegal, known in particular through the work of Donal Cruise O'Brien (1971, 1975). The Mouride order is striking for its success in creating political and economic order, including its successful peanut farming enterprise. As Mourides have emigrated from Senegal, they have taken this work ethic with them and have created islands of economic success in New York and in Europe. Of course, Islam in Africa is more diverse than this focus suggested, but by the 1980s we knew a lot more about saints than about ʿulama, and about miracles than about laws (see below for more on the Mourides).

If most Muslims acknowledge the existence of special "friends of God" (awliyâ, sing.: waliy), the "pious ones" (sâlihîn) mentioned in the Qur'an, they are not at all in agreement as to what powers these friends have and how ordinary humans ought to relate to them, if at all. Those who do enter into a relationship with them might bring offerings in exchange for spiritual and material benefits. The shrines built around the graves of dead saints, and the homes of living ones, have become Sufi centers. Although one finds both shrines and living saints in many parts of the world, in northern and western Africa they have attained particular political significance as lodges, some of which have mosques, schools, and centers of agriculture and commerce associated with them.

A signal anthropological contribution to understanding Sufism has been the focus on specific lodges and their practices. One of the early key texts was Eickelman's (1976) study of the Sherqawi lodge in a town in western Morocco. Whereas Evans-Pritchard and Gellner had placed North African Sufism firmly within a framework of segmentary lineage structures, Eickelman stressed the religious basis for the political authority enjoyed by the leaders of the order.

In the western Moroccan town of Boujad, the key religious place is the shrine or zawya (zâwîya) founded in the sixteenth century by a saint, here called a marabout, Sidi Muhammad Sherqi. By Eickelman's count (Eickelman 1976: 6), one-third of the town's eighteen thousand people claimed descent from this holy man, who continued to serve as an intermediary between God and those who sought his aid. Marabouts, living or dead, are the North African Sufi, "friends of God," who are in a position to pass along God's grace (*baraka*) to those who seek it. This privileged spiritual position became the basis for political power across North Africa, and particularly in Morocco, where, as Eickelman writes (Eickelman 1976: 7), "maraboutism" was the prevailing sociopolitical form of Islam until the late nineteenth century.

The rise of politically powerful lodges and orders beginning in the fifteenth century had to do with the growing practice of tracing a genealogy from a holy man upward to the Prophet Muhammad. The royal dynasties of Morocco, including the present king, also trace such a Prophetic genealogy, and this dual set of such claims has probably added to the legitimacy of each. By the late nineteenth century, the Sherqawi lodge and its subsidiary marabouts – including anyone locally considered to be able to transmit baraka and possessing a kin tie to the founder – extended over a large area and received gifts of grain and valuables in return for those blessings. The Moroccan ruler in effect devolved some of his authority to the lord (*sid*) of the zawya, granting to him the right to propose a local king's deputy or *qaid* (*qâ'id*) and relying on the order to resolve local disputes (Eickelman 1976: 31–64).

As of the late 1960s, the town of Boujad had twenty-three Sherqawi shrines; in 1969, during one two-week period during the celebrations of the founder, twenty-five thousand tribesmen visited the shrine (Eickelman 1976: 84). The conceptions of spiritual power that motivate and animate these visits draw on the broadly distributed notions of wali mentioned above but also, through the term marabout, on notions of the social order characteristic of Morocco. The term marabout comes from the Arabic root r-b-t, meaning to tie or bind, and indicates that the saint is "tied to God" in a dyadic relationship, just as human clients are "tied to" those on whom they depend.

As analyzed by Eickelman, Lawrence Rosen (1984), and Clifford Geertz (1968), Moroccan society is structured around such social dyads, which may multiply either into networks or into hierarchies, depending on the broader social configurations in which they are located. The root n-s-b is central to understanding these ties. The root gives rise to words that translate as "relationship," "to link," "to trace one's ancestry," and "proportionate," and is used to indicate ties and relationships that provide an identity: to ancestors, to birth place, to occupation, or to any social group, or category. People cement these ties by exchanging obligations through gifts and services (Rosen 1984: 18–30).

Eickelman echoes Émile Durkheim in arguing that people structure their social relations in particular ways and then project those structural relations onto the supernatural world. Just as individuals shape their social world through gifts and obligations to others like them, so too they shape their ties to marabouts through exchanges: they have obligations (to give grain, for example) and they can expect to receive blessings (baraka). This obligation to give things and to reciprocate with blessings then generates a general social rule that any person should offer hospitality to those who arrive at one's house with gifts.

The Sherqawi case provides an opportunity to see how the broad Islamic tradition shapes practices and ideas across widely different societies, but is in turn shaped by local ideas. In examining western Moroccan ideas that bear on social and religious life, Eickelman emphasizes the idea of the wali, the importance of reason `aql (from the root [`-q-l]), and the central place of obligation. Each concept, or rather each collection of ideas, can be found in, say, Pakistan and Indonesia as well as in Morocco, but with distinct emphases in each place. The idea of the saint or wali, the "friend" of God, spread along with Sufism across Muslim-majority societies. But if in parts of Africa it underpinned the development of hierarchical social orderings, in South and Southeast Asia it shaped worship practices around graves of individual saints and a general sense of the power of the "inner" (*bâtin*) world of spiritually powerful beings.

By contrast, the idea of reason, while also part of a universally acknowledged set of Islamic values, tends to be discursively highlighted in those times and places where Muslims are urging the reform of older institutions. Movements to reform Islamic practices and institutions often invoke an appeal to reason over and against superstition, polytheism (shirk), and illegitimate innovation (*bid`a*), whether in Africa, Asia, or elsewhere.

The logic of distribution of each of these ideas, then, has its own particular form: ideas of sainthood are mapped onto local cultural forms, while ideas of rationality emerge with reform movements. The idea of right and social obligation (*haqq*), by contrast, seems to be linked to regional ways of creating social networks. In much of Africa, social ties are formed through obligations of open-ended hospitality and defense of the honor of a kin group. But nothing is inevitable about the form and practices that will characterize any particular Sufi order. By the 1960s, for example, an order called the Budshishiyya, a branch of the Qadiriyya founded in 1942 in western Morocco, had become an urban proselytizing order, increasingly appealing to the French-speaking elite (Haenni and Voix 2007). One of its more prominent teachers, Sheikh Abdessalam Yassine, became the spiritual leader of the Moroccan Justice and Charity (*al-`Adl wa-l-Ihsân*) movement, linking the Sufi order to a politically oriented, urban religious organization.

But the order developed out of a "diasporic" network as well. The noted intellectual Faouzi Skali, also the founder in 1995 of the Fès Festival of World Sacred Music, developed training sessions in France for the Budshishiyya order. In these sessions he emphasized the general spiritual qualities of Sufism, and then transported these ideas back to Morocco. At the same time, the new Moroccan leader of the order, Sidi Hamza, transformed the order from a highly localized, rural institution to one more adapted to a delocalized, urban clientele. As part of the effort to generalize the order, he replaced celebrations of local saints' birthdays with the birthday of the Prophet Muhammad. He also started a summer Sufi university near the town of Madagh.

Elsewhere, the same order has taken on a corporatist character. In Casablanca it features social groups organized around professions, thus the "zawiya of medical doctors." Those who join the order include many who come by way of other spiritual journeys, by way of Buddhism or a general New Age set of pathways; some adherents come from the community of Moroccans studying in France. But this opening up of the order to a more generic sense of spirituality has had an immediate consequence for its mode of authority, in that some of the new recruits see no reason to think of Sidi Hamza as a particularly important mediator between them and God. For them it is the practices that are important, not the relation of pupil to master. Encouraging this tendency are associations that have emerged to link together what had been distinct Sufi practices and even non-Islamic spiritual traditions. One convert to the Budshishiyya order wrote a book called *Maghribi Yoga* (North African Yoga), which claims that yoga originated from North African Sufi practices! Sufism, then, becomes reduced to its spiritual disciplines and physical exercises, free or devoid of a sense of hierarchical ties of haqq to a sheikh or to his predecessors.

Political economies of salvation

Sufi orders thus seem especially good subjects for comparative social analyses that ask how and why orders differ in their ways of structuring the local social world. After his early work in Egypt, Michael Gilsenan studied Sufism in a second field site, this time in Lebanon. This contrastive study allowed Gilsenan (1982) to see how deeply two configurations of spiritual power and temporal ordering – albeit both called "Sufism" – could differ. He had begun work in Cairo in the 1960s, in an order that provided the urban poor ways to have access to miracles (*mu`jizât*). These miracles constituted signs of grace or power from the divine, or *karâmât*, coming as God's blessing (baraka). The low-paid workers who formed the core of the order drew on these three key ideas – miracles, grace, and blessing – to find order and meaning in what might otherwise seem to be accidental events of everyday life: sickness or fortune, marriage or death, finding a small amount of money, or losing it. Here is where the Sufi order comes in: the order's officers made sure that followers understood that God's blessings were channeled by way of the founder, the long-deceased saint who acted as intermediary between God and the faithful. The stories attesting to his powers depicted the saint as an illiterate, untutored man who nonetheless was able to best the ulama in erudition, regarding complex problems of mathematics or matters of theology. In this regard, they resembled the understanding of the Prophet Muhammad as the vehicle for divine revelation, revelation in the form of beautiful, inimitable poetry, revealed through a man whose very illiteracy proves that the Qur'an *was* of divine origin, as he could not possibly have created the verses himself.

When Gilsenan (1996) turned to working among Sufis in northern Lebanon, he found a very different conceptual and political organization. Little mention was made of grace or blessings; rather, everything was couched in terms of the opposition between the land-owning governing clan and the men of religion, the *beys* (or "lords of the marches"), and the sheikhs. On the one side was temporal power and force; on the other, knowledge and spiritual authority. "Sufism" here was part of a generalized opposition between two categories of powerful men. All stories of miracles and spiritual power were framed by that political opposition: a lord once insulted a sheikh, and subsequently lost his wealth, while another could not stand up straight until a sheikh willed it.

But this division was not strictly one of earthly versus divine power; villages were run by sheikhs or by lords, and in the former case, the sheikhs were themselves the landowners. Furthermore, the beys subsidized the lives of the sheikhs, and the sheikhs preached that the political order should not be upset. In a fashion redolent of Martin Luther's comments on the German peasant revolts, sheikhs taught that peasants were potential sources of disorder, and disorder was to be avoided.

Gilsenan finds that the highly structured nature of power in northern Lebanon means that to speak of a free-floating baraka would not have had an "elective affinity" (Max Weber's borrowing from Goethe) with the political order, whereas in the more loosely structured world of proletariat Cairo, such an affinity develops, in that grace comes via the saint, and is found in any number of events in everyday life.

Here is one time-honored contribution of the anthropologist, in showing how political ties reshape and reweight religious ideas: not producing them as simple reflections of material conditions, but transforming them into a locally specific set of ideas and practices. Lebanon and Cairo – and for that matter Senegal and Morocco – share ideas of God's grace, but everyday ways of talking about divine power differ markedly.

West Africa presents a different set of possibilities for combining local political power and access to divine blessing. West African scholars have argued that Islam fits into a pre-existing set of ideas about power and knowledge, the "esoteric episteme" in Louis Brenner's words (2001). Both power and knowledge are seen as inherently hierarchical and as esoteric, with some elements of knowledge kept secret. Thus the use of amulets, and ideas of mystical knowledge and sainthood, while present in Islamic formulations worldwide, became especially prominent in West Africa. Non-Islamic people held similar ideas: that power resided in secret objects or secret knowledge, and that sorcerers or witches held concealed sources of power.

If power/knowledge is intrinsically linked to secrecy in West Africa, then it is unsurprising that Muslim leaders who succeeded in anti-colonial jihads would be seen to hold esoteric powers that might be passed on to their descendants, or that Sufi leaders would be particularly successful in this region in forging political or economic enterprises on the bases of their special access to the divine. Sufi emphasis on esoteric knowledge and leadership presented an elective affinity with West African ideas.

The military and spiritual leader Umar Tall (d. 1864) provides a case in point. Tall was affiliated to the Tijaniyya order, named after Ahmad al-Tijani (d. 1815), who claimed that he had received revelations directly from the Prophet Muhammad and that those who recited his order's prayers gained special access to heaven. As Tall conquered neighboring peoples and attacked the French, his followers saw his military success as due to his access to esoteric knowledge. Colonial rule over a large geographical area had facilitated the emergence of this kind of leader, by making it easier to move around and establish spatially broad affiliations (Soares 2005). France's Muslim policies also favored Sufis because they represented a relatively orderly, and thus safe, form of Islam, in contrast both to local Muslims who traveled and hence could spread danger-ous pan-Islamic ideas, and to the Islam of North Africa. (This French view that West African Islam is more domesticated than North African Islam continues to shape French media treatments of Muslims.) French policies encouraged division within religious orders, a variant of the usual divide-and-rule strategy. Thus when a Tijani leader, Muhammad al-Akhdar, arrived from Morocco at the turn of the twentieth century claiming that he had the correct teachings that had been transmitted from the Prophet through al-Tijani, and also that the way local Sufis prayed was incorrect, he was arrested and detained by the French. But he suc-ceeded in appointing a successor, Hamallah, who attracted people who were not part of the religious establishment and those who rejected pre-vailing social hierarchies (Soares 2005: 78–9). The French came to see the Tijani branch, which followed the descendants of Umar Tall, as the safer bet, and repressed the branch associated with Hamallah. Exiled in 1941, Hamallah died in France, although many of his followers, who became members of the Hamawiyya, believe that he lived on and would return someday.

The current representatives of these lineages now occupy key roles in the "prayer economy" of this part of Mali. When Benjamin Soares conducted fieldwork in the late 1990s in Nioro, the central town for Tijani, Hamallah's son, Muhammadu, was referred to as "the sharif" in the region, using a term for a descendant of the Prophet Muhammad. Others recognized Umar Tall's descendant, Cerno Hady Tall, as Tall's successor. Followers of each of these figures considered their leader to be the saint, and gave them gifts, which enabled both men to amass substantial fortunes. Each maintained a religious center (*zawiya*), to which followers made annual pilgrimages. Both were thought to be closer to God than were ordinary people, and to have powers that came from God, including the power to predict events. Malians living elsewhere in Africa, or even in France, would visit Nioro to ask the two leaders to intercede on their behalf through prayers to God. Soares emphasizes that the lineage of these men was necessary, but not sufficient, to ensure their reputation as saints. People discussed the miracles and wealth of these men, and even their ability to change physical appearance, as signs that confirmed their saintly status, seeing them as blessings that they receive directly from God – and rightly so, given their proximity to Him.

Ordinary people sought out these leaders for religious instruction or for aid in resolving a dispute. An entire lineage might ally itself with one or the other of the two leaders. And such alliances became visible on Fridays. People might perform their Friday congregational prayers at the Hamallah lodge in order to make clear that their loyalties lie with that branch. The Tall lineage has just a small mosque, but some people would make daily trips there to pray. (Recall that in Chapter 3 we discussed the use of congregational salat in many regions to clarify ritual or social allegiances.)

Soares tells us how the prayer economy works in its own terms: ordinary people give gifts to these saintly leaders so that they in turn will distribute them to the poor. These gifts range from a bit of grain to a new car. People call these gifts by the Arabic word *hadiya*, and thereby distinguish them from alms (sadaqa), even though these gifts, too, eventually benefit the poor. They use hadiya only for gifts made to those of saintly lineage, and they have a specific conception of the logic of such gifts. Hadiya gifts create merit, and by giving them to saints, or at least to people closer to God than are ordinary folks, the gift-givers receive this merit, called *baraji*, which was as important as baraka (Soares 2005: 167). Givers receive the merit through blessings and prayers, or perhaps as a hand placed on their shoulder, which is understood to be directly transmitting blessings.

The hierarchy of saintliness is translated into physical distance and separation in Nioro. On the annual visits to the religious sites in the town, visitors line up in the hope, often unrealized, of seeing, or even touching, the saintly men. But even for people who live in the town, boundaries are maintained: Hady Tall travels the short distance between home and mosque in a car, so as not to have to mingle with ordinary folk. Muhammadu, his rival, prays in a separate space, even on Fridays. And at the same time that the leaders' sanctity is reaffirmed through their separation from ordinary people, so too their followers remind themselves of their shared status as the saint's followers when they see each other gathering near one or the other of the sacred sites.

The reach of Tijani saintly power is not limited to Mali. By reproducing images and even events on photographs, tapes, and disks, followers can expand the sacral catchment areas of these and other saints – although in doing so they risk being accused of polytheism, or shirk, by other Muslims. Moreover, the two Nioro religious leaders have attracted interest and gifts from high-ranking political leaders, including the presidents of Mali, Mauritania, and Gabon, as well as well-off merchants throughout western Africa. These prestigious visitors would arrive in private planes and cars; some even bought villas in Nioro to accommodate them on their visits. The religious figures received them privately, gave them blessings, and probably employed forms of divination and amulets for them.

Next door in Senegal, there arose the best-known of the West African Sufi orders, the Murîdiyya or Mourides (O'Brien 1971). The Mouride order differs in one key religious respect from other orders we have considered, a difference that has had political–economic repercussions: it is not strictly speaking an order. Other orders, such as the Tijaniyya and Qadiriyya, distinguish themselves through their particular sacred genealogies and their recitations (dhikr, *wirid*). A line of spiritual ancestors transmitted a specific set of practices down to the current faithful, and this genealogy is recited and often displayed prominently in spaces associated with the order. It is often differences over the recitation practices that lead to, or are used to justify, divisions among orders. For example, the division within the Tijaniyya that led Hamallah to found a new branch order began when his promoter, al-Akhdar, argued that the correct form of a certain prayer developed by Ahmad al-Tijani involved twelve recitations, rather than the eleven recitations practiced in Nioro.

The Mourides work in a different way. Founded by Sheikh Amadou Bamba (1850–1927) in the late nineteenth century in Senegal, they are best known for their astute combination of rigorous prayer activities and successful peanut trade. Unlike those we have been discussing, the order is based not on the exclusive use of a set of recitations, but on the founder's insistence that each of his followers submit to a sheikh and practice Islam. They could recite prayers he had written, but they were also free to recite prayers from other orders, provided by other sheikhs. The unifying idea for the Mourides was that everyone should submit to an order, an emphasis contained in the order's name, for *murîd* means follower or pupil or, in the Sufi context, disciple. The focus of the order was not on a long lineage of spiritual transmission, but on obedience in everyday affairs to the order's leader or "Khalifa-General." After Amadou Bamba's death, his followers focused their worship activities on his tomb in the Senegalese city of Touba, and on the mosque that was completed there in 1961.

This difference in the definition of the order has had social consequences, for other sheikhs have disputed the spiritual superiority of
Amadou Bamba's son and successor, but have acknowledged his role as
Khalifa-General, as the head of an enterprise (O'Brien 1971: 123). And
quite an enterprise it was: followers not only gave gifts to the leader, as
with other orders, but they also were required to work for several days
each year on his fields and on those of other sheikhs. The leader turned
this free labor into an enormously successful cash-crop enterprise, particularly in peanuts. Although initially the French had suspected Bamba of
disruption, they supported the peanut industry of his successors, giving
them land, machinery, and credit.

Global movements

These orders are tailor-made for extending nodes of authority around
the globe, because a sheikh can delegate authority to a disciple, who
then becomes leader of a branch established in a new place. Indeed,
Sufi orders played major roles in spreading Islam into much of Asia and
Africa by drawing on this logic of segmentary authority. But since the
late nineteenth century, the increased ease of travel and communication
has made it possible for teachers to directly monitor and control their
followers' activities.

From the center in Touba, Senegal, the Mourides have been particularly
active in constructing religious–commercial networks throughout the
world. In Marseilles, for example, Mourides developed a local network
at the beginning of the twentieth century, owning small hotels and cafes.
In the 1970s, after drought in Senegal and the worldwide economic crisis
pushed many Mourides into new transnational trade, they began to
move in larger numbers to Paris, New York, and elsewhere. Marseilles has
maintained an important place in this network, both because of its port
history and because it once was a stop on the route to Mecca. Today the
Marseilles Mourides are most likely to gather on those occasions when the

sheikh of their order arrives from Senegal. After the Mourides had settled in far-flung places, the Touba sheikh transformed the pattern of visiting (*ziyâra*): whereas adepts once visited the sheikh to pay homage, now it is the sheikh who circulates around the globe to visit his followers (compare Blank 2001). As of the 1980s, and in more public fashion by the 2000s, the several thousand Senegalese Mourides in Marseilles welcomed regular visits by the descendant of the order's founder. The members of the many Mouride worship circles, the *dâ'ira*s, where adepts regularly meet to recite religious poems and pray, come together to welcome the sheikh. He, in turn, brings signs of his blessings, his baraka, in forms of images and cassettes. When, for example, the Sheikh Sérigne Mourtada Mbacké visited Marseilles in 2001, he urged his followers to build a "Sérigne Touba house," as he did at each stop on his circuit; taken together, these houses demarcate the Mouride global space (Bava 2003: 161).

Many other West Africans in France belong to other Sufi orders and participate in their respective global circuits of travel and study. The Tijaniyya order is represented by the Sheikh Tierno Mansour, who lives south of Dakar but makes regular visits to his followers in the Paris region and elsewhere in France. He makes his French base in an apartment in a high-rise building outside of Paris. For many of his Pulaar-speaking followers in France, he stands as a moral exemplar (and indeed as a saint, wali) in a land where upholding and transmitting Islamic values is seen as extremely difficult. Many of these Muslims credit his visits for returning them to the proper practice of Islam (Soares 2004).

An Iranian order, the Shahmaghsoudi, illustrates another geographical possibility: centering an order *in* the diaspora. Founded in California, the order includes over seventy-five lodges throughout the world and was created to provide alternative forms of Islam to those promoted by the Iranian Revolution. At the same time, it taps into the centuries-old Oveyssi Sufi tradition. Whereas Senegalese Mourides take their affiliation with them as they move out into other parts of the world, Iranians already in exile came to the Shahmaghsoudi order as a way to recapture something of their Iranian spiritual heritage (Werbner 2003). In similar fashion, a lodge of French men called the "Sufi and Cultural Association" is housed north of Paris and acknowledges a Sufi master living in Tunisia who is part of the al-Alawiyya order. The active participants are French men whose origins lie in diverse Muslim-majority countries who grew up together and converted to the Sufi path as an alternative to drugs and delinquency.

Sufi organizing has always had the possibility of expanding and extending outward to trace its reach through visits to shrines or, as in Marseilles and New York, through visits by saints to those who await his arrival. The faster and more affordable global travel becomes, the more easily sheikhs and adepts can employ this feature of Sufism, and the higher the velocity and the greater the reach of their networks.

Sufism reminds us sharply of the inward and outward dimensions of Islamic lives which I have underlined throughout these chapters. On the one hand, tasawwuf regards an inner pathway toward knowledge and spirituality; on the other hand, the Sufi lodges constructed around spirituality have served as powerful vehicles for political and economic, as well as religious, objectives. In that sense it is unsurprising that, early on, anthropologists found these orders enticing objects for further study.

SEVEN

ℚ

Judging

The first Islamic polity emerged when the Prophet Muhammad became ruler of the city of Medina. He transmitted God's words, resolved disputes among his followers, and responded to questions about all manner of concerns: how to worship, how to treat one's spouse, how to dress in public. Through his words and his deeds, Muhammad was the source of Islamic norms, the judge of human conduct, and the ultimate recourse for those with puzzles or problems.

The memory of this unity, in Muhammad, of ruling, judging, teaching, and worshipping, underlies the frequently expressed idea that Islam does not distinguish the religious from the secular. After Muhammad's death this unity began to come apart; some people ruled, others led prayers, still others collected and examined hadith, some taught, some judged disputes among the people, and some commanded armies. But the Prophet's example of how to do each of these things retained its stature as an authoritative model for correct Islamic conduct, and, as we have seen, the transmitted reports, hadith, of what he did and said remain one of the two main sources for knowing shariah.

But right after the Prophet's death new problems needed to be resolved. One man, Abu Bakr, was selected to lead the community, but other people who had known the Prophet personally, his Companions, also engaged in responding to questions from Muslims (*futyâ*) and delivered legal opinions, fatwas. Certain men of this generation were particularly productive, among them the former secretary to the Prophet, the governor of the Yemen, and Muhammad's uncle, Ibn `Abbas. These and other individuals were called muftis. The three Arabic words futyâ, muftî, and fatwa share the triliteral root f-t-y, "opinion," which in its different morphological forms can convey the meaning of consultation, or questions and answers, about norms and law (Masud, Messick, and Powers 1996).[1]

Although anyone with a reputation for knowledge and piety might issue fatwas, not all muftis had the same relationship to political power. Even during the Umayyad period (661–750), certain muftis became part of the administration of a territory and acted as advisors to judges and rulers. Others became independent sources of criticism and correction to the ruler. Increasingly, rulers sought to appoint their own official muftis in order to exercise a degree of control over fatwa giving. To this day, the tension persists between the mufti as advisor to the state and the mufti as independent provider of religious legal opinion.

By the eighth century, several distinct categories were used to refer to men who were knowledgeable in Islam. Some were designated as possessing Islamic knowledge or `ilm, by being referred to as ulama (`ulamâ') or scholars, a term that does not specify any particular branch of knowledge. Others specialized in learning about substantive law or fiqh and were known as fuqahâ', or "jurists." These men did not necessarily hold office or exercise specific powers.

The office empowered to resolve disputes was that of the judge or qâdî. Like the mufti, the judge drew on the model of the Prophet for his authority, but his task was quite different. The mufti's major challenge was to determine what the law was in light of competing interpretations of the pertinent scriptural texts. The judge faced two challenges. First, he had to determine what the facts were, in light of competing testimony. Then he had to make a judgment, a hukm, in light of the law.

---

[1] On contemporary practices of muftis in more informal settings, which address the personal and ethnical concerns of ordinary persons seeking fatwas, see Agrama (2010) and Caeiro (2011).

Judges were appointed by rulers and depended on them for the execution of their judgments, but they based their judgments on the available Islamic jurisprudence from across the Muslim world. It is not surprising that judges would have recourse to muftis to inform them about jurisprudence and to supply an additional source of legitimacy for their rulings. It is also not surprising that from the earliest period Muslims have expressed an ambivalence about judges, often repeating such hadith as "Of three judges, two are in Hell."

In general, then, there developed two fundamental practices of shariah interpretation. The realm of binding decisions belonged to the judge, who heard disputes among claimants following established legal procedures and issued his rulings with the broader political and legal environment in mind. The realm of non-binding legal opinions, fatwas, belonged to the mufti, who responded to questions posed to him in person or, more likely, in the form of a letter. These questions might issue from anyone: ordinary Muslim, judge, or state ruler.

Sifting through competing claims in Morocco

Now let us consider a series of examples of how judges did their work. I stress here that, like judges everywhere, Islamic judges interpret the law, search their consciences, study the claimants and witnesses before them, and bear in mind the social and political constraints on what they can do. Only by capturing these reasoning processes, as some anthropologists and historians now are trying to do, can we properly understand how judges negotiate among these constraints.

I begin with a pre-modern case, from a time when state-issued Islamic legal codes and Western-style law courts did not yet exist. We know of some such cases from documents written by judges or muftis summarizing facts and procedures, which, in the hands of able and imaginative historians, allow us to achieve something like an ethnographic perspective on judicial practices. And doing so allows us to understand how judges acted before the advent of colonial regimes and modern codified laws.

The historian David Powers (2002) has analyzed a case from early fourteenth-century Morocco that reveals the importance of rules of evidence and proof in Islamic law, and the important role played by muftis as well as judges in courts. Around 1313, a man named Salim brought suit in a town in northern Morocco to a judge named al-Tirjâli. Salim said that he was the son of `Alî, a local notable now deceased, that his mother was a slave girl, and that he wanted his share in his father's inheritance (specifically, a share of the rent received by properties once seized by the state).

Salim's problems were twofold: `Ali had not explicitly recognized Salim as his son, and `Alî's eldest son, `Abd al-Rahmân, denied that Salim was his brother. Salim needed evidence. He must have looked far and wide for help, for he submitted statements from ninety people. The pertinence of these statements varied, but some did state that `Alî had acknowledged Salim as his son and that Salim's sister had acknowledged him as her brother.

It was not enough to amass such statements, however, without evidence as to the credibility of each such witness. As in the science of hadith, the character of a source directly affects the reliability of a report. For legal proceedings, this principle has produced a category of "professional witness," a person whose probity and reliability earn him a spot at a judge's court. There were a number of them attached to the court of the judge, al-Tirjâli, and some of these witnesses entered statements in support of Salim's claim. Even though some of these statements merely alleged that rumors in circulation in the marketplace attested to Salim's paternity, the credibility of these professional providers of truth rendered this evidence acceptable to the judge, who made it clear that he was likely to side with Salim.

However, `Ali's son `Abd al-Rahmân submitted his own counterclaims, and these had to be assessed as well. `Abd al-Rahmân even visited a mufti in the capital city of Fez in hopes that the mufti would find irregularities in the judge's reasoning and instruct him to change his position, as muftis could do. In this case the mufti declined to issue such an instruction, but in his letter to`Abd al-Rahmân he pointed out a procedural problem. According to the law regarding professional witnesses, said the mufti, if two such witnesses testify to a rumor, then the judge must seek confirmation from a third such witness. Moreover, if other such witnesses deny the existence of such a rumor, then the original testimony does not stand. To make his point, the mufti referred to a court case included in an authoritative commentary on Moroccan law. Although judges' decisions do not themselves have the value of precedent in Islamic law, a mufti may refer to a case to support his opinion as to what the law has to say on a particular topic.

In his written decision, al-Tirjâlî denied that the case mentioned by the mufti had any bearing on Salim's problem. In this case, but not in the other, the professional witnesses lived in the same town as the parties to the case, and thus could be assumed to have particularly reliable knowledge about the state of affairs prevailing in the town, including the veracity of prevailing rumors. (Rumors, like hadith, can be more or less sound.) This response was a standard part of judicial reasoning – as it is in Western courts – whereby one party dissociates two cases that someone else has tried to link.

Al-Tirjâlî evidently became nervous about points of weakness in his reasoning, however, for he sought out legal opinions from muftis attached to his own court, from a mufti living long ago in Spain, and from a prominent mufti in Fez. The Fez mufti confirmed all of al-Tirjâlî's reasoning, specifying, among other things, that the professional witnesses' testimony concerning rumor enjoyed a high level of epistemological certainty.

We do not know precisely why al-Tirjâlî, early on in the judicial process, decided that Salim's claims were valid, but we do know that, having done so, he followed a complex process of ascertaining the law and the facts. He

drew on generalized knowledge in the community to determine whether
`Alî ever had acknowledged Salim as his son. He made use of earlier
cases, decided long ago and far away, as precedent (but dissociated the
case at hand from the cases advanced by `Abd al-Rahmân). He sought
out confirming opinions from muftis, both in his town and at the capital,
especially concerning the relative weight to be accorded different kinds
of testimony.

The case shows how pre-modern Islamic judges drew on local knowledge about facts and also on the principles of evidence and reasoning
widely shared by jurists and judges across a wide area of Muslim gov-
ernance. Here we see the main lines of classical Islamic reasoning and
procedure, against which we can then compare examples of contemporary Islamic legal practices, each illustrating a particular way in which
judges and jurists have responded to cultural differences and to the
political and legal transformations characterizing the rise of modern
nation-states.

Ethnographic studies by Lawrence Rosen (1989) show that judges
in twentieth-century Morocco worked much as did their fourteenth-
century predecessors. Now, as then, it is oral testimony that carries the
day. Rosen explains that notaries determine and certify that a particular witness is the sort of person who tells the truth, something to be
ascertained by considering his or her reputation. If he or she is such a
person, and only then, should the judge accept the witness's testimony.
The testimony might come to the court as a written statement, but it
would have first been delivered orally to the notary, who would have had
the opportunity to assess the character of the witness. More witnesses
are better than fewer, since with more people claiming such-and-such,
the likelihood of the claim's being true is increased. Witnesses who live
close to the parties to a dispute are more reliable than those living farther
away, because they are considered more likely to have accurate knowledge
about the parties and their affairs.

Bargaining for a divorce in Iran

Contemporary Iran differs from our other examples in that the lawgivers and jurists of the Islamic Republic draw on the jurisprudence of Shi'ite Islam, the minority stream of worship and judging that followed the leadership of 'Ali and his descendants. Our focus is not on the differences in doctrine, however, but on the common problems and possibilities that Muslim men and women face in court, and in this dimension an Iranian court resembles those in Morocco, Indonesia, or Zanzibar.[2]

We are in a small courtroom in Teheran, Iran, located near the Ministry of Justice, where Ziba Mir-Hosseini carried out fieldwork in the late 1990s.[3] A religious judge (*hakim-i shar'*) sits at a high desk, and a clerk, a woman, at her own desk by his side. The two officials, both appointed by the state, hear claimant after claimant. The judge questions the parties and often their relatives, usually in sessions separated by weeks or months. Laws enacted after the 1979 Islamic Revolution established these "special civil courts," which exist alongside the general civil courts and which have jurisdiction over family law cases, i.e., those involving marriage, divorce, and child custody. Women bring the majority of cases. Most cases brought by either men or women involve a demand for divorce.

Understanding divorce in Islam requires understanding that marriage in Islam(*nikâh*) is a sacred contract. It is sacred, and can be viewed as part of 'ibadat, worship and service of God, because it follows divine rules that render sexual relations between the two parties licit (halal) for purposes of sexual enjoyment and procreation. It is a contract because

---

[2] On the workings of a Zanzibar divorce court, see Stiles (2009), and see Michael Peletz's (2002) analysis of divorce cases in a Malaysian court. Peletz makes an important argument about the role of these courts in encouraging the expression of individual sentiments and interests, and in that sense as part of modernity.

[3] The account of a Teheran divorce court is drawn from Ziba Mir-Hosseini (2001); see also her superb film on the court (Longinotto and Mir-Hosseini 1998) and the more recent study by Arzoo Osanloo (2009), which also examines more broadly the struggle for women's rights in Iran.

it is a conditional agreement freely entered into by the two parties, and can be broken if those conditions are not fulfilled.

Such is the bare-bones definition of marriage. In most Muslim societies the way people carry out a marriage emphasizes its dual nature, as worship and as contract. A marriage usually involves reciting al-Fatihah, the first verse of the Qur'an, and may be presided over by a religious official. The husband gives his wife (or promises to give her) a payment called mahr, consisting of a valuable or a sum of money.

In both classical and contemporary Islamic jurisprudence, husbands and wives do not have the same rights to divorce, but both can initiate divorce proceedings, and in most countries, modern legislation has increased a wife's capacities to bring about a divorce. A husband seeking to divorce his wife will probably follow a unilateral procedure called talaq. In many Muslim societies (and in classical Islamic jurisprudence) it is sufficient that he pronounce the words "I divorce you" in order to divorce his wife. Her consent is not needed. However, many countries require that a husband obtain the permission of a judge before he may pronounce the divorce formula, and that he do so in court. The role of the judge varies considerably according to national law codes. In Indonesia, the judge requires the husband demonstrate sufficient cause for divorce before granting him permission to pronounce the divorce formula. In Iran the judge is required to seek reconciliation of the parties, but cannot, in the end, prevent the husband from divorcing his wife.

A wife who seeks to divorce her husband is likely to request either a khul divorce, an annulment, faskh, or dissolution (tafrîq). In the first case the wife induces the husband to agree to a divorce by promising to pay him a sum of money (or, if he has not paid the mahr in full, by foregoing that which is owed her). She declares her reluctance to continue with the marriage. Either a husband or a wife may obtain an annulment, but husbands rarely do so because they have the easier option of pronouncing the talaq. A judge may annul a marriage on grounds that it had a defect right from the start, for example, that the husband and wife were close kin, or that there was no agreement to pay mahr. A judge also may declare the marriage dissolved because one or both parties failed to meet a condition of the marriage, for example, because the husband was impotent, or failed to provide sufficient material support for his wife, or harmed his wife.

In many Muslim societies, jurists or legislators have taken an important step toward gender equality by adding to the marriage contract a clause by which the husband agrees to abide by certain rules. By signing this clause he agrees to a "delegated divorce," ta`liq talaq, which delegates to a judge at some subsequent moment the right to declare that the husband, because he has failed to abide by one of these rules, in effect has repudiated his wife. Among typical "triggers" for divorce are: his prolonged absence, his failure to provide for the material or sexual needs of his wife, or his marriage to a second wife without the consent of the first wife. Although nothing in Islamic law requires a groom to sign this clause, social pressure from the bride's family, or broadly accepted social norms, may make it difficult for him to refuse.

These broad outlines of marriage and divorce provide a legal background against which Muslim societies have developed specific judicial practices, creative legal responses to local social norms and state policies. In Iran, judges cannot prevent men from divorcing their wives, but women make use of the law to obtain as favorable an outcome as possible. Iranian religious judges act in accord with Shi'ite jurisprudence and with the relevant statutes, most importantly the Iranian Civil Code (which sets out principles of Shi'ite jurisprudence in codified form), and the Special Civil Courts Act. They may exercise discretion in order to align their sense of equity with the rights of both parties; these efforts may (but do not always) help these women in their efforts.

In the Teheran courtroom studied by Mir-Hosseini in the late 1980s, a religious judge heard the divorce (talaq) application brought by Hassan, a civil servant, who after seven months of marriage stated that he and his wife Nahid were "incompatible." At the first session the judge asked

Nahid if she consented to the divorce. She declined to consent. Now, although Iranian law (and Shi'ite jurisprudence more generally) gives to a husband the right to divorce his wife without her consent, an act passed just seven months after the 1979 Revolution limits that right. In order to divorce his wife, the husband must appear before a judge (which is why Hassan was in court at all), and if the wife does not agree to the divorce the judge must refer the case to arbitration. In this case, the judge appointed as arbiters a brother of Nahid and a brother of Hassan. The two men sent a written report to the judge, in which they stated that Hassan was to blame. He had just taken a second wife, they explained, and this wife had insisted that he divorce Nahid.

At the second court hearing, Nahid at first refused to consent to the divorce, and then agreed to give her consent on the condition that Hassan pay in full the 250 gold coins of mahr promised at the time of marriage. Nahid was resorting to a bargaining strategy often used by women in middle-class urban Iran. In such circles, a woman always demands a higher amount of mahr than her prospective groom can conceivably afford to pay, with situations such as this one in mind. Hassan did not have the means to pay the full mahr, and Nahid's demand created an effective, if temporary, roadblock to the divorce.

The judge tried once more to convince the two parties to come to an agreement, but failing at that, he called a third session at Hassan's insistence. At this session Nahid added to her earlier demands a new one, that Hassan pay her maintenance for the period since he left her house to move in with his new wife. The judge continued his quest for a resolution between the parties, and appointed a new set of arbiters. Their report was similar to that delivered by the initial pair, adding that they also supported Nahid's request for maintenance.

Frustrated by the judge's (and the arbiters') apparent agreement with Nahid's position, Hassan sent letters to the three leading jurists in Iran (including the Ayatollah Khomeini) asking if it was not against Islamic law to require full payment of the mahr as a condition of divorce. The three responded with legal opinions, in each case stating that Hassan should be allowed to pay the mahr in installments, and that his ability to pay should not stand in the way of his right to divorce. Hassan forwarded these letters to the judge and demanded another hearing. The hearing was held, and the two parties reached an agreement. Nahid agreed to the divorce, and Hassan agreed to give her full custody of their two-year-old son and to pay the full mahr, in monthly installments, along with current and past maintenance. The case had taken two years to resolve. Hassan got his divorce, and Nahid had received what was by the standards of this time and place a favorable settlement.

According to Mir-Hosseini (2001: 77), from the beginning Nahid had crafted her actions in order to shape the terms of an inevitable divorce rather than to prevent it from occurring. Nahid was able to obtain custody, her mahr, and maintenance by using her strong bargaining position (her clear right to mahr) to full advantage. She benefited from the judge's evident sympathy for her position, from the reports of the two sets of arbiters, and from the fact that her husband had very little room to maneuver. Hassan had to win a divorce in order to live peacefully with his new wife, and the pressure on him doubtless grew as the judicial process dragged on. In this case time was on Nahid's side.

Hassan was not without legal acumen, however, as his appeal to the leading jurists of Iran demonstrates. As in fourteenth-century Morocco, the Iranian judge and mufti of today occupy distinct roles, the one finding facts and issuing judgments, the other finding the law and issuing opinions. In practice, however, their activities intertwine. The mufti may subvert or strengthen the statements of law issued by the judge in support of his judgments. But the judge has his own sphere of autonomy, in that he decides when to delay and when to proceed, and can accept or reject evidence (a power whose importance we shall see in the next case).

These two cases, one from fourteenth-century Morocco and one from contemporary Iran, differ in key respects apart from their locations in time and space. The Moroccan case turned entirely on a finding of fact: had the father ever acknowledged Salim as his son? The Iranian case had more the character of a bargaining session, where the question was which party would be the first to give way. But in both cases the judge evinced a sentiment for one side over the other, and made use of his judicial capacities to push the case in that direction, even though he worked within established procedures and traditions.

Arguing for a fair division in Indonesia

Now let us turn to a third case, this one from contemporary Indonesia. The juxtaposition of Iran and Indonesia brings up several of the many dimensions of contrast that run through the contemporary Muslim world. Iran is part of the Shi'ite Muslim world, whereas Indonesians follow the larger Sunni tradition. Since 1979 Iran has been an Islamic Republic; since 1945 Indonesia has been a non-confessional (though not a secular) one. The area that is now Iran was part of the early expansion and development of Islam, and much of what we may think of as Islamic civilization came from Persian writers, artists, and scholars. By contrast, Islam came much later to Indonesia, and largely by trade. Today, most Muslim Indonesians see themselves as living on the periphery of the Muslim world, rather than in the Islamic heartland.

These contrasts make the many similarities in judicial practices between Iran and Indonesia all the more striking. Let us look at the religious court for Central Aceh, on the northern end of Sumatra. There, as in Iran, state-appointed judges hear cases regarding family law. Women bring the majority of cases to the court, and they usually involve divorce. Judges urge disputants to reach agreement on their own. In divorce cases they appoint two arbiters, chosen from among the relatives on each side, to attempt reconciliation. In their recourse to substantive law, they follow a state-issued code but also draw on older jurisprudence, as well as on their own notions of fairness and justice in interpreting the law and in interpreting the facts of the case. In these respects they operate as do judges in Islamic courts throughout Indonesia.

At any one time since the 1990s, the Central Aceh court has had between three and six judges, and most of the judges have come either from local Gayo society or from neighboring regions of Aceh province. Nearly all the judges have graduated from the Islamic Law faculty of one of Indonesia's state Islamic colleges (IAIN, Institut Agama Islam Negeri), and some also have degrees from university law schools.

Most of the cases heard by these judges involve divorce requests, but litigation related to inheritance or gifts takes up large portions of their time because of the need for multiple hearings, investigations in the field, and follow-up actions to enforce their judgments. One case from the 1990s shows how Indonesian judges, like judges in Teheran or in fourteenth-century Morocco, draw on their own values in interpreting the law and in responding to orders and interpretations given to them by other authorities. The case involved a dispute over the division of an estate among heirs, and turned on claims made by the defendant that the deceased had bequeathed land to them with the consent of all the heirs (Bowen 2005).

The case takes us into the realm of the "science of shares" (`ilm al-farâ'id), the fixed rules for dividing the property of a deceased Muslim. These rules guarantee the rights of heirs, whose shares are explicitly set out in the Qur'an. One of the major innovations of Islamic law was its insistence on these fixed shares, in keeping with the saying attributed to the Prophet Muhammad that "the laws of inheritance (farâ'id) constitute one-half of all knowledge and are the first discipline to be forgotten" (Powers 1986: 8).

This "science" brought about a sharp shift in how wealth was transferred – students of Islamic law and history agree on this point if on no other (Coulson 1971). In the societies of pre-Islamic, seventh-century Arabia, wealth was passed down from senior male to senior male as a fund for provisioning the group. By contrast, Islamic rules dictate awards in fixed proportions to individuals, women as well as men, in accord with their precise kin ties to the deceased. Under Islamic law, individuals could make absolute claims on wealth by virtue of their birth or marriage, claims that did not depend on the good will of an elder or a chief. Moreover, these claims were portable, i.e., they did not depend on residing in the place of one's birth. Finally, the claims derived their normative force from the eternal word of God, not from the good will of an elder male. The new legal framework thus was a useful way to unite diverse tribes and peoples, and to expand the realm of Islam into new lands.

Islam did not prevent property owners from disposing of their property before death, however. Under Islamic law as commonly practiced – whether in the early modern Middle East or in twentieth-century Indonesia – Muslims may leave a bequest (*wasiyya*) or make a gift or donation (*hiba*) during their lifetime, or they may establish an endowment or trust (waqf) to be managed by designated persons. Each of these three mechanisms – bequest, gift, endowment – has its own attractions and limitations as a means of transmitting wealth outside the contours of the fixed rules.

Let us consider first the case of bequests. You make bequests during your life, but they only take effect after your death. You may not bequeath more than one-third of your estate, nor may you leave a bequest to your heirs unless – and here is the important qualification – all the heirs consent to the bequest. This heirship strategy thus has the advantage of giving you control of your wealth during your lifetime, instead of relying on the generosity of your children, but it is not a convenient way to dole out shares to relatives.[4]

Gifts are quite different. You must give them during your lifetime. You may give away all of your wealth to anyone: for example, you could give

---

[4] See Coulson 1971: 143–50, 255–7; for a detailed ethnographic study of women's access to property in Palestine, see Moors (1995), and for a recent overview of family law and women's interests see Tucker (2008).

all your land to one daughter, or to one son, leaving other children and other heirs without any inheritance, although Muhammad did condemn parents who apportion gifts so as to favor some children over the rest. Giving property is a contract, and you lose all rights over the property after giving it, which reduces your bargaining power with respect to your heirs.

This domain of Islamic law in effect contains two quite distinct ideas about how people should transmit property: either as they wish, or according to fixed formulae. In particular societies, the tension between those two ideas may map onto a social tension between different heirs. For example, in Central Aceh, the social norms once generally adhered to by the Gayo people allowed for parents to give and bequeath their land to their children. Quite often parents would give land to children as they married and reserve some land as a bequest to the child who cared for them in old age (as an heirship strategy of reserving some property to ensure proper filial attention). The other children were not asked for their consent to these bequests. These arrangements often left effective control of property in the hands of eldest sons, who acted as guardians of the estate after the parents' death; these sons sometimes claimed that gifts or bequests had been made to them, and they could effectively delay the division of an estate for a full generation. Some of those daughters have seen in the legal idea of "fixed shares" a way for them to receive land quickly through the mediation of the Islamic court.

Cognizant of these rules and practices, judges on the Central Aceh Islamic court have acknowledged gifts and bequests, but they also have tried to ensure that elder brothers did not deprive other heirs of their rightful shares. They have been motivated by a concern for ethics and equity: for a *fair* process of distribution as well as a *legal* one. Beginning in the 1990s, the judges frequently refused to recognize some bequests as valid, even if those holding the property had all the requisite paperwork, because they suspected coercion by elder brothers. They could do so because of the rule that bequests require consent of all the heirs. The gifts and bequests were seen as departures from the Islamic system of fixed shares and thus worthy of the equivalent of what is called "strict scrutiny" in American jurisprudence.

In 1987, a woman named Samadiah brought a claim in the court against two of her sisters and two of her nephews. Her parents, Wahab and Maryam, had left a good deal of wealth when they died, including a house and good farmland. Samadiah had received none of the land, and she asked that the wealth be divided among the heirs according to Islamic law (Bowen 2003: 126–34).

Why had Samadiah received nothing? The two nephews said that Wahab had divided the land among his children except for three land parcels that he had left as a bequest to the child or children who looked after him in old age. The children had quarreled over who among them had the right to the land – probably Wahab had spent time with more than one child, and so they all thought they could claim part of the bequest. According to the nephews, in 1969 all the children had taken part in a village assembly, under the aegis of the village headman, and had agreed that one of the daughters, Egem, had done the caring and had the rights to the bequest. (Her son was one of the nephews who was a defendant in the suit.) The defendants produced a document attesting to the bequest, a document that the civil court had acknowledged as valid in 1970.

The history of the family followed a predictable storyline for Central Aceh. The two nephews' parents had remained living in the village after marriage, and they had taken control of family affairs. The nephews inherited this de facto control over the family land, refusing to divide it further. Two sisters of the plaintiff appeared as co-defendants with the nephews, but only because they each had received a small amount of property at the 1969 village meeting, and Samadiah wanted this land redivided along with the larger portions controlled by the men. Under the judges' questioning, the two sisters contradicted the story told by the nephews, stating that they knew nothing about a bequest, and that the village headman had divided the estate. He had given them a small part of it but had left the rest in the hands of the two nephews. They agreed with Samadiah that the rest of the land should be redivided.

At first glance the plaintiff did not appear to have much of a case. After all, the headman had presided over a meeting at which a division of the land was accepted by all concerned, and a written document to this effect already had been upheld by the civil court. Nonetheless, the Islamic court judges ruled otherwise, stating that, despite the document, the very fact that some heirs now contested the case showed that they never could have sincerely agreed to the division. Ruling in favor of Samadiah's request, the judges ordered all the wealth to be divided according to Islamic rules.

Why did the Islamic court judges choose to find that there had not been an agreement about the bequests even though there was an apparently valid document attesting to the contrary? Judge Kasim, a native of the area, explained to me in 1994 that the other heirs, principally the two daughters, could only have sincerely accepted the 1969 agreement if it had been in accord with their Islamic rights. That agreement was clearly in contradiction with the contents of scripture, he said, because it did not award them their rightful share, and he could not imagine them freely agreeing to it. He and the other judges had felt that the two daughters had been pressured into signing the 1969 document, even though such pressure could not be proven. Because no one would freely sign such an agreement if it were so clearly against her interests, he reasoned, there must have been pressure. Moreover, even if such an agreement had been legal, "it deviated too far from justice" (*keadilan*, from `*adil*, fair, just).

Observe in both these cases how easy it would have been for the judge to say that the agreements were valid. After all, the letters of agreement had been signed by all the parties concerned, and no proof was offered of coercion. But the judges said that they disbelieved these documents. They contrasted sincere agreement (*ikhlas*), which could only be obtained if the division had been fair, with mere procedural correctness. They drew on their intuitions about the reasoning processes of the parties to the case to find as they did, against the strength of a written document.

Each of these three cases highlights a different area of Islamic law: rules of evidence, the laws of marriage and divorce, and the "science of shares." These judges were working in very different social milieu and from different sets of legal rules. In all three cases, however, the judges drew on their ideas about human nature, their sympathies and sentiments for one or the other party to the case, and their sense of equity and fair play. All drew on scripture, previous judgments, law codes, and local social norms. Here we see again the recursive nature of Islamic reasoning: from a shared tradition, through the particulars of time and place, to a judgment, which then can change the shared tradition. We also see that it would be impossible to understand judicial reasoning were we only to read a judge's written opinions. It is through interviews, observations, and careful study of other documents that we can build an adequately complex picture of a complex reasoning process.

We also understand that a decision in an Islamic setting, as with judicial decisions generally, concerns ethics and equity as well as the law. Judging ends up being far more capacious than a narrow notion of law might suggest. This breadth of judging becomes particularly important in understanding how Muslims have sought to adapt their normative traditions to new settings in Western Europe and North America, a topic to which I now turn.

EIGHT

Migrating and adapting

As Muslims have moved recently in large numbers to new countries, particularly in Western Europe and North America, they have adapted Islamic norms and traditions to new social and political spaces. As a result, Muslim institutions and orientations show marked differences across different Western countries; the challenge to anthropologists is to study in *contrastive* fashion these processes of adaptation. In this chapter, I take the example of Islamic divorce to illustrate how we can understand processes of Islamic adaptation by contrasting several country cases and then examining the mechanisms that can explain the contrasts.[1]

Although the Muslim presence in Western Europe and North America is an old one, particularly in south-eastern and south-western parts of Europe, new streams of Muslim workers and their families arrived in Europe during the mid-twentieth century – earlier in some places, such as France and Britain, and later in others, such as Sweden and Spain. Most came from South Asia, North and West Africa, and Turkey, although

---

[1] This approach differs from other possible approaches, in two ways. First, rather than looking at state-driven policies (as in Laurence 2011), I look at how Muslims have created new religious institutions and new modes of religious reasoning. Second, I look for explanatory elements that may be shared across countries, rather than starting from explicit, often stylized national models (as in Fetzer and Soper 2005).

increasing numbers have arrived more recently from other places (Bowen 2008). In the same period, new waves of Muslims came to North America from South Asia and the Middle East (Leonard 2003).

Although it is tempting to discuss "Islam in the West," taking any two pairs of countries reminds us how divergent these processes have been. Take, for example, France and Germany. Most French Muslims come from countries once colonized by France, and so they arrive with some degree of familiarity with the French language and with the colonial and post-colonial institutions shaped by France; not so in Germany, where Turks arrived as part of circular labor migration policies that sought to minimize any such contact (Schiffauer 2000). France has combined universalistic civic principles with racism and post-colonial bitterness; Germany has moved at glacial speed from ethnic notions of national belonging to entertaining the idea that immigrants could become citizens (Kastoryano 2002). Other pairs of countries differ along other dimensions, including the specifics of colonial legal practices, notions of religion's place in public life, and whether immigrants are encouraged to form civic associations. All these host-country differences lead to different responses by Muslim immigrants.

How do we then construct illuminating contrasts? One starting point is to look at who migrated and how they settled. Did people tend to come from concentrated pockets or from widely scattered areas? Do they now live largely with people like them? In Britain there are streets and neighborhoods of multiple similarities, such as a street I have visited in Leicester where everyone is a Sufi-oriented Muslim trader of Gujarati origin who arrived in Britain by way of East Africa. In France more often we find broad mixtures of North Africans, West Africans, native French, and other Europeans in the large council housing units called *HLMs* or *cités*. The contrast arises from very different situations in the countries of origin – much more fine-grained ethnic and religious distinctions in South Asia than in North Africa – and also from how migrants arrived – chain migrations of entire villages in South Asia to neighbor-hoods in British cities, versus French policies of recruiting workers from across North Africa.

These facts of migration and settlement shape the sense of "commu-nity" among migrants in very practical ways. How important is it to learn the language of the host country? Less so if you live surrounded by others speaking Urdu or Bengali in a neighborhood of Birmingham or East London; more so if you live in a mixed-origins housing area in a French city; somewhere in between if you live in certain Chicago neighborhoods. How much authority do religious leaders from the "old country" have here? More authority if ties of village and mosque are reproduced in a Bradford neighborhood; less so if Muslims in Paris find themselves sharing only a broad sense of North African identity and obligation to worship (Bowen 2009a; Lewis 2002).

Although there are many studies of migration and politics, we are just beginning to construct the anthropology of these recent Muslim adaptations. I will try to illustrate how we can approach broad questions of migration and adaptation through fieldwork, in much the same way as we approached comparable divergences and changes in modes of salat and sacrifice. I do so by asking: how does a Muslim woman get a religious divorce?

Shariah councils in localizing Britain

Alone among Western countries, Britain has a range of institutions that mediate or arbitrate conflicts among Muslims (Bano 2004). Only one of them, the Muslim Arbitration Tribunal, headquartered at the Hijaz College north of London, arbitrates in commercial or, less often, family conflicts. The director is a barrister in the eyes of the English legal system as well as a pir in the eyes of Sufis residing in Britain, and he has tried to run the Tribunal as a way of bringing about decisions that are both religiously valid and legally relevant (Bowen 2011).

Other institutions offer various forms of non-binding mediation, where the documents produced are not enforceable in civil court. Some of these institutions are quite informal, in that a relative or local imam may be called upon to resolve a dispute. But in many cases involving family issues, the parties may seek the aid of a Shariah council. Muslims can easily find such councils in London, Birmingham, Bradford, Manchester, and elsewhere. They provide downloadable forms on their websites, charge set fees for service, and meet on scheduled days of the month.

Why do these tribunals exist primarily in Britain? The answer lies in the story of how Muslims have come to live in Britain and the particular English habits of dealing with ex-colonial minorities. Muslims make up perhaps 3 percent of the overall British population today; about half of this number are born overseas and half in Britain. Most are from South Asia, and tend to come from particular districts. The Mirpur district of Pakistani Kashmir accounts for most of the Pakistanis in Britain today, as does the Sylhet district for Bangladeshis (Gardner 1995; Shaw 2000). Parts of Birmingham, Bradford, or Leeds are mainly lived in by people speaking Urdu. Most families who came from South Asia try to arrange marriages between their British-born sons or daughters and close relatives back home.

Until the mid-1960s, migration was mainly "circular"; that is, men came and worked and then returned, often to be replaced by close kin or someone else from the same lineage or village. In Britain, they lived with others from the same lineage or who followed the same religious school. They thought of themselves as transient residents, and they regarded marriage and divorce as matters to be handled in the community with little or no involvement from the English courts. In addition, the government provided aid to local ethnic associations, who then became the primary agents in realizing Muslim demands regarding schooling, halal foods, and so forth. Muslims learned to resolve problems "in the community."

Things changed when in the late 1970s both new migration and government aid were severely curtailed, and some Muslims began to see the mosques as their new bases and to ask for the creation of Muslim institutions, regulated by "shariah." These calls increased after Muslims' 1989 protests against Rushdie's *Satanic Verses*, and counter-protests against religious censorship, heightened the sense of being different as Muslims rather than as members of ethnic groups. Given the divisions among British Muslims, the calls for nationwide shariah never amounted to much. But some Muslims saw Islam-based mediation as a way of keeping things in the community and as a way of proclaiming allegiance to an increasingly beleaguered faith. One young woman told the legal scholar Samia Bano (2004) in the 2000s: "I'm a Muslim. I identify as one and anything that helps to validate and enhance my role as a Muslim in British society obviously I welcome and I will support it."

Thus, Muslims developed habits of resolving issues locally, as others residing in England always had. Because marriage and divorce in England are largely private, contractual matters, mediation fits well into the English socio-legal context. Although there are clear legal limits on what may be contracted for – a judge will reopen any agreement if the interests of children or the fairness of financial settlements are at issue – privately dealing with marriage and divorce does not raise legal objections.

One of the largest councils today is the Islamic Shariah Council, London, which began work in the early 1980s and today has offices in a large house in a quiet residential area of Leyton in the eastern London suburbs. People gather in the front office to speak with members of the staff, and eventually with the Islamic scholars (they don't call themselves "judges"). Mediations may begin in a home or mosque, at the request of the husband or wife or family members, or at the council office. The religious scholar will hear the dispute and probably encourage the couple to resolve their differences. If the dispute leads to divorce, the mediator may suggest arrangements for childcare, the disposition of the bridal gift (mahr) and support for the wife and the children, all according to their interpretation of shariah. Sometimes the couple signs such an agreement, but it has no legal value.

Once a month a handful of the scholars affiliated with the council meet in a room next to the large Regents Park Mosque in Central London and review case files and, when they have enough information, grant divorces. The assembled scholars come from Pakistan, Bangladesh, and Palestine, and they also rely on colleagues from Somalia, Sudan, and elsewhere to interview petitioners in their own languages. Among themselves, the scholars deliberate in English, Arabic, and sometimes in Urdu, depending on who is sitting at the table.

Each of these cases presents its own complicated history, but many, if not most, involve transnational journeys and pleas by women to receive religious divorces from their absent or misbehaving husbands. At the February 2008 monthly meeting, the council considered seven cases, all wives' petitions for divorce. The women had been born in Pakistan, Somalia, and Mauritius. One had married in Abu Dhabi and another in Yemen, and husbands were living in Italy, Pakistan, Mauritius, and, in two cases, in places unknown. The council either dissolved the marriage in question or asked for further information to determine the husband's whereabouts.

Amina's story is typical of such cases (Bowen 2009b). In 2006, she approached a Muslim religious teacher near her home outside London. She wished to divorce her husband. They had married in Pakistan, moved to England, had been separated for several years, and she intended to file for divorce in court. But she wished to have proof that she was divorced religiously as well, in case she wished to remarry. The teacher recommended that she approach London's Islamic Shariah council, and the six Islamic scholars sitting as the council agreed to take up her case. They saw their first task as trying to save the marriage, as would Islamic judges in other countries, but because the husband had failed to answer earlier entreaties to appear before them, they agreed to dissolve the marriage and sent Amina a letter to that effect. With the letter in hand, she now will be able to remarry in a country practicing Islamic law – Pakistani judges will require it for a marriage in Pakistan,and if she remarries in England, she will be able to satisfy relatives and neighbors (and perhaps herself) that she has not sinned.

These spaces of marriage and divorce continue to be transnational and to involve brokering across "religious" and "secular" institutions. About half the time, British Bangladeshis or Pakistanis look to their home country, and sometimes to their home village or lineage, for a marriage partner. So the scholars must craft their decisions with the probable reception abroad in mind, if they are to ease a woman's quest to remarry. And, indeed, what right do these scholars have to dissolve marriages? They reiterate that, in a land without Islamic institutions, it is the duty of those with knowledge to undertake this and other tasks for the community.

How do the scholars settle disputes? To a great extent, they try to draw from the repertoire of Islamic rules to try to shape and direct the behavior of constituents, with the problems of adapting to England in mind. The council's secretary, Suhaib Hasan, tends to focus on the need to pressurise husbands into acting correctly. For example, his council starts by urging the husband to deliver a talaq (and he includes a khula' as a kind of talaq) even if his wife initiated the action. To do that, the husband must fill out, sign, and have witnessed a "talaq nama," on which he agrees to pay the mahr in full along with a *mut'a*, a small payment sometimes called a divorce "remedy."

But most of the time we end up dissolving the marriage because of his pride; the men rarely are willing to grant the divorce if the woman initiated the proceedings. If he initiates it we send him a talaq nama. We issue it to make sure that the wife gets her mahr back – all of it if the marriage was consummated and half if it was not. So it gives us some leverage over the husband. The husband wants the talaq nama because he may need a paper to prove he was divorced. (Suhaib Hasan, personal communication, 2007)

The scholars can flexibly interpret various terms of this set of claims so as to put pressure on men to behave in accord with British expectations, as in the following case, explained to me by Suhaib Hasan:

SH: In a case we decided recently, the couple had married in Karachi. He had been living in England, and went back there to get a wife. His parents were pressuring him to marry this girl; they were upset he was dating girls, and Muslim parents will get upset and find a wife, but he did not want her. When they came to us, he said that they had not consummated the marriage and so she was due only one-half the mahr, but she said they had consummated it. Well, some scholars wrote that if the couple is in khalwat [isolation] and could have touched each other's bodies, then that constitutes consummation, and we ruled that such was the case and that she was due the entire amount.

JB: But surely other scholars said the opposite, so why did you choose this opinion?

SH: Well, what was he doing marrying her if he did not want to do so? He had already married another woman by the time she came to us, never wanted her. England is about to pass a new law against forced marriages, which will penalize parents if they force a girl – it usually is girls – to marry, meaning that they did not want the marriage. Because in those cases the marriage rarely works out; it must be in the heart to work. It must be as they say here a "love marriage." (ibid.)

By interpreting rules for determining consummation of marriage in this way, the council is able to (1) maximally award mahr to the wife, (2) structure the incentives so as to add a bit more reason not to engage in the kind of please-the-parents marriage described here, and (3) anticipate the direction of English law. Of particular interest, and consistent with many other such instances, is that Hasan justifies his selection of this view of consummation not in terms of Islamic first principles, allegiance to a particular legal school, or a particular fiqh methodology, but rather in terms of his own ethical view of the behavior of the young husband: "What was he doing marrying her if he did not want to do so?" This comment has nothing to do with judging the likelihood of consummation, or choosing among alternative scholarly opinions, but rather imputes improper motives to the husband (and indirectly to his parents), and judges it appropriate to punish him by granting all the mahr to the wife.

In practice, the Leyton council finds itself constrained to respond to local social and legal conditions and at the same time to maintain an international Islamic credibility – all the more so in that many of the divorces in question are transnational. Thus this council finds itself working in both domestic and transnational spaces, and having to develop modes of justification that can mediate between them.

North Africans in centralized France

In Britain, how Muslims migrated reinforced their transnational ties to their places of origin. Settlement in France took place in somewhat different ways than in Britain. Most Muslims in France come from North Africa, and they settled in relatively mixed neighborhoods, in part because of the role of the state and of private industries in building housing near factories. (Turks have settled in ways that more closely resemble the British pattern.)[2]

Moreover, the French political and legal context prevents the development of institutions such as the Shariah councils. French Republicanism is hostile to intervening institutions in general, and the idea of Islamic law taking hold is shocking to anyone in France. In December 2008, at the end of a French television program on the dangers posed by increasing religious influence on European politics, the narrator asked: where will this all lead? The answer was to show footage from the Islamic council in the British community of Leyton, where the music and the long beard on the scholar were chosen to scare the audience: if we go down this path, we will end up like Britain, where imams rule society.

---

[2] I discuss specifics of immigration and settlement in Bowen (2009a).

The French historical starting point is, of course, not community control and private arrangements, but a Republican set of theories and assumptions that state institutions provide the best way to construct a society (Bowen 2007). Religion was the main obstacle to the Republic, and over the past century, laws were passed to keep religion out of the public sphere. Marriage and divorce are "public things" in the French civil law tradition, not matters of private contract, and thus the idea of contracts constituting part of the marriage makes no French legal sense. Furthermore, many in France see Islamic marriages as a way of refusing to fully enter into the "common life" that binds citizens together. Marrying people Islamically who have not married at city hall can land an imam in jail. In 2010, two ministers sought ways to remove the French nationality of a man on the grounds that although married legally to only one wife, he had married in Islamic fashion to others. (The man in question replied that if having a mistress means you're thrown out of France, the government will soon be a few ministers short of a Cabinet.[3])

Although from time to time two or more respected Islamic scholars might gather to dissolve a marriage (particularly among immigrants from West Africa), no institutions exist that are similar to the Islamic Shariah Council in Britain. But of course women do find themselves in difficult marriages and do seek advice from scholars. One such scholar, from Tunisia, told me what he then does:

I look into their marriage and try to calm things down, asking the husband to come, and I see him too. If the husband refuses to divorce her or if the wife brings witnesses about abuse, then I say to her: "Go to the civil court and get a divorce, and you will be doing nothing wrong in terms of religion." I just say this on my own behalf; no one has authorized me to pronounce anything; it is psychological, assuring the woman that she is doing nothing wrong. If she asks me to write it down, I do so. I usually refuse such

---

[3] "Voile intégral, polygamie: Comment un fait divers devient une controverse politique," *Le Monde* on-line, April 26, 2010.

requests – if I accepted all of them I would be doing nothing but that – but a few slip through! Other women either find other imams to do so, or they just go to the courts without troubling themselves further. (Dhaou Meskine, interview, 2008)

Those French religious scholars and authorities with a public role urge Muslim men and women to use the available civil institutions for marriage and divorce, saying that French courts already do all that Muslims need in this regard. Another prominent scholar from Tunisia was surprised to hear from me that in Britain women wanted to have separate religious divorces, as, for him, a judicial divorce takes care of the matter. Indeed, he argued that Muslims should consider the civil marriage at city hall to be *required* on Islamic terms:

Some people think that having to go to city hall and fill out forms is too much work, and moreover they consider marriage to be a religious matter – and they do so all the more because some Islamic authorities say that marriage is religious. They say that the Prophet, in his time, did not have laws about registering marriage, so it is not necessary for Muslims to do so. But then you can say – and this may make you laugh but there is something to it – that back then, the society was composed of tribes, and if someone married he never would just leave his spouse because his life would be in danger, everyone knew each other then, so there was no need for these regulations. But now it is different. That is reasoning according to the purposes (maqâsid) of Scripture. (Hichem El Arafa, interview, 2007)

Marrying in city hall is thus indicated by scripture, because the purpose of scripture's passages on marriage is to make marriage a stable contract.

The imam at the main mosque in Lyons explained why he refuses to perform Islamic marriages if couples are not legally married:

It causes problems when they do this if the couple separates and the husband will not give the wife a divorce. She has nowhere to turn to divorce. The state does not recognize the marriage. I have nothing to recommend, because I am not a judge, so I cannot divorce a couple, apply a khula' divorce with payment, which would be the wife's right. I tell them that marriage is for life. (Bowen, 2009b : 163)

The imam's account is a pragmatic one: because France lacks the religious judicial institutions that could apply a religious divorce, a woman should ensure her future ability to free herself from an unsuccessful marriage by marrying in civil fashion. The state not only provides legal force to preserve the marriage, but also provides the mechanism to leave the marriage that, in other societies, might be provided by an Islamic judge. But he and other imams do not see it as appropriate or necessary to create Islamic tribunals in France. I think that this position is shaped by three factors that make the perceived benefit less and the potential cost higher than is the case in Britain.

First, the issues to be resolved are less critical because high "promised" mahr is less often a feature of marriages among North and West Africans than it is among South Asians. If finances are not at issue, then one element of bargaining and dispute is removed. Second, the French Muslim leaders come mainly from North Africa; many of the most influential come from Tunisia, where marriage and divorce are handled by a single court system and marriage is considered to be a public matter: the idea of separate civil and religious courts therefore makes little sense to them. Finally, the potential cost of arguing for the creation of councils is higher than in Britain because of the strong disapprobation of French officials of any intermediate religious institution not under state control. If you risk expulsion for voicing unpopular religious opinions or appearing with your wife in a full covering, you are hardly likely to campaign for creating shariah councils.

Religion–state ambiguities in the United States

On the dimensions we have been considering, the United States resembles more closely Britain than France, but with sparser Islamic settlement, and more cross-ethnic mixing. But there are also concentrated pockets of people with similar origins in larger cities, such as Yemenis in Dearborn (Michigan), Hyderabad Indians in Rogers Park (Chicago), and Bosnians in St. Louis. In addition, American courts are somewhat more reticent than English ones to pronounce on religious matters unless such matters can be translated into non-religious terms (Quraishi and Syeed-Miller 2004).

As a result, one finds in the United States a few shariah councils but they are far less developed and less generally known than in Britain. In northern California, the Islamic Shari'a Council, California was created by a former associate of the founders of the Islamic Shariah Council in London. But, as is indicative of their relatively low profile, this and some other shariah councils in the United States follow only one of the four Sunni legal schools, the Hanafî, and for that reason only serve people from South Asian backgrounds, where that school predominates. (By contrast, their English counterparts will draw on the legal school followed by the parties to a dispute, and have created their own traditions by drawing from several such schools.) Although the California council carries out its proceedings in English, another, the Chicago-based Shariah Board of America, works entirely in Urdu. Their procedures also were modeled after British councils.

But in most American cities, individual imams or well-educated community leaders are approached in matters of marriage and divorce. Most refuse to dissolve a marriage but try to persuade the husband to deliver a talaq; such is the case for the imam of the Islamic Foundation of Greater St. Louis (Mufti Minhajuddin, interview, 2008). In other cities, some people have taken the step of organizing ad hoc panels to grant divorces to wives, but with some hesitancy and concern about the legitimacy of their actions.

In Columbus, Ohio, Mouhamed Tarazi, who trained in medicine in Syria, directs a charter school with entirely Muslim students, most of them Somalis. He is mandated by the state to marry couples, and perhaps once a month he is approached in matters of divorce. He always endeavors to involve the imam from the couple's mosque (there are about fourteen mosques in Columbus). Although he tries to reconcile the couple, usually the husband does not live in Columbus or will not attend the mediation session, so he awards a khula'.

MT: Recently, a Somali woman from Kenya came to see me. When still living in Kenya, her father married her to a man from Kenya living in California. She went to California but refused to live with the man; he already had another wife. A year later work attracted her to Columbus, and she came to see me. I got two other men to decide with me, a committee, as I usually do, and gave her the divorce.

JB: What authority do you have to issue the divorces?

MT: If we don't do something we effectively push these women to leave Islam or to find another man, and then they feel that they are going against Islam if they marry him, because they never were divorced Islamically. God gives me the courage to do this, and I hope I will get my reward from Him in heaven. I will get my reward . . . because these men they act as males not men, they don't realize that to be a man, to have dignity, is if the marriage does not work, you let your wife go, that is a "true man." (Interview, 2009)

In his words you can hear both his pleading with the husbands to pronounce a divorce and obviate the need for these councils, and his experience of failure in getting local imams to cooperate with him.

The disputes these men hear usually concern assets, and their hope lies in contracts that would be enforceable in civil court and that would guarantee the wife her share of the assets and also the full payment of the mahr. Tarazi's son happens to be a lawyer and he is at work on a model pre-nuptial agreement. When Tarazi marries a couple (in civil and religious fashion) he has them sign a letter (what the South Asians would call a "nikah nama") that specifies the amount of mahr.

He does not encourage people to draw up additional contracts because he is unsure if they would be honored in court. He learned about these uncertainties through his own role as an expert witness in a 2008 Ohio case, where the appellate court ruled that to enforce the mahr provision of a marriage contract would be to violate the Establishment clauses of both the United States and the Ohio Constitutions (Zawahiri v. Alwattar, 2008-Ohio-3473).

In the United States, jurisprudence varies from state to state on the question of whether a mahr agreement may be enforced. In a 2002 New Jersey case, for example, judges treated the marriage contract specifying mahr as a contract, rather than as a pre-nuptial agreement (which usually is subject to heightened scrutiny), and approved its enforcement (Odatalla v. Odatalla 810 A.2d 93 (NJ Super.Ch. 2002)). Muslims are increasingly focusing on obtaining enforcement of mahr provisions in marriage contracts, according to a recent analysis of Islam-related jurisprudence in the United States (Quraishi and Syeed-Miller 2004). For multi-ethnic Muslim communities, such as that in Columbus, no effective informal enforcement mechanisms exist to compel a husband to pay the mahr (or for that matter maintenance). For those groups accustomed to figuring a high "promised" mahr into the marriage contract, the civil courts become critical players in the overall process of regulating marriage and divorce. In the absence of a functional equivalent to the British shariah councils, American imams are trying to refine a legal instrument that courts will enforce.[4]

Muslim immigration to the United States has resulted in weaker, or rather sporadic, concentration effects than in Britain, and the Muslim landscape is more fragmented. Despite the existence of a national organization led by South Asian immigrants, the Islamic Society of North America, Muslim activities in cities and towns tend to be organized locally. Moreover, South Asians represent a much smaller proportion of American Muslims than is the case in Britain (African Americans

---

[4] A trend recently confirmed by Chicago-area divorce lawyer Azam Nizamuddin, who handles issues of mahr repayment through a combination of appropriate pre-marital contracts and, should divorce take place, pre-trial hearings (interview, February 2011).

and Arabs represent the other major groupings). The American legal response to Islam-related court cases suggests a somewhat greater wariness to refer to religion in judgments than one finds in Britain. Thus we find the development of secular legal instruments – contracts – as a way for courts to intervene.

Islamic ideas of marriage and divorce travel transnationally, in that the same basic concepts appear in Britain, France, and the United States. Experiences with judicial systems in countries of origin travel also: South Asians in Britain are used to khul'a divorces conducted in private; North Africans in France are used to divorces conducted at the state courts. But Islamic scholars and authorities draw from Islamic texts and traditions with local possibilities in mind, and because those local features differ across countries, so do the dominant directions of views and practices. How that happens involves the degree to which Islamic scholars take account of how their counterparts in Islamic countries will assess their decrees (quite a lot in Britain, very little in the United States); how far these leaders can go in creating Islamic social or legal institutions to act alongside civil courts (not at all in France, quite far in Britain); and the issues that surface as most sensitive in public opinion (marriage in France, divorce in Britain, and contractual enforcement in the United States).

The Islamic scholars operating in Britain, France, and the United States are innovating. More or less explicitly, they recognize that their interpretations and decisions cannot simply reproduce opinions and decisions given in Cairo or Karachi. They also are responding mainly to the concerns of the Muslims around them, and not relying on the major regional Islamic organizations in Europe and North America. Their worries are practical more than doctrinal: how to maintain legitimacy with respect to the ordinary Muslims who seek their services and how to shape procedures and decisions that will be effective in social and legal terms.

As we have seen, ideas of "effective" differ across countries. For the Shariah council scholars in Britain, it means gradually gaining recognition by the legal system, although what "recognition" might mean is far from clear. For their counterparts in France, it means working within the rather more constraining French legal system and under its increasingly assimilationist political pressures. For those in the United States, who are less assured in their roles than are their British cousins, it means trying to devise contracts for mahr that will be enforceable, leaving only the question of marriage dissolution to be solved in-house.

More broadly, and in the broader context of comparative social and political studies, these three cases suggest we ought to look at two general dimensions of change: pathways of migration and the path dependencies of state institutions. On the one hand, migrants bring past experiences with them as they travel along migration pathways: experiences in Karachi or Tunis shape how Islamic leaders think and act in Birmingham or Lyon, and they do so more strongly to the extent that communities in origin countries reproduce themselves in host countries. On the other hand, state legal and political institutions create "structures of opportunity" for these immigrants, which dictate what can be entertained in law and in public space. The result is complex processes of differentiation.

I do not think that the anthropology of Islam in Europe or North America ultimately should differ in questions and methods from anthropologies of Islam in countries with long-standing Islamic institutions. The field of Islamic studies generally has followed dominant Muslim forms of discourse in distinguishing between the "Islamic world" and the rest. But from an anthropological perspective, observant Muslim men and women living in France or Canada work through many of the same issues facing their cousins in Morocco or Pakistan: how to develop a proper attitude toward God through prayer or in dressing, how to find schools for their children that will train them for the modern world and perhaps also build their character, and how to carry out obligations to pay the zakat or go on the pilgrimage. Their available institutions will differ from one country to the next, but the basic set of personal and practical tasks they set themselves share the features we have studied in this book: concerns for piety, practice, and relations to others, whether Muslims or non-Muslims.

Islamic leaders face other challenges as well: how to organize an Islamic school, ensure that meat is properly prepared, and mediate in conflicts that may arise in marriage or in non-religious domains of everyday life. These challenges are no less difficult in countries with Islamic social and legal institutions than elsewhere; they are just different. We often forget that most "Muslim countries" are in fact religiously pluralistic countries, with legal systems of European origin, characterized by ongoing, lively internal debates about how to articulate Islamic norms with international norms of gender equality. A judge in Egypt or Nigeria must think about how a range of religious and political actors will respond to a court decision, just as does an Islamic scholar in Canada or Germany. Teachers in Islamic secondary schools in Malaysia or in the United States hope that their pupils will advance to posts in biology or history in national universities at the same time that they acquire religious knowledge.

NINE

Mobilizing

Although the practices we have examined in previous chapters – learning, worshipping, judging – form the center of Islamic religious preoccupations, in their daily lives, Muslims, along with other humans, have other worries as well, such as jobs, peace, and respect. It is here that religious appeals often are directed at mobilizing Muslims to improve their social lot, by organizing, preaching, or fighting. It is also here that most of us have the most difficulty sorting out motivations and actions. How do religious beliefs, social loyalties, and political passions interrelate? The role of the anthropologist has been to try and articulate the individual's passions and actions, on the one hand, and his or her role in broader (sometimes transnational) social movements, on the other.

Predication and politics in Egypt

Our starting point will be the da`wa, the "call" or "summons," that Muslims are urged to make to their fellow Muslims, asking them to pursue their faith in a pious and proper way. In the twentieth and twenty-first centuries, the organizers of Islamic social movements have used da`wa as the way to spread their message and to recruit followers. In the years following the dismantlement of the Ottoman Empire (the last pretender to the status of Caliphate), Muslim leaders throughout the Muslim-majority world sought to reinvigorate the *umma* and restore an Islamic society.

In Egypt in 1928, Hassan al-Banna founded the Muslim Brotherhood for this purpose. The Brotherhood began with the goal of encouraging Muslims to become better Muslims by performing their ritual duties and helping one another. The movement expanded to become a major social and political force, one that took on the goal of creating a new Islamic society (Mitchell 1969).

The Brotherhood illustrates the intertwined and shifting relationships among three goals of raising personal piety, improving society, and reshaping government. In his early years, al-Banna delved deeply into Sufism and retained a lifelong active role in Sufi circles, but he also led groups dedicated to stamping out immoral behavior among fellow Muslims and resisting Christian missionary activities. In Cairo he organized students from his own teacher-training college Dar al-`Ulûm and from al-Azhar University to train people in preaching and da`wa, offering their services not only through mosques but also in the coffee houses that dotted the city. Here was the analogue to the eighteenth-century European coffee-house culture described by Jürgen Habermas as the source of modern political thinking outside both the family and the state – the "bourgeois public sphere." In Cairo this sphere was a site for discussions oriented toward improving the piety of Muslims, not rethinking the nature of the state. The Brotherhood quickly established a pattern for expansion: they would establish a headquarters in a neighborhood or a new city and immediately undertake a project, building a mosque, school, or club, which brought neighborhood residents into contact with the Islamic message.

In the late 1930s, al-Banna defined the Brotherhood as "a Salafiyya message, a Sunni way, a Sufi truth, a political organization, an athletic group, a cultural-educational union, an economic company, and a social idea" (Mitchell 1969: 14). Some members of the Brotherhood felt that it also must become a fighting organization within Egypt, and they quoted the hadith that: "He among you who sees an abomination must correct it with his hand; if he is unable then with his tongue; if he is unable then with his heart. The last of these is the weakest of faith"; they argued that physical responses to oppression were the best. Al-Banna countered with a Qur'anic verse (16: 125): "Call unto the way of thy Lord with wisdom and fair exhortation, and reason with them in the better way," which would favor reasoning.

The Brotherhood has had tumultuous relations with successive governments. They were dissolved in 1948 for fear that they were plotting revolution, and al-Banna was assassinated the following year. Although they welcomed the 1952 revolution that brought Nasser to power, and were allowed to emerge once more into public view, they were once again banned in 1954, after a Brotherhood member made an attempt on Nasser's life. In the 1970s, Anwar Sadat courted them as allies against the left, but the long period of suppression and imprisonment, which included the execution of Sayyid Qutb in 1966, had radicalized a wing of the group. This wing intensified its violent attacks on the state at the same time that a centrist wing was rebuilding itself as a mainstream political party as well as a social services organization. Members gained control of university student associations and professional unions. The late 1980s were the apogee of the Brotherhood's influence, as a number of preachers associated with the organization gained national prominence. In 1987, they won a majority of seats in the parliament and then were banned from politics as a party, although members of the Brotherhood continued to run as independent candidates. None gained a seat in the 2010 elections, reducing the election's legitimacy and contributing to the outrage at political repression that produced the revolution of the "Arab Spring" in early 2011. The Brotherhood played a secondary role in the movement that centered on Cairo's Tahrir Square, but gradually became an important element in negotiations toward political change and became a legal party that June.

Brotherhood-related organizations stand alongside many other non-profit religious organizations that receive financing locally, through the apportionment of zakat or the voluntary contributions of merchants and others to the poor. These organizations blossomed in the late 1980s, after Egypt had begun its program of economic liberalization and consequent reductions in state support for social welfare. Realizing that these policies would create a vacuum in services, the government issued permits for these organizations, which were tied to mosques that functioned outside the direct control of the state (despite the government's plans, so far unrealizable, to eventually control all mosques and preachers). Members of the Brotherhood went to coffee shops, schools, and mosques to speak about Islam, using the forms and idioms of the sermon to win over their fellow Muslims. They also printed, and distributed widely, short books and magazines.

Although some have tried to explain Islamic movements as reactions against threats to collective identity or government neglect and repression and have minimized their Islamic content, anthropologists and other social scientists have focused on the ideas and practices within the movements that have encouraged participation and mobilized support. It is not enough that grievances exist; successful mobilization has social prerequisites and it depends on motivating people (Bayat 2010).

In the case of Islamic social movements, leaders have successfully engaged in "summoning" through da`wa. Among the causes of grievance were the increases in higher education under Nasser without the provision of adequate opportunities for work, the perception of overwhelming Western cultural and economic power, and the failure of established political parties to respond to real needs. The responses included the creation of new mosques and social networks to provide services. The number of private mosques more than doubled during the 1970s (Wickham 2002: 98). Remittances from the Gulf states and the local collection of zakat funded the mosques. The mosques provided hospitals, schools that tutored students in secular subjects (increasingly necessary as the quality of public school teaching declined from the 1970s on), charity distribution centers, and lending libraries for Islamic books and sermon cassettes. Thousands of private Islamic voluntary associations provided similar social and religious services. When the Labor party newspaper al-Sha`b turned toward Islamism, under the editorial leadership of `Adil Hussein, it provided a major daily outlet for opinions of Brotherhood members and activists in other branches of the Islamic revival, *al-Sahwa al-Islâmiyya.*

These organizations were not "political" in the ordinary sense of the term; they focused on improving the quality of life for those in their neighborhoods and on increasing the piety of individual Muslims. But the very fact that private Islamist organizations were providing the schooling, health care, welfare aid, and other services that the state claimed to provide had political results, undermining the state's claims to legitimacy and supporting the claims of Islamic parties that the form of government would need to be changed in order to establish a just and prosperous society.

The activists in the informal sector who staffed mosques and hospitals, schools and day-care centers often were not affiliated with any formal organization, not even the NGOs described above. Carrie Wickham (2002) carried out fieldwork in three poor Cairo neighborhoods, where activists spoke of what they were doing across all these domains as forms of da`wa. These activists quoted Hassan al-Banna, to the effect that reform would spread from the individual through the neighborhood to the society at large, and only after that would the state change. Imams preaching at small, independent mosques called on ordinary young men and women to adopt a more self-consciously Islamic mode of life, which meant changing their appearance (for example, wearing more modest clothes, growing a beard), praying regularly, and spending more time listening to religious lessons at a mosque or on cassette tapes. These lessons, delivered to groups of women or groups of men, particularly concerned social questions, about finding a spouse or creating a Muslim family. Many young people also bought da`wa pamphlets and short books in kiosks and Islamic bookstores. Most of these reflect a Brotherhood perspective, in stressing how a full commitment to Islam results in observant religious practice, but also in a concern for improving society. Central is the idea that Islam is a complete program (*manhaj*) for organizing society, but the writings direct the reader to begin by reforming him- or herself through the struggle against desires (*al-ijtihâd ma`a al-nafs*), and then to engage in outreach, or da`wa, to others in his or her own neighborhood (Wickham 2002: 130–49). Some books direct the da`i to tailor the message to the audience, and to begin by building a personal relationship with the addressee, then build that person's sense of God's wonders, providing simple books on one's obligations to God, and only later expanding the sense of obligation to include other domains of life.

Wickham (2002: 150–75) points out that these calls were effective because the Islamic networks already were embedded in neighborhoods, so that one might come to know a da`i through one's participation in informal lessons or study groups at a mosque, participation that entailed few risks and built up a sense of trust between the newcomers and those already in the network. The da`i came from that neighborhood or had strong local ties. Furthermore, involvement in an Islamic network offered tangible benefits – one could gain help in getting a visa, finding work, or meeting a potential spouse – as well as such emotional benefits as a sense of solidarity and security. This involvement also had a coercive side, as when the norms of dress were impressed on young women and men, appropriate dress was provided, and the recruits were reminded frequently of what they ought to do.

Why were these particular normative messages appealing to so many young people? Many ordinary Muslims saw the basic problems of Egyptian society as stemming from the breakdown of social norms, a loss they saw in their everyday encounters with corrupt officials and teachers. Islamic calls for social justice resonated powerfully with these youth. Moreover, the Islamic call provided an alternative theory of worth. For young people who saw little use or value for their secular school degrees, a call that stressed the greater value of religious knowledge was attractive. The downgrading of material things also comforted those who did not stand to gain many through secular paths of study and work. Pointing out that this shift in values comforted those in dead-end careers does not diminish the importance of the call's content; it helps explain how the call held particular appeal for people who had moved into higher education, or who might have done so.

Anthropological studies of how people talk, read, and listen in a da'wa vein give us a better understanding of how some Muslims have organized and mobilized others around themes of reform, piety, and social justice. Many people know the story of how the Ayatollah Khomeini sent cassette tapes of his sermons throughout Iran before he himself returned on a triumphal flight from Paris, but such tapes have played a role in mobilizing support for Islamic movements much more widely. Charles Hirschkind (2009) describes the circulation of tapes of sermons by popular preachers, including Shaykh Abd al-Hamid Kishk (d. 1996), a popularity heightened by the broad perception that the state-controlled radio and television hid the real truth from citizens.

These media of da'wa – speeches and sermons, books, cassettes, and now the internet – bring together the personal and the political, or, more precisely, the development of one's piety with the duty to create a society that will be closer to Islamic norms. In contemporary Cairo, as described by Hirschkind (2009), this dual call to piety and civic duty is now supranational. Ordinary Muslims listen to taped sermons from Saudi Arabia and Jordan. The biggest crowds at the major annual French Islamic assembly at the Salon du Bourget turn out for high-profile speakers from Cairo or other Muslim-majority countries, whose fame has preceded them via electronic media. As in Egypt, French Muslims may listen to these tapes at home or in taxis, private cars, or cafes. The speeches take the form of sermons or draw on sermon techniques of persuasion, in that they seek to move the listener to change his or her everyday life. But like the sermon in the mosque, they also respond to the state's actions, criticizing efforts to ban headscarves from schools and the broadcasting of "indecent" television programs.

What relationships do these networks of mosques, sermons, cassettes, and listeners have to political processes and state forces? As Hirschkind (2009) demonstrates, the leading preachers have been affiliated at one time or another with state institutions and with the Muslim Brotherhood or other oppositional groups. Shaykh Kishk, for example, during the 1960s and 1970s regularly denounced the state in his sermons in Cairo and was imprisoned twice, but during this entire period he preached for the Ministry of Religious Affairs at his Cairo mosque. The government finally banned him from preaching, but he continued to air his opinions in a newspaper published by the government party.

The Brotherhood offers a particularly important instance of a widespread phenomenon, namely, the rise of organizations with religious messages and social functions in response to perceived social needs, and the ambivalence they encounter or experience with respect to their political activities. In Indonesia, the Muhammadiyah and Nahdlatul Ulama (NU) grew out of different institutional bases, but under Suharto's New Order, both became important bases for politicians seeking to challenge an oppressive state. Robert Hefner (2000) argues that both organizations became sources of commitment to democratic pluralism in Indonesia and thus attest to the potential of a "civil Islam."

Hefner's argument serves as an important check to assumptions bundled into the term "Islamism," which lumps together movements seeking to change everyday behavior through da`wa with those seeking violent overthrow of regimes. "Islamism" remains an unquestioned category of instant political analysis in many countries, thus in early 2011 the question posed after the flight of Ben Ali from Tunisia was: would the Islamists return? (They did.)

These same careful case studies also show that Islamic "civil society" organizations can assume a range of stands with respect to toleration and pluralism. The very same Nahdlatul Ulama that in the 1990s nurtured democratic aspirations had nurtured participation in army-initiated massacres of suspected "Communists" in 1965–6 (Hefner 1990:

193–227). Religion-backed movements can generate a wide variety of political positions – a point made by Irfan Ahmad (2009) by contrasting the fates and fortunes of the Jamaat-e-Islami parties in India and in Pakistan. The Indian Jamaat transformed itself in order to convince a secular and multi-confessional public of its proper place in a democratic India. Its story resembles that of the Indonesian organizations described by Hefner. Its Pakistani counterpart continued to advocate an Islamic state and to support criminal laws based on Islam. There is nothing inevitably democratic about civil society organizations – Hitler's brown-shirts meet all the criteria for membership in that category – nor is there anything inevitably anti-democratic about Islam-inspired organizations (Eickelman and Piscatori 2004).

Islamic mobilization occurs in a wide variety of settings. Daromir Rudnyckyj (2010) traces the genesis of a spiritual motivation program in Indonesia from a mosque in Bandung to implementation in a nearby steel factory. The template for Islamic revival in the factory was based on an engineer's views of Islam, combining spiritual guidance, business success training, and a vision of Islam as predictive and encompassing of science and technology. The key is raising the work ethic to a level of piety, and reminding workers that God is the accountant par excellence. These programs have a marked effect on ideas of citizenship, however, implicitly equating civic participation with Islamic faith and pointing up the quandary of reviving Islam as a central motivating force in institutions that must remain religiously pluralistic.

Schools and transnational Islamic movements: the Deobandi case

The modern seminary gave rise to many contemporary Muslim social movements. As we saw in Chapter 2, until the nineteenth century religious education was mainly about learning enough classical Arabic to be able to recite verses of the Qur'an and, at higher levels, to engage in

jurisprudential reasoning and hadith sciences. One studied with a particular teacher, and one's diploma was from that teacher. Modern religious
schools sprung up across Muslim societies in response to colonial secular education, and they followed the model of the colonial schools. The
new madrasa, as Muslims in much of the world called the new Islamic
schools, featured a paid teaching staff and a sequence of courses. A
change in the spatial organization of learning marked the shift: students
now sat in benches facing a teacher rather than in circles around him
or her.

Earlier we learned of the influential madrasa founded in 1867 in the
town of Deoband, near Delhi in northern India. The school did not teach
English (unlike some others), but its use of Urdu allowed it to attract
boys from a wide area of northern India and Central Asia. The school's
teachers emphasized the importance of learning hadith and using them
to combat deviations from the correct path. They and their students
became a new class of learned men, ulama (in Arabic, `ulamâ'), who
claimed the right to speak up on issues of the day, to issue fatwas, and
to start new schools elsewhere. Thus was born a network of teachers and
schools labeled "Deobandi" (Metcalf 2002). They preferred to pursue
their religious activities outside of government, and most opposed the
creation of Pakistan as a state specifically for Muslims. But on these and
other issues, they found themselves in competition with other schools
and teachers, some of whom advocated stricter interpretations of scripture, while others urged more toleration toward such practices as saint
worship.

The Deobandi school has spawned not only other schools but also
other Islamic social movements, which differ among themselves in the
emphases they give to jurisprudential debate, teaching, or missionary
work. A particularly influential offshoot of the Deoband movement
has been the Tablighi Jama`at, the "Society for Conveying the Faith,"
a movement for spreading word of correct Islamic practice throughout
the world, which has been discussed in earlier chapters. The Tabligh

began in the 1920s when a Deobandi-trained scholar, Maulana Muhammad Ilyas Kandhlawi (1885–1944), urged followers to go out and remind Muslims of their religious obligations, but to refrain from entering into conflict and debates. The missionaries were trained in the hadith and life of the Prophet Muhammad. They tried to organize their lives around self-improvement as well as teaching, both based on the Prophet's example. Muhammad Ilyas concentrated on expanding the Tabligh's activities within India in order to reach nominal Muslims, and in particular those in danger of being attracted to Hinduism.

In 1944, Muhammad Ilyas was succeeded by his son, Muhammad Yusuf, who began to build the movement outside of India; he also permitted his followers to approach non-Muslims. The Tabligh spread along the pilgrimage route to Mecca and along trade routes leading to eastern Africa and Southeast Asia. In 1965, Muhammad Ilyas's great-nephew, In'am-ul-Hassan, became the third leader or amîr, and the movement expanded into Europe and North America. In 1995, the grandson of Muhammad Yusuf, Saâd, succeeded to this position, and continued the emphasis on expanding and strengthening Tablighi networks worldwide.

These missions of tabligh – conveying divine guidance – are regularly required of the men and women who adhere to the movement. Followers should travel as teams (jama`ats) to invite other Muslims to join them in worship. Men are supposed to give to such missions one night a week, three days a month, forty days a year, and one period of 120 continuous days once in a lifetime. The longer tours may take them far afield, stretching outside the Tablighi network to other countries and continents.

The Tablighi seek to create as little hierarchy as possible. Each group chooses a leader and gives him advice. Ideally, roles shift from one member to another during a tour, so that someone may lead prayer on one occasion and cook on another. The overall structure also downplays hierarchy, and has zones and divisions to facilitate communication and gatherings. In India, the center (markaz) is at Nizamu'd-din, where leaders from zones throughout India gather for periodic meetings. Gatherings in Pakistan, Britain, and North America attract large crowds, and are occasions for men and women from around the world to make contact. Metcalf (2002) describes three kinds of network along which Tablighi travel and communicate. First, Tablighis often travel together to make the pilgrimage to Mecca, and once there, they reach out to other Muslims as a group. Second, one religious school, the Nadwatu'l-'Ulama in Lucknow, northern India, provides a scholarly center for the Tablighi and sends students out across the world (see Chapter 2). Finally, as traders or workers travel, they create a third network among them. In particular, Gujaratis have spread the Tablighi message from South Asia to Britain through their work-related travel.

The Tablighis seek to perfect themselves as well as to convince others to return to proper Islamic practice. They state that even if they do not persuade Muslims to change their practices, they will have succeeded by conveying God's message, and in the process remaking their own lives. Their basic teaching is faithful religious worship and service, `ibâdât, and in particular the regular performance of salat worship. Indeed, the first two of their six basic points are the confession of faith and observance of salat, followed by knowledge, obtained through reading of texts, ideally aloud and in public. These three tenets form the foundations of piety, best realized in a group. Subsequent tenets concern respect for Muslims, sincerity (ikhlâs) of intention in all one's acts, and freeing up of time for missionary work.

The French name for the group, Faith and Practice (*Foi et Pratique*), underscores these emphases. The adept seeks to organize his or her everyday life with the example of the Prophet in mind, starting with the growing of a beard and the wearing of a white garment (the djellaba) and turban. A focus on the correct performance of salat fits well with this emphasis, for the salat is supposed to be an exact replica of the Prophet's practice. Not only is any deviation from this model prohibited, but correct performance purifies the world. Muhammad Ilyas cited the Prophet's statement that "each of the five salats expiates the sins committed since the previous salat," and a follower in Paris told an investigator that "the salat removes all the world's evils" (Kepel 1991: 183).

As Barbara Metcalf (2002) writes, the Tablighis took from their Deobandi teachers three elements. They took the emphasis on the hadith as the source of religious knowledge that for the Deobandis had been a weapon against "Hindu" practices, and turned it into a method for reaching out to fellow Muslims to remind them of their religion. They also followed the Deobandis in their emphasis on personal purity, and converted it from a characteristic of a holy man, a pir, to a characteristic of the entire body of adherents, the *jama'at*. They see themselves as a group endowed with a divine mission, in effect "democratizing" the notion of authority to carry on a struggle for personal purification, which they refer to as a jihad. Finally, they continued the Deobandi avoidance of politics.

Although in their early years Tablighis worked through existing structures, increasingly they have their own centers and mosques, including a seminary in Dewsbury in Britain, a mosque in Paris, and a network of twenty-five mosques in the United States (Metcalf 1996: 113). Gilles Kepel (1991: 177–209) provides us with a detailed account of one Friday collective worship at the main mosque affiliated with the Tablighi in Paris, the Omar mosque on Jean-Pierre-Timbaud street in the north-east of Paris. The street is lined with shops catering to Muslims, such as halal butcher shops, Islamic bookstores, and pilgrimage travel services. Tabligh followers continually buy up properties belonging to non-Muslims, in order to make the quarter entirely Muslim.

During the morning of the worship service, men and women recited praise to God, the dhikr, literally "remembrance" of God. These recitations form an important element of knowledge, `ilm, the third Tabligh principle. After the call to prayer, the sermon began around 2 p.m., given by the amir of the movement in France, Mohammad Hamammi, who spoke in colloquial Tunisian Arabic to an assembly of men and women from many different origins, including Algerians, West Africans, Comorians, and so forth. Many would have had difficulty with colloquial or classical Arabic, but the style of the sermon was telegraphic, emotional, and physical, according to Kepel, and certain words and phrases would have come through adequately to the listeners. His sermon lauded the virtues of a Muslim life and held as reprehensible the alternatives: a woman failing to wear headcovering was "naked," he said; men who have their wives and daughters work outside the home are not Muslims, and so forth.

Afterwards, a small number of the worshippers remained to study portions of a book with the imam. The book was the Riyadh as-Salihin of Imam Nawawi, a compilation of hadith written in the thirteenth century and used today as a guide to correct practice by Muslims throughout South and Southeast Asia. As Kepel points out, it is attractive because it is organized by theme (clothing, eating, etc.) and because it is compact, omitting the long chain of transmitters of the hadith. It also responds to a general demand I have encountered frequently among Muslims in France, that is, for a straightforward list of dos and don'ts, to make the task of living a pious life as simple as possible.

Later that afternoon, groups of men assembled to go out on "tours" of Tablighi activity to destinations in Paris or the suburbs. Their leaders would have chosen places for them to spend the night, usually a mosque or prayer house in a place where immigrant workers live. The arrival of these groups would have been at the behest of the leadership of the local prayer house. Given the shortage of books, teachers, and other resources, prayer house organizers generally were quite happy to have the free assistance of the Tabligh in teaching about religion. Kepel argues (1991: 205–9) that the timing of the Tabligh's expansion in France during the 1980s was perfect: at the moment when Muslim immigration ceased to be seen (by everyone, Muslim and non-Muslim) as a temporary phenomenon, families arrived to join working men, and these men and women began to raise difficult questions of morality and social norms in a new country.

To them, the Tabligh offered the assurance of simple and clear answers: maintain a pious religious life, stay out of the public and political eye, and you will be saved. The organization also offered the possibility of a life organized around pious practices of worship, tabligh, recitation, and lessons that could reorient the disoriented. The Tabligh also appealed to young French men, out of work and without a cause, who found an all-encompassing life in community-based life, as part of a jama'at.

When, in the early 2000s, I carried out fieldwork in Islamic schools in Paris, I found many men, and fewer women, who had begun their active interest in religion by joining the Tabligh after being approached by one of these "tours" and invited to participate in worship services. Most of those invited in came from Muslim backgrounds, but some did not. Eventually all of them left the Tabligh (or I would not have encountered them in the places I did), in all cases because they grew tired of the simplicity of the Tabligh teaching, which remained limited to a small number of hadith. They looked for other sources of knowledge.

Other movements also were inspired by the Deobandis but developed their teachings in a different direction. Whereas the Deobandi leadership advocated a secular state structure within which they could carry out their activities, a minority broke with them over this issue and founded the Jamaat-e-Islami, to support the creation of an independent Pakistan for Muslims. Although a small minority party, they were successful in shaping the teachings in Pakistani madrasa, including those where the future Taliban leadership of Afghanistan were trained.

The Taliban emphasized a different side of Deobandi teaching, namely, their willingness to correct other Muslims' deviations from correct Islamic practices. In the 1980s, some three million Afghan refugees flooded western Pakistan. For many of the boys among them, Islamic madrasas provided the only available schooling. One school, the Madrasa Haqqaniya near Peshawar, trained a number of the future leaders of the Taliban. These "taliban," or students, carried to an extreme the criticism of customary practices common to Deobandis, and made the seclusion of women a central element in their vision of a properly Islamic society.

Barbara Metcalf (2002) argues that the Deobandis, the Taliban, and the Tablighi share a pragmatic attitude toward political life, a willingness to seek allies nearly anywhere, that bespeaks the absence of a positive political program. Of course, specific political doctrines are also shaped by other elements of the society. For example, when, in the mid-1990s, the Taliban developed their political "creed," it resembled Pashtun ideas of political rule, in being based on allegiance to a particular individual, either a tribal ruler or an "*amîr al-mu'minîn,*" Commander of the Faithful (Marsden 2005). When Afghans have fought wars in the past two centuries, even when accompanied by ideological statements regarding Marxism, nationalism, or Islam, they have always been motivated by personal loyalties to clan or ethnic groups, or to individuals. The creation of "Afghanistan" involved wars by the British-backed Pashtun leader Abdur Rahman Khan in the late 1880s against non-Pashtun tribes, and especially against Hazara, Uzbek, Turkmen, and Tajik groups, and Pashtun attacks against these groups persisted through the course of the twentieth century. The Pashtun domination of the Communist government of the 1980s led Uzbek and Turkic groups to join the mujahidîn, just as the Taliban Pashtun were opposed by the Uzbek-led Northern league.

The Taliban also modeled their institutions of consultation (*shura*) after the Afghan *loya jirga,* a grand council that was expected to ratify the conclusions and desires of a leadership body. When a thousand ulama were convened after September 11, 2001, to decide whether to surrender Osama bin Laden, they understood their role as one of ratification, not one of giving a fatwa. Nor did the Taliban "sharia courts" appear to draw on Islamic procedural requirements or the jurisprudence of any legal school. The village councils they employed were indigenous Afghan institutions. Even after the defeat of the Taliban regime in late 2001, several of the Pashtun men who had been ministers in that regime successfully approached Hamid Karzai and found places in the new government, exchanging their turbans for the *pokhol* wool hat worn by Karzai.

Varieties of jihad

Anthropologists insist upon viewing the role of ideas in a specific social context. Nowhere is this tenet more important than when treating ideas of great public significance, such as that of jihad (*jihâd*) within Islam. The root j-h-d means "effort," and the verb *jâhada*, to struggle or strive. The root also generates the word ijtihâd, or the struggle to arrive at an interpretation of a text, which is used across Islamic contexts to designate the act of directly interpreting a scriptural passage rather than relying on the findings of a legal school (Hallaq 1984). In the Qur'an, words deriving from j-h-d occur forty-one times with the general sense of struggle; ten times with the sense of armed struggle; and on other occasions with the sense of acting righteously and sacrificing for God (Bonner 2006: 22). From the beginning, the idea that jihad can concern struggles against inner temptations as well as against outer foes finds textual support.

The term jihad continues to provide a socio-religious framework for presenting socially active work as religious work. For example, the Shi'ite women Lara Deeb studied in Beirut spoke of their community service as "women's jihad" (2006: 204–5). In Bangladesh, debates continue as to whether the "lesser jihad" to establish an Islamic state is still relevant and obligatory (Huq 2009).

The Qur'an contains two kinds of verses with respect to combat. One set of verses explicitly limits legitimate war to situations where Muslims are first attacked, such as chapter 2, verse 190, which says "and fight in the way of God with those who fight you, but aggress not: God loves not the aggressors." Another set mentions no such conditions, such as chapter 9, verse 29, "Fight those who believe not in God and the Last Day and do not forbid what God and His Messenger have forbidden – such men as practice not the religion of truth, being of those who have been given the Book – until they pay the tribute out of hand and have been humbled." Even this second set, however, links fighting to the expansion of the Muslim political and religious community, the umma, and the subjugation and payment of tribute by neighboring peoples. Indeed, maintaining control over armies before and after the beginning of Islam required periodic raiding of neighboring tribes, if not expansion of a community's borders, in order to retain soldiers' loyalty by redistributing wealth.

Early jurists confirmed the idea that the umma, led by a caliph, a rightful successor to Muhammad, had the collective obligation to urge other peoples to convert or, if they would not do so, force them to submit to Muslim rule and to pay tribute. This obligation gave rise to the idea that the world was divided into the dar al-Islâm, the world of submission to God, and the dar al-harb, the world that was subject to warfare and conquest. These jurists also developed laws of just war, including the rights of enemy combatants and of non-combatants, when attack was permitted, and how to fairly divide the spoils.

In the modern period, jurists have developed several quite distinct sets of ideas about jihad (Peters 1996). Modernist Muslim thinkers writing from the late nineteenth century onward drew on the first set of Qur'anic verses mentioned above to argue that the normal state of relations among nations, Muslim or non-Muslim, is the state of peace. War is justified only when necessary to defend oneself. Furthermore, they said, God wants people to come to Islam out of study, reflection, and conviction, and not under force of arms. The Qur'anic verse "there is no compulsion in matters of religion" (2: 256) is often quoted to buttress this argument. This line of thinking has been continued by such influential Muslim figures as the Egyptian jurist Sheikh Yûsuf Qardâwî, and by sheikhs of al-Azhar University in Cairo.

A second, opposed line of reasoning was put forth by Islamic groups seeking to fight their own Muslim governments and seeking religious justification for their attacks. In Egypt, for example, the Muslim Brother-hood figure Sayyid Qutb (d. 1966) argued that armed aggression against the government was justified because Egyptian leaders, although they professed Islam, in fact had left the faith and thus were legitimate targets for attack.

As in so many matters, Islamic texts and traditions may be cited to support a wide range of actions. Many contemporary Muslim scholars underscore this quality of Islam. Although some Muslim public figures claim that scripture has a single, unambiguous meaning, this has not been an important position among Muslim jurists, who generally have held that either there is no single correct Islamic position on legal matters, or that there is, but humans, imperfect as they are, cannot be expected always to arrive at it. Under these two views, differences in interpretation of the Qur'an and the hadith either are planned by God, or are forgiven by Him (Abou El Fadl 2004). In this, Muslims are somewhat less likely than contemporary Fundamentalist Protestants to claim that scripture has a single "literal" meaning.

One saw this "retreat to literalism" practiced, very understandably, by Muslims in the United States just after the destruction of the World Trade Center towers on September 11, 2001. Some scholars were featured in media coverage as saying that "Islam is a religion of peace" and that it "could never approve of such attacks." Similarly, verses from the Qur'an promoting peaceful coexistence among peoples and attacking those who kill were cited as if they, and not the statements coming from terrorists, represented true Islam. Rare were the authorities who stated that scripture contains lots of messages, and that one can find verses and interpretations of them that support attacks on unbelievers, as well as the peace-oriented verses more widely quoted.

Of course, the weakness of this approach was immediately apparent when others quoted verses that urged Muslims to fight infidels, and others that spoke in a highly negative fashion of the Jews. The appropriate response to this practice of citing out of context was to speak of the historical circumstances in which these verses were received, and of the interpretive traditions and alternatives built up around them. But this way was closed to those who had begun the debate by their own acontextual reciting of scripture.

The problem in searching for a single "Muslim position" on jihad, or even regarding particular actions, is that legal opinions, fatwas, are produced in response to a specific question. The choice of question can select the answer. For example, shortly after the invasion of Afghanistan in the fall of 2001, influential US Muslim scholars posed a question to Sheikh Yûsuf Qardâwî, the Egyptian scholar living in Qatar, whose broadcasts on the television station al-Jazîra are followed by Arabic-speaking Muslims throughout the world. The scholars asked whether Muslims serving in the US armed forces ordered to fight in Afghanistan ought to obey orders. Qardâwî answered that they should, because they had taken an oath to do so. Subsequently, others put a different question to him: should Muslims bombard women and children in Afghanistan? Qardâwî answered that they should not (Kurzman 2003, Netzer 2004).

Throughout Islamic history, jihad has provided a justification for unifying against an enemy, and in many cases it has provided the basis for a new political system. In West Africa, for example, the norm of jihad was instrumental in expanding the realm of Islamic rule and constructing stable and prosperous communities. The "chain" of jihad spread through the region over two centuries, from the 1670s in the far western Sahara, to anticolonial movements of the late nineteenth century.

West African jihad movements responded to a difficult question for Muslims then and now: in the absence of a single Muslim ruler, a caliph, who has the authority to create an Islamic polity, or to declare jihad? In West Africa in the eighteenth century, established Muslim political authority was weak and distant: there was an Ottoman Empire, effectively confined to the Mediterranean, and an independent Moroccan authority, with little reach below the Sahara (Robinson 2000).

What has been the relationship between Islam and war in recent conflicts in Afghanistan? From the beginning of the resistance to the Soviet-backed regime in the 1970s, to the victory of the Taliban in 1996, Islam has provided a repertoire of ideas of authority, on which various individuals and groups could call in order to rally people behind them. In this respect, the question of jihad has been subsumed in broader questions of political authority.

David Edwards (2002) examines the role of Islamic authority in shaping the lines of resistance to Soviet rule in Afghanistan. The traditional social forms for armed combat in Afghanistan were tribal. Tribes fought under their own leaders, and perhaps allied with each other, particularly if they spoke the same language. In a place with many different ethnic groups and language families, centralized authority never has been easy to develop, nor has large-scale unity against someone wielding central power. When, in the late 1970s, Afghan tribes began to form armed groups or *lashkar* to attack the troops of the Soviet-backed government, the most effective rhetoric for gaining inter-tribal unity was that of Islam. Various actions taken by the regime could be cited as defiling Islam, and thereby provide a rallying cry for all groups. An inter-tribal "jihad council" took collective responsibility for actions, preventing tribal rivalries from fractioning the anti-government coalition.

Eventually, tribal and larger ethnic rivalries stymied efforts to mount a unified military front, as they prevented any coalitions from lasting. But in the process, rival claimants to lead the resistance or to govern Afghanistan called on different elements of Islamic tradition to justify their claims. The three most important kinds of religious claims were saintly lineage, the prestige of a foreign religious education, and the promise of a "return to village religion." None was decisive, but each was Islamically legitimate.

Claiming descent from a saint or, better yet, from the Prophet Muhammad, attracts followers in most, if not all, Muslim societies. Continuity through direct contact over the generations is a general feature of Islam, as we saw above: the Prophet's statements are only valid if an unbroken chain of reliable witnesses has transmitted them; relations of teachers to students create a chain of spiritual learning; and descent from parent to child is a particularly accepted basis for claiming to have inherited a mantle of religious authority. In Afghanistan, the strong tribal norms that bind people together based on patrilineal descent reinforce the appeal of these claims.

One man making such claims was Hazrat Sibghatullah Mujaddidi, whose family claimed to have descended from Sheikh Ahmad Sirhindi, a central figure in the development of Indian Sufism in the seventeenth century. The family was invited to Afghanistan in the late eighteenth century by the first Afghan king, and established a political base among Pakhtun tribal groups (the largest ethnic category in Afghanistan). These tribesmen became their disciples in a Sufi order (Edwards 2002: 253). The family enjoyed considerable power in making and breaking subsequent kings. Mujaddidi increased his own authority when in 1953 he earned a degree in Islamic jurisprudence from al-Azhar University in Cairo. This combination of lineage and a prestigious degree gave him considerable legitimacy in the eyes of Pakhtun Afghans. In 1979, he sent letters out to his followers in a number of places calling for mass uprisings against the government. In Herat, two hundred thousand people responded to his call, saying, as he himself recalled it, "Oh, this man is the right man. We shall start." The uprising was brutally suppressed by Soviet troops, a failure that considerably lessened his capacity to mobilize people for jihad. In any case, ties of loyalties to Sufi leaders (pirs) had weakened considerably in the course of the twentieth century.

The chief beneficiaries of this weakening in the struggle to lead the jihad were the new Islamic political parties. The legitimacy of claimants to lead these parties rested on their early involvement with party organization and their foreign Islamic credentials. A key source of legitimacy was a professor of Islamic Law at Kabul University, Ghulam Muhammad Niazi, who in the late 1960s was the principal sponsor of the Muslim Youth

Organization, the origin of later Islamic movements. Two of the most important contestants for Afghan jihad leadership, Ustad Burhanuddin Rabbani and Engineer Gulbuddin Hekmatyar, based their claims in large part on their respective ties to this professor. Rabbani claimed that he had been Niazi's chief assistant at the university. Hekmatyar countered that it was another man from the Niazi tribe, Abdur Rahim Niazi, and not Rabbani, who was Professor Niazi's true heir, and that Abdur Rahman Niazi had worked closely with Hekmatyar in the early days of the Muslim Youth Organization. The Rabbani–Hekmatyar rivalry was ethnic, as well as purely political: Rabbani was a Persian-speaking Tajik; Hekmatyar a Pakhtun. Their respective parties became increasingly polarized along ethnic lines in the late 1970s and 1980s.

Why were their ties to a university professor so important to these two rivals? Professor Niazi was acknowledged to be the first Afghan to have studied with members of the Muslim Brotherhood in Cairo, and to have brought their ideas to Afghanistan. It was Ustad [a religious honorific] Rabbani who had translated works by the Brotherhood figure Sayyid Qutb into Persian, but Professor Niazi's status as the first to have learned the new ideas of Brotherhood underscores the importance of precedence in determining authority in Afghan society. It also shows how the older ties to Sufi teachers and other Afghan scholars had diminished in importance, supplanted by the prestige of foreign, and presumably better, Islamic knowledge (Edwards 2002: 239).

The rivalries among Hekmatyar, Rabbani, and other leaders led to the destruction of Kabul, murder and plunder in towns and villages throughout the country, and the rise in the mid-1990s of a new movement, the Taliban or "students." Their claims to legitimacy in leading a jihad against the tribal rulers and party leaders were, again, based on religious norms, but this time those norms were based on the ideals of an indigenous Islam, the Islam of Afghan villages – ideals that had been corrupted, they said, by the work of the parties and by the predominance of Kabul University. The Taliban warriors had grown up in refugee camps along the frontier and in Pakistan, and had attended religious schools in Pakistan. They held out the possibility of a restoration of an earlier Afghan Islam, and the rejection of all foreign influences, whether Soviet, Western, or Arabic. Ironically, it was their subsequent naïve welcoming of Saudi and Egyptian members of al-Qaeda that led to the destruction of the Taliban government and a return to power of the regional tribal leaders. But much of their original appeal to Afghans was their refusal to follow either tribal loyalties or city-based party politics.

Edwards' scholarship shows how we can understand calls for jihad as part of specific struggles for autonomy and power. The traditions and literature around jihad form part of a number of distinct cultural repertoires on which Muslims can call; these repertoires differ across societies, so that the resonances of, and alternatives to, jihad are quite different in Afghanistan than, say, in Indonesia. Edwards shows that in Afghanistan that repertoire includes the alternative complex of values and actions around honor and tribal loyalty. Elsewhere, the term developed other webs of meaning: in Indonesia, for example, jihad has associations with long-standing Christian–Muslim tensions over missionary activities and with conflicts over power and resources in local contexts.

In these cases – the Muslim Brotherhood in Egypt, Deobandi schools and movements across Asia (and beyond), and tribe-based factions in Afghanistan – the Islamic tradition provides elements of a repertoire of idea and ideals, goals and norms. Local actors, the product of particular histories and structures, select from that repertoire and formulate calls to action that resonate with others. With respect to social movements and armed struggle, as with respect to prayer and courts, Muslims create versions of the Islamic tradition that suit those audiences and are relevant at a certain time and in a certain place.

The major contributions of a new anthropology of Islam to Islamic studies come in large part from anthropology's insistence on bracketing, in the phenomenological sense, some of the certainties we have about the world: what constitutes "law," what a headscarf means to its wearer, the existence of an "Islamic world." We can then start from the practices and statements of individuals as they make their way through, and sometimes construct, social institutions of worship, education, law, or politics, and examine the multiple meanings they create as they do so. Along the way anthropologists build in analyses of villages and lineages, languages and stories, and modes of meaning that characterize regions and classes. The Islam we construct in anthropology is in this sense from the ground up, and highly contextualized.

But precisely because it takes seriously how Muslims view their worlds, the anthropology of Islam also incorporates into its analyses of practices and meanings the sense of a global Islamic tradition. The Muslim at prayer presupposes knowledge of how to read and recite scripture; the anthropology of prayer must then begin with knowledge of scriptures and their uses, interpretations, and histories. The judge at his or her desk draws on myriad sources of normativity, including the texts and traditions of a legal school, and of national law, which must then become part of the anthropologist's object of study as well. The family sacrificing a sheep reflects on the Prophet Abraham's sacrifice, on the ethics of giving away, and also perhaps on the contribution of the sacrificed animal to the family's afterlife. The anthropologist must bring to that moment a sense of these traditions as well, and of their permutations and combinations across the Islamic world, which make the highly varying forms of sacrifice recognizable across societies where Muslims live.

Anthropologists studying Islam have, through this double reflection on contextualized practices and global traditions, reshaped many of the habitual concerns both of social anthropology and of Islamic studies. They have reshaped social anthropology by challenging more or less explicit normative assumptions about gender, religious law, and knowledge. To the extent that we come to understand how veiled women, Islamic judges, and religious pupils see their world and advance through it, we find it more difficult to assume that each is merely the object of oppressive ignorance. They have reshaped Islamic studies by arguing that even socially and educationally marginal Muslims draw on the Islamic tradition when thinking through prayer, healing, or sacrifice. Far from being part of an illiterate body of "receptors" of Islamic knowledge, they are producers of such knowledge as well as practitioners.

Both these contributions return us to the major methodological imperative of social anthropology, which also is an ethical imperative: to show as fully as we can the lives of ordinary, and not only ordinary, people as they work through the dilemmas and opportunities of every day, and not only everyday life.

Glossary

I have included here major Arabic terms and some other widely used terms, but not all foreign words. For Arabic terms I provide a common transcription here and on the first occasion each word appears in the book, but thereafter I use a simplified transliteration, thus Qur'an (*Qur'ân*), shariah (*sharî`a*), ulama (`*ulamâ'*). I do not seek to distinguish between heavy and light consonants (h, d, s, etc.).

adhân: the call to prayer.

`*âdil*: just, fair.

ahl al-kitâb: "people of the book," a category generally applied to Christians and Jews, to indicate the history of revelation and worship they share with Muslims, but sometimes extended to other religious groups.

`*âlim*: scholar, someone with knowledge, pl., `*ulamâ*`; cf. `*ilm*, knowledge.

amîr: leader, "commander."

`*aql*: reason.

awliyâ' (**sing.: *walîy***): "friends of God," saints, those close to God, spiritual beings.

barakât: God's blessings.

bid`a: innovation, usually illegitimate from the speaker's point of view.

da`wa*: "call," instruction to other Muslims about religion, practiced by *dâ`iy.

dhikr: "remembrance"; repeated chanting.

du`â': prayer.

faskh: annulment of a marriage.

fatwa (**pl.: *fatâwâ***): a legal opinion provided by an Islamic scholar (in the role of *muftî*) to questions.

fiqh: (the science of) jurisprudence, carried out by jurists, *fuqahâ'*.

fitna: disorder, in the sense of civil strife.

hadîth (pl.: *ahâdîth*): reports, of saying or deeds by the Prophet Muhammad.

hadîya: gifts.

halâl: permitted.

Hanafî: belonging to the *Hanafîya* legal school.

haqq: obligation, right.

harâm: forbidden.

hijâb: head covering for women.

`ibâda* (pl.: *`ibâdât): act of worship and service to God.

`îd:* religious feast day, especially the *`îd al-adhâ, Feast of Sacrifice, and the *`îd al-fitr*, at the end of Ramadan.

ijmâ`: consensus of previous generations of scholars; one of the four sources of Islamic jurisprudence.

ijtihâd: interpretation by individuals of Islamic sources.

ikhlâs: sincerity.

`ilm: knowledge.

isnâd: chain of transmitters.

jâhilîya: state of ignorance, pre-Islamic times.

jihâd: struggle.

jilbâb: Islamic dress for women, usually consisting of a loose dress and head covering.

jinn: spirits.

khalîfa: deputy or vice-regent of God.

khatîb: preacher or sermon-giver.

khula': divorce initiated by the wife.

madhhab: legal school or tradition.

madrasa: "school," often religious school.

mahr: gift made directly from the groom to the bride.

Mâlikî: belonging to the *Mâlikîya* legal school.

ma`rifa: gnosis.

mu`âmal,* (pl.: *mu`âmalât): the conduct of humans toward each other, as distinct from *`ibâda*, the conduct of humans toward God.

muftî: someone who issues a fatwa.

mu`jizât: miracles.

murîd: follower, pupil.

nikâh: marriage.

niyya: intention.

nizâm: system, ordering.

pîr: spiritual leader, guide.

qâdî: judge.

Qur'ân: the Qur'an, revelations from God to the Prophet Muhammad; cf. *qirâ'a*: recitation.

sadaqa: voluntary offering.

Salafi (from *salaf*): ancestors, designating movements urging Muslims to return to the religion's origins and the practices of the first generations of Muslims.

salâh: the main Islamic ritual of worship or prayer; *salât jamâ`ah*: congregational worship.

shalwar kamiz: South Asian-style long tunic over trousers.

Shâfi`î*: belonging to the *Shâfi`îya legal school.

sharî`a: path pointed out by God for humans; the norms and rules that guide a Muslim on that path; a body of positive laws putatively reflecting those norms and rules.

shaykh: spiritual leader, knowledgeable person.

shirk: polytheism.

silsila: chain (e.g. of transmitters); cf. *silsilat al-nasab*: chain of ancestors, genealogy.

sûra: chapter, of the *Qur'ân*.

tablîgh: conveying divine guidance; cf. Tablighi Jama'at: movement to do same.

talâq: divorce pronounced by husband.

tanzîl: the sending down of revelation.

taqlîd: in jurisprudence: the (unquestioning) adoption of a legal opinion of a scholar or school (*madhhab*), rather than engaging in *ijtihâd*.

taqwâ: piety or fear of God.

tarîqa: the Sufi path, a Sufi order.

tasawwuf: meditative practices, mysticism, Sufism.

tawhîd: unity of God.

`ulamâ'*: see *`âlim.

umma(h): the worldwide Muslim community.

waqf: endowment or trust.
wasîya: bequest.
zakâh: obligatory annual payment of alms.
zâwîya: lodge, shrine.
ziyâra: visit, usually to shrines.

Bibliography

Abou El Fadl, Khaled. 2004. *Islam and the Challenge to Democracy*. Princeton University Press.

Abu-Lughod, Lila. 1986. *Veiled Sentiments: Honor and Poetry in a Bedouin Society*. Berkeley: University of California Press.

    1989. "Zone of Theory in the Anthropology of the Arab World." *Annual Review of Anthropology* 18: 267–306.

Agrama, Hussein Ali. 2010. "Ethics, Tradition, Authority: Toward an Anthropology of the Fatwa." *American Ethnologist* 37: 2–18.

Ahmad, Irfan. 2009. *Islamism and Democracy in India*. Princeton University Press.

Ahmed, Leila. 1992. *Women and Gender in Islam: Historical Roots of a Modern Debate*. New Haven: Yale University Press.

Antoun, Richard. 1989. *Muslim Preacher in the Modern World*. Princeton University Press.

Asad, Talal. 1986. *The Idea of an Anthropology of Islam*. Washington, DC: The Center for Contemporary Arab Studies, Georgetown University.

Austin, J. L. 1975. *How to do Things with Words*. (2nd edn.) Cambridge, MA: Harvard University Press.

Bano, Samia. 2004. "Complexity, Difference and 'Muslim Personal Law': Rethinking the Relationship between Shariah Councils and South Asian Muslim Women in Britain." Doctoral thesis, University of Warwick, Department of Law.

Basedow, Jürgen, and Nadjma Yassari (eds.). 2004. "Iranian Family and Succession Laws and their Application in German Courts." *Beiträge zum ausländischen und internationalen Privatrecht*, 43. Tubingen: Mohr Siebeck.

Baumann, Gerd. 1996. *Contesting Culture: Discourses of Identity in Multi-Ethnic London*. Cambridge University Press.

Bava, Sophie. 2003. "Les Cheikh-s Mourides Itinérants et l'Espace de la Ziyâra à Marseille." *Anthropologie et Société* 27 (1): 149–66.

2004. "Le Dahira Urbain. Lieu de Pouvoir du Mouridisme." *Les annales de la recherche urbaine* 96: 135–43.

Bayat, Asef. 2010. *Life as Politics: How Ordinary People Change the Middle East.* Stanford University Press.

Berkey, Jonathan. 2002. *The Formation of Islam: Religion and Society in the Near East, 600–1800.* Cambridge University Press.

Blank, Jonah. 2001. *Mullahs on the Mainframe: Islam and Modernity among the Daudi Bohras.* University of Chicago Press.

Boddy, Janice. 1989. *Wombs and Alien Spirits: Women, Men, and the Zâr Cult in Northern Sudan.* Madison: University of Wisconsin Press.

Boellstorff, Tom. 2005. *The Gay Archipelago: Sexuality and Nation in Indonesia.* Princeton University Press.

Bonner, Michael. 2006. *Jihad in Islamic History: Doctrines and Practices.* Princeton University Press.

Bonte, Pierre. 1999. "Sacrifices en Islam: Textes et Contextes," in Pierre Bonte, Anne-Marie Brisebarre, and Altan Gokalp (eds.). *Sacrifices en Islam: Espaces et Temps d'un Rituel,* pp. 21–61. Paris: CNRS Editions.

Bowen, John R. 1989. "Salât in Indonesia: The Social Meanings of an Islamic Ritual." *Man* (N.S.) 24: 600–19.

1993. *Muslims through Discourse: Religion and Ritual in Gayo Society.* Princeton University Press.

2003. *Islam, Law and Equality in Indonesia: An Anthropology of Public Reasoning.* Cambridge University Press.

2005 "Fairness and Law in an Indonesian Court," in M. Khalid Masud, David S. Powers, and Ruud Peters (eds.). *Dispensing Justice in Muslim Courts: Qadis, Procedures and Judgments,* pp. 117–41. Leiden: Brill.

2007. *Why the French Don't Like Headscarves: Islam, the State, and Public Space.* Princeton University Press.

2008. "Europe," in Andrew Rippin (ed.). *The Muslim World,* pp. 118–30. London and New York: Routledge.

2009a. *Can Islam Be French? Pluralism and Pragmatism in a Secularist State.* Princeton University Press.

2009b. "Private Arrangements: Recognizing Shari`a' in England," *Boston Review,* March/April.

2011. "How Could English Courts Recognize Shariah?" *St. Thomas Law Review.*

Brenner, Louis. 2001. *Controlling Knowledge: Religion, Power and Schooling in a West African Muslim Society.* Bloomington: Indiana University Press.

Brenner, Suzanne. 1996. *The Domestication of Desire: Women, Wealth and Modernity in Java.* Princeton University Press.

Bibliography

Brisebarre, Anne-Marie. 1998. *Fête du Mouton: Un Sacrifice Musulman dans l'Espace Urbain.* Paris: CNRS Editions.

Brown, Daniel. 1999. *Rethinking Tradition in Modern Islamic Thought.* Cambridge University Press.

Bulliet, Richard W. 1994. *Islam: The View from the Edge.* New York: Columbia University Press.

Caeiro, Alexandre. 2006. "The Social Construction of Shari'a: Bank Interest, Home Purchase, and Islamic Norms in the West." *Die Welt des Islams* 44 (3): 351–75.

2011. "Fatwas for European Muslims: The Minority Fiqh Project and the Integration of Islam in Europe." PhD Dissertation, University of Utrecht, Netherlands.

Callan, Alyson. 2008. "Female Saints and the Practice of Islam in Sylhet, Bangladesh." *American Ethnologist* 35 (3): 396–412.

Caton, Steve Charles. 2005. *Yemen Chronicle: An Anthropology of War and Mediation.* New York: Hill and Wang.

Cohen, Abner. 1969. *Custom and Politics in Urban Africa.* Berkeley: University of California Press.

Combs-Schilling, M. E. 1989. *Sacred Performances.* New York: Columbia University Press.

Coulson, N. J. 1971. *Succession in the Muslim Family.* Cambridge University Press.

Cruise O'Brien, Donal B. 1971. *The Mourides of Senegal: The Political and Economic Organization of an Islamic Brotherhood.* Oxford: Clarendon Press.

1975. *Saints and Politicians: Essays in the Organisation of a Senegalese Peasant Society.* Cambridge University Press.

Daudy, Abdurrahim. 1950. [Untitled manuscript.]

Deeb, Lara. 2006. *An Enchanted Modern: Gender and Public Piety in Shi'i Lebanon.* Princeton University Press.

2009. "Piety Politics and the Role of a Transnational Feminist Analysis." *Journal of the Royal Anthropological Institute* (N.S.): S112–S126.

Dresch, Paul, and Bernard Haykel. 1995. "Stereotypes and Political Styles: Islamists and Tribesfolk in Yemen." *International Journal of Middle Eastern Studies* 27 (4): 405–31.

Edwards, David B. 2002. *Before Taliban: Genealogies of the Afghan Jihad.* Berkeley: University of California Press.

Eickelman, Dale F. 1976. *Moroccan Islam: Tradition and Society in a Pilgrimage Center.* Austin: University of Texas Press.

1985. *Knowledge and Power in Morocco.* Princeton University Press.

and James Piscatori. 2004. *Muslim Politics.* (2nd edn.) Princeton University Press.

Eisenlohr, Patrick. 2006. "As Makkah is Sweet and Beloved, So is Madina: Islam, Devotional Genres, and Electronic Mediation in Mauritius." *American Ethnologist* 33 (2) 230–45.

El Guindi, Fadwa. 1999. *Veil: Modesty, Privacy, Resistance.* Oxford: Berg.

El Zein, Abdul Hamid. 1974. *The Sacred Meadows: A Structural Analysis of Religious Symbolism in an East African Town.* Evanstown, IL: Northwestern University Press.

Evans-Pritchard, E. E. 1949. *The Sanusi of Cyrenaica.* Oxford: Clarendon Press.

Ewing, Katherine Pratt. 1997. *Arguing Sainthood: Modernity, Psychoanalysis, and Islam.* Durham, NC: Duke University Press.

Fetzer, Joel, and J. C. Soper. 2005. *Muslims and the State in Britain, France and Germany,* Cambridge University Press.

Fischer, Michael M. J. 1980. *Iran: From Religious Dispute to Revolution.* Cambridge, MA: Harvard University Press.

and Mehdi Abedi. 1990. *Debating Muslims: Cultural Dialogues in Postmodernity and Tradition.* Madison: University of Wisconsin Press.

Flueckiger, Joyce Burkhalter. 2006. *In Amma's Healing Room: Gender and Vernacular Islam in South India.* Bloomington: Indiana University Press.

Gade, Anna. 2004. *Perfection Makes Practice: Learning, Emotion, and the Recited Qur`ân in Indonesia.* Honolulu: University of Hawai'i Press.

Gaffney, Patrick D. 1994. *The Prophet's Pulpit: Islamic Preaching in Contemporary Egypt.* Berkeley: University of California Press.

Gardner, Katy. 1995. *Global Migrants, Local Lives: Travel and Transformation in Rural Bangladesh.* Oxford University Press.

Geertz, Clifford. 1968. *Islam Observed: Religious Development in Morocco and Indonesia.* University of Chicago Press.

Gellner, Ernest. 1969. *Saints of the Atlas.* University of Chicago Press.

1980. *Muslim Society.* Cambridge University Press.

Gilsenan, Michael. 1973. *Saint and Sufi in Modern Egypt: An Essay in the Sociology of Religion.* Oxford: Clarendon Press.

1982. *Recognizing Islam: Religion and Society in the Modern Arab World.* New York: Pantheon.

1996. *Lords of the Lebanese Marches: Violence and Narrative in an Arab Society.* Berkeley: University of California Press.

Gräf, Bettina, and Jakob Skovgaard-Petersen (eds.). 2009. *Global Mufti: The Phenomenon of Yûsuf al-Qaradâwî.* New York: Columbia University Press.

Graham, William A. 1987. *Beyond the Written Word: Oral Aspects of Scripture in the History of Religion.* Cambridge University Press.

Bibliography

1993. "Traditionalism in Islam: An Essay in Interpretation." *Journal of Interdisciplinary History* 23: 495–522.

Haenni, Patrick, and Raphaël Voix. 2007. "God by all means . . . Eclectic Faith and Sufi Resurgence among the Moroccan Bourgeoisi," in Martin van Bruinessen and Julia Day Howell (eds.). *Sufism and the "Modern" in Islam*, pp. 241–56. London: I. B. Tauris.

Hallaq, Wael B. 1984. "Was the Gate of Ijtihâd Closed?" *International Journal of Middle Eastern Studies* 1: 3–41.

2009. *Shari`a: Theory, Practice, Transformations*. Cambridge University Press.

Hammoudi, Abdellah. 1993. *The Victim and its Masks: An Essay on Sacrifice and Masquerade in the Maghreb*. (Orig. French 1988.) University of Chicago Press.

Haniffa, Farzana. 2008. "Piety as Politics amongst Muslim Women in Contemporary Sri Lanka." *Modern Asian Studies* 42 (2/3): 347–75.

Hefner, Robert W. 1985. *Hindu Javanese: Tengger Traditions and Islam*. Princeton University Press.

1990. *The Political Economy of Mountain Java: An Interpretive History*. Berkeley: University of California Press.

2000. *Civil Islam: Muslims and Democratization in Indonesia*. Princeton University Press.

and Muhammad Qasim Zaman (eds.). 2007. *Schooling Islam: The Culture and Politics of Modern Muslim Education*. Princeton University Press.

Hirji, Zulfikar (ed.). 2010. *Diversity and Pluralism in Islam*. London: I. B. Tauris.

Hirschkind, Charles. 2009. *The Ethical Soundscape: Cassette Sermons and Islamic Counterpublics*. New York: Columbia University Press.

Ho, Engseng. 2006. *The Graves of Tarim: Genealogy and Mobility across the Indian Ocean*. Berkeley: University of California Press.

Hourani, Albert. 1962. *Arabic Thought in the Liberal Age, 1798–1939*. London: Oxford University Press.

Houtsonen, James. 1994. "Traditional Qur'anic Education in a Southern Moroccan Village." *International Journal of Middle Eastern Studies* 26: 489–500.

Hubert, Henri, and Marcel Mauss. 1964. *Sacrifice: Its Nature and Functions*. University of Chicago Press.

Huq, Maimuna. 2009. "Talking Jihad and Piety: Reformist Exertions among Islamic Women in Bangladesh." *Journal of the Royal Anthropological Institute* (N.S.): S163–S182.

Johansen, Julian. 1996. *Sufism and Islamic Reform in Egypt: The Battle for Islamic Tradition*. Oxford University Press.

Jones, Carla. 2010. "Materializing Piety: Gendered Anxieties about Faithful Consumption in Contemporary Urban Indonesia." *American Ethnologist* 37 (4): 617–37.

Karamustafa, Ahmet T. 2007. *Sufism: The Formative Period.* Edinburgh University Press.

Kastoryano, Riva. 2002. *Negotiating Identities: States and Immigrants in France and Germany.* Princeton University Press.

Kepel, Gilles. 1991. *Les Banlieues de l'Islam: Naissance d'une Religion en France.* Paris: Seuil.

Kurzman, Charles. 2003. "Pro-U.S. Fatwas." *Middle East Policy* 10 (3): 155–66.

Lambek, Michael. 1981. *Human Spirits: A Cultural Account of Trance in Mayotte.* Cambridge University Press.

    1993. *Knowledge and Practice in Mayotte: Local Discourses of Islam, Sorcery and Spirit Possession.* University of Toronto Press.

Lapidus, Ira M. 1988. *A History of Islamic Societies.* Cambridge University Press.

Laurence, Jonathan. 2011. *The Emancipation of Europe's Muslims.* Princeton University Press.

Leonard, Karen Isaksen. 2003. *Muslims in the United States: The State of Research.* New York: Russell Sage Foundation.

Lester, Rebecca. 2005. *Jesus in Our Wombs: Embodying Modernity in a Mexican Convent.* Berkeley: University of California Press.

Lewis, Bernard. 1988. *The Political Language of Islam.* University of Chicago Press.

Lewis, Philip. 2002. *Islamic Britain: Religion, Politics, and Identity among British Muslims.* (2nd edn.) London: Palgrave.

Longinotto, Kim, and Ziba Mir-Hosseini. 1998. *Divorce, Iranian Style.* Film. Twentieth-Century Vixen.

Lukens-Bull, Ronald. 2005. *A Peaceful Jihad: Negotiating Identity and Modernity in Muslim Java.* New York: Palgrave Macmillan.

MacLeod, Arlene. 1991. *Accommodating Protest: Working Women, the New Veiling, and Change in Cairo.* New York: Columbia University Press.

Mahmood, Saba. 2005. *Politics of Piety: The Islamic Revival and the Feminist Subject.* Princeton University Press.

Marsden, Magnus. 2005. *Living Islam: Muslim Religious Experience in Pakistan's North-West Frontier.* Cambridge University Press.

Masquelier, Adeline Marie. 2001. *Prayer has Spoiled Everything: Possession, Power, and Identity in an Islamic Town of Niger.* Durham, NC: Duke University Press.

Masud, Muhammad Khalid, Brinkley Messick, and David S. Powers. 1996. "Muftis, Fatwas, and Islamic Legal Interpretation," in Muhammad Khalid Masud, Brinkley Messick, and David S. Powers (eds.). *Islamic Legal Interpretation: Muftis and their Fatwas,* pp. 3–32. Cambridge, MA: Harvard University Press.

Maududi, A. A. n.d. *Towards Understanding Islam.* Kuala Lumpur: Murtaza Sdn. Bhd.

Bibliography

McIntosh, Janet. 2004. "Reluctant Muslims: Embodied Hegemony and Moral Resistance in a Giriama Spirit Possession Complex." *Journal of the Royal Anthropological Institute* 10 (1): 91–112.

Messick, Brinkley. 1993. *The Calligraphic State: Textual Domination and History in a Muslim Society.* Berkeley: University of California Press.

Metcalf, Barbara Daly. 1982. *Islamic Revival in British India: Deoband 1860–1900.* Princeton University Press.

2002. *"Traditionalist" Islamic Activisim: Deoband, Tablighis, and Talibs.* Leiden: ISIM Papers, no. 4.

(ed.). 1996. *Making Muslim Space in North America and Europe.* Berkeley: University of California Press.

Mir-Hosseini, Ziba. 2001. *Marriage on Trial: A Study of Islamic Family Law.* (Revised edn.) London: I. B. Tauris.

Mitchell, Richard P. 1969. *The Society of the Muslim Brothers.* London: Oxford University Press.

Moors, Annelies. 1995. *Women, Property and Islam: Palestinian Experiences, 1920–1990.* Cambridge University Press.

Mottahedeh, Roy. 1985. *The Mantle of the Prophet.* New York: Random House.

Munson, Henry. 1993. *Religion and Power in Morocco.* New Haven: Yale University Press.

Muslim, Imâm. n.d. [1971?]. "Kitâb al-Adâhî," in *Sahih Muslim*, vol. III, pp. 1080–94. Beirut: Dar al Arabia.

Nadwi, Mohammad Akram. 2007. *Madrasah Life: A Student's Day at Nadwat al-Ulama.* London: Turath Publishing.

Navaro-Yashin, Yael. 2002. *Faces of the State: Secularism and Public Life in Turkey.* Princeton University Press.

Netzer, Miriam. 2004. "One Voice? The Crisis of Legal Authority in Islam." *Al-Nakhlah*, The Fletcher School, Tufts University. Spring 2004, article 6.

Noor, Farish A., Yoginder Sikand, and Martin van Bruinessen (eds.). 2008. *The Madrasa in Asia: Political Activism and Transnational Linkages.* Amsterdam University Press.

Ortner, Sherry B. 2005. "Resistance and the Problem of Ethnographic Refusal." *Comparative Studies in Society and History* 37 (1): 173–93.

Osanloo, Arzoo. 2009. *The Politics of Women's Rights in Iran.* Princeton University Press.

Osella, Filippo, and Caroline Osella. 2008. "Islamism and Social Reform in Kerala, South India." *Modern Asian Studies* 42 (2/3): 317–46.

Paden, J. N. 1973. *Religion and Political Culture in Kano.* Berkeley: University of California Press.

Parkin, David, and Stephen Headley (eds.). 2000. *Islamic Prayer Across the Indian Ocean: Inside and Outside the Mosque.* London: Routledge.

Pearl, David, and Werner Menski. 1998. *Muslim Family Law.* (3rd edn.) London: Sweet & Maxwell.

Peletz, Michael. 1996. *Reason and Passion: Representations of Gender in a Malay Society.* Berkeley: University of California Press.

2002. *Islamic Modern: Religious Courts and Cultural Politics in Malaysia.* Princeton University Press.

Peters, Rudolph. 1996. *Jihad in Classical and Modern Islam.* Princeton: Markus Wiener Publishers.

Powers, David S. 1986. *Studies in Qur'an and Hadîth: The Formation of the Islamic Law of Inheritance.* Berkeley: University of California Press.

2002. "Kadijustiz or Qâdî-Justice? A Paternity Dispute from Fourteenth-Century Morocco," in David S. Powers, *Law, Society, and Culture in the Maghrib, 1300–1500*, pp. 23–52. Cambridge University Press.

Quraishi, Asifa, and Najeeba Syeed-Miller. 2004. "No Altars: A Survey of Islamic Family Law in the United States," in Lynn Welchman (ed.). *Women's Rights and Islamic Family Law*, pp. 177–229. London: Zed Books.

Robinson, David. 2000. "Revolutions in the Western Sudan," in Nehemeia Levtzion and Randall L. Pouwels (eds.). *The History of Islam in Africa*, pp. 131–52. Athens: Ohio University Press.

Rosen, Lawrence. 1984. *Bargaining for Reality: The Structure of Social Relations in a Moroccan City.* University of Chicago Press.

1989. *The Anthropology of Justice: Law as Culture in Islamic Society.* Cambridge University Press.

Rudnyckyi, Daromir. 2010. *Spiritual Economies: Islam, Globalization, and the Afterlife of Development.* Ithaca: Cornell University Press.

Schielke, Samuli. 2009. "Being Good in Ramadan: Ambivalence, Fragmentation, and the Moral Self in the Lives of Young Egyptians." *Journal of the Royal Anthropological Institute* (N.S.): S24–S40.

Schiffauer, Werner. 2000. *Die Gottesmänner: Türkische Islamisten in Deutschland.* Frankfurt-am-Maine: Suhrkamp Verlag; Auflage: Erstausgabe.

Schimmel, Annemarie. 1975. *Mystical Dimensions of Islam.* Chapel Hill: University of North Carolina Press.

Sells, Michael. 1999. *Approaching the Qur'ân: The Early Revelations.* Ashland, OR: White Cloud Press.

Shaw, Alison. 2000. *Kinship and Continuity: Pakistani Families in Britain.* London: Routledge.

Ash-Shiddieqy, T. M. Hasbi. 1950. *Tuntutan Qurban.* Jakarta: Bulan Bintang.

Bibliography

Shryock, Andrew. 1997. *Nationalism and the Genealogical Imagination: Oral History and Textual Authority in Tribal Jordan*. Berkeley: University of California Press.

Siegel, James T. 1969. *The Rope of God*. Berkeley: University of California Press.

Silverstein, Michael. 1977. "Cultural Prerequisites to Grammatical Analysis," in M. Saville-Troike (ed.). *Linguistics and Anthropology: Georgetown University Round Table on Languages and Linguistics*, pp. 139–51. Washington, DC: Georgetown University Press.

Silverstein, Paul A. 2004. *Algeria in France: Transpolitics, Race, and Nation*. Bloomington: Indiana University Press.

Simpson, Edward. 2007. "The Changing Perspectives of Three Muslim Men on the Question of Saint Worship over a 10-Year Period in Gujarat, Western India." *Modern Asian Studies* 42 (2/3): 377–403.

and Kai Kresse (eds.). 2008. *Struggling with History: Islam and Cosmopolitanism in the Western Indian Ocean*. New York: Columbia University Press.

Singer, Milton B. 1972. *When a Great Tradition Modernizes: An Anthropological Approach to Indian Civilization*. New York: Praeger.

Smith, Wilfred Cantwell. 1957. *Islam in Modern History*. Princeton University Press.

Smith, W. Robertson. 1894. *Lectures on the Religion of the Semites*. London: A. C. Black.

Soares, Benjamin F. 2004. "An African Muslim Saint and his Followers in France." *Journal of Ethnic and Migration Studies* 30 (5): 913–22.

2005. *Islam and the Prayer Economy: History and Authority in a Malian Town*. Edinburgh University Press.

Souilamas, Nacira Guénif. 2000. *Des "Beurettes" aux Descendantes d'Immigrants Nord-Africains*. Paris: Grasset.

Starrett, Gregory. 1998. *Putting Islam to Work: Education, Politics, and Religious Transformation in Egypt*. Berkeley: University of California Press.

Stiles, Erin. 2009. *An Islamic Court in Context: An Ethnographic Study of Judicial Reasoning*. New York: Palgrave Macmillan.

Tambiah, Stanley Jeyaraja. 1970. *Buddhism and the Spirit Cults in North-East Thailand*. Cambridge University Press.

Tapper, Nancy and Richard Tapper. 1987. "The Birth of the Prophet: Ritual and Gender in Turkish Islam," *Man* (N.S.) 22: 69–92.

Tapper, Richard. 1984. "Holier Than Thou: Islam in Three Tribal Societies," in Akbar S. Ahmed and David M. Hart (eds.). *Islam in Tribal Societies*, pp. 244–65. London: Routledge & Kegan Paul.

Tarlo, Emma. 2010. *Visibly Muslim: Fashion, Politics, Faith*. Oxford: Berg.

Taylor, Charles. 2007. *A Secular Age*. Cambridge, MA: Harvard University Press.

Tucker, Judith E. 2008. *Women, Family, and Gender in Islamic Law.* Cambridge University Press.

Van der Veer, Peter. 1988. *Gods on Earth: The Management of Religious Experience and Identity in a North Indian Pilgrimage Center.* London School of Economics Monographs on Social Anthropology, no. 59. London: Athlone Press.

Venel, Nancy. 1999. *Musulmanes Françaises: des Pratiquantes Voilées á l'Université.* Paris: Harmattan.

Werbner, Pnina. 1990. *The Migration Process: Capital, Gifts and Offerings among British Pakistanis.* Oxford: Berg.

2003. *Pilgrims of Love: The Anthropology of a Global Sufi Cult.* Bloomington: Indiana University Press.

Wickham, Carrie Rosefsky. 2002. *Mobilizing Islam: Religion, Activism, and Political Change in Egypt.* New York: Columbia University Press.

Winkelmann, Mareike. 2008. "'Inside and Outside' in a Girls' Madrasa in New Delhi," in Farish A. Noor, Yoginder Sikand, and Martin van Bruinessen (eds.). *The Madrasa in Asia: Political Activism and Transnational Linkages*, pp. 105–22. Amsterdam University Press.

El Zein, Abdul Hamid. 1974. *The Sacred Meadows: A Structural Analysis of Religious Symbolism in an East African Town.* Evanston: Northwestern University Press.

Index

Index

Index

Qur'an, 2, 4, 6, 11–19, 22–7, 29, 35, 37,
    39–40, 43, 45–7, 56, 60, 62–3, 67,
    71, 77–8, 86, 88, 103, 108, 122, 124,
    129, 145, 150, 182, 190, 192, 200,
    202, 211
Qur'anic schools, 25

reason, 126
recitation, 11, 13, 16, 18, 24, 26, 29, 31, 36,
    45, 70, 84–5, 88, 104, 111, 120, 122,
    134, 188, 202
reformism, 14
revelation, 11, 13, 17–18, 65, 102, 108, 129,
    200, 202
ritual, 50–8
ritual meals, 14, 83, 84, 89,
    104
Rosen, Lawrence, 6, 143
Rudnyckyj, Daromir, 182

sacrifice, 42, 50, 52, 75–101, 102–4, 158,
    198, 199, 206
Sacrifice, Feast of, 49, 76, 80, 83–7, 89,
    91–2, 98, 104, 201
sadaqa, 103, 113, 133, 202
saint, 29, 38, 39, 44, 107, 109–10, 114, 120,
    124–6, 128, 129–30, 132–3, 136,
    183, 194
Salafi, 57, 175, 202
salâh, 13. *See also salât*
salât, 13, 22, 34, 42, 44–5, 48, 50–8, 59, 80,
    87, 103, 132, 158, 185
samadîyah, 15
Saudi Arabia, 1, 2, 180
Sayyid Qutb, 33, 176, 192, 196
school, 13, 22–34, 35–7, 39, 54, 57, 68, 70,
    72–3, 86, 90, 120, 123, 159, 163,
    168, 173, 175, 177, 179, 182–3, 185,
    188–90, 198, 201–2
    in Afghanistan, 35–7
scripture, 2, 4, 5, 12, 15, 17, 22, 25, 28, 31,
    57, 62, 67, 76, 86, 92, 154–5, 183,
    192–3, 198

secular, 18, 23, 26, 30–2, 35, 43, 89, 138,
    149, 162, 171, 177, 179, 182–3, 188
Senegal, 99, 124, 130, 134–5, 206
sermon, 60–6, 80, 89, 177, 180, 186, 201
Shâfi'i, legal school, 54
shariah (*sharî`a*), 28, 112, 122–3, 138, 140,
    160, 167–8, 170, 200
sheikh, 28, 31, 65, 110, 119–23, 127–9,
    134–36, 191, 193, 195
Shi'ite, 35, 59, 107, 111, 120, 144, 146–7,
    149, 190
shirk, 13, 40, 102, 112, 115, 127, 133, 202
shrines, 111–12, 124–5, 137, 203
Siegel, James, 6
silsila, 111, 120, 202
Soares, Benjamin, 131–3
social movements, 4, 49, 112, 174, 177,
    182–3, 197
song, 37–40
souls, 54, 106
South Asia, 9, 26, 29, 37, 72, 109, 156–7,
    159, 185
spells, 15, 102–3, 105, 106
spirit possession, 115–18
Starrett, Gregory, 25, 34, 48, 212
Sudan, 116, 161, 205, 211
Sufi, 202, 207–8, 213
    orders, 52, 55, 107, 116, 119–37, 195
        Alawiyya, 137
        Budshishiyya, 127–8
        Muhammadiyya Shadhiliyya, 122
        Naqshbandi, 120–2
        Qadiriyya, 111, 120
        Shahmaghsoudi, 136
        Sherqai, 124–7
        Tijaniyya, 131, 134, 136
    poetry, 35, 38, 48
    shrines, 5
Sufi theories of being, 106, 107
Sufism, 5, 28–9, 38, 107–15, 119–37, 175,
    196
Sunni, 19, 20, 28, 35–6, 38–9, 46, 53, 57,
    107, 120, 149, 168, 175